My Story

MICHAEL CLARKE

Also by Michael Clarke

The Ashes Diary
Captain's Diary
Ashes Diary 2015

My Story

MICHAEL CLARKE

MACMILLAN
Pan Macmillan Australia

First published 2016 in Macmillan by Pan Macmillan Australia Pty Ltd
1 Market Street, Sydney, New South Wales, Australia, 2000

Cataloguing-in-Publication entry is available
from the National Library of Australia
http://catalogue.nla.gov.au

Typeset in 13.5/16.5 pt Bembo by Midland Typesetters, Australia
Printed by McPherson's Printing Group
Jacket, case and endpapers design by Debra Billson
Internal photo sections by Mark Thacker, Big Cat Design
Front endpaper image: Hamish Blair/Getty Images
Back endpaper image: Ryan Pierse/Getty Images

Aboriginal and Torres Strait Islander people should be aware that this book may contain images or names of people now deceased.

FSC www.fsc.org MIX Paper from responsible sources FSC® C001695

The paper in this book is FSC® certified.
FSC® promotes environmentally responsible, socially beneficial and economically viable management of the world's forests.

CONTENTS

Fight one more round. When your feet are so tired you have to shuffle back to the centre of the ring, fight one more round. When your arms are so tired that you can hardly lift your hands to come on guard, fight one more round. When your nose is bleeding and your eyes are black and you are so tired you wish your opponent would crack you one on the jaw and put you to sleep, fight one more round – remembering that the man who always fights one more round is never whipped.

– James 'Gentleman Jim' Corbett
Bare-knuckle Heavyweight Champion 1882–1892

FOREWORD
by Brian Lara

Sometimes in life you happen upon a 'game changer', a person or thing that can dramatically change the course of events, or alter perceptions and outcomes. Meeting Michael Clarke, getting to know him and witnessing his achievements on and off the field of play, was one of those game changers for me.

Quietly confident while possessing a demeanour and presence that commanded notice and respect, he made a vivid impression on our first encounter. I had just arrived in Guyana for the start of the 2003 West Indies versus Australia series and was looking for the first available car from the airport into Georgetown. With permission, I jumped into the back seat of a taxi carrying one other passenger. Immediately, I thought *Australian journalist . . . here we go.* I expected a long trip to the hotel with endless questions. I enquired, but the young man replied, 'No, I am Michael Clarke, I'm replacing Damien Martyn. Nice to meet you, Mr Lara.' I shook his outstretched hand and from that point onwards, hearing from Michael has been hearing from a friend.

Michael and I became close, perhaps even to the chagrin of his Australian teammates who may have felt that such a closeness with an opponent was unhealthy. Michael related how much he enjoyed watching me play during his youthful days, and I saw his as a very special talent coming out of Australia. He absolutely loved his cricket and dreamed of playing at the highest level for his country. This he did with great success and flair. In my mind, what set him apart was his sponge-like outlook and keenness to listen and learn from whomever could make him a better cricketer.

One memory which stands out is when, after a win by Australia over the West Indies in Hobart, my teammates and I went to the Australian dressing room to offer congratulations and have the usual after-match drink with the opposition. I moved around the room and eventually settled next to Michael. One by one, all the young Australian players moved in on our conversation with that same willingness to learn that Michael had when we first met. Michael already knew he was dropped for the next Test match, but he never allowed that disappointment to spoil the atmosphere created in that moment. I knew then the manner of man that Michael is and the high regard and openness he had for our friendship.

Michael became a fierce competitor on the field of play, the only way you should be when competing for your country. As a captain, Michael led by example on and off the field. One could look at all the players on the field, and picking Michael as the leader was a simple task. His antics, aptitude and confidence made him stand out among his peers.

As a cricketer, one lives a hectic, high-energy and sometimes overwhelming life, and balancing one's personal and professional life is not always easy. But Michael achieved this balance with what always seemed to be a calm and happy ease. He has left a very strong legacy in the cricketing world. Here is a man who grew up watching his countrymen become the number one team in the world, dominating the opposition at home and away. He dreamed about playing with and against his childhood heroes, which he did with great accomplishment. He led his country bravely and at all times showed great sportsmanship.

'Pups!' Sir Vivian Richards would shout when he wanted my attention. Today I say to you, Pup, that you have shown the world your true self: strong, committed, confident, fearless, honest, loyal to your family and many more great character traits; but most importantly to me and many others, a true friend. I couldn't be prouder of you or happier for you. This book is a wonderful testament to your life thus far, but remember, my friend, your journey continues. I am confident that you will continue to be a game changer and I look forward to witnessing it.

1

THE DAY LIFE CHANGED

It's a beautiful morning for cricket: today is the semi-final of the 2007 World Cup and we are in St Lucia to play South Africa. Although we have had an unbeaten run in the tournament so far, this is knock-out time, and the whole world knows how much the Proteas and their countrymen want a World Cup.

A light sea breeze is blowing through the window of my hotel room. I'm starting to get my head around today's game when my mobile phone rings. The screen says it's an overseas call.

My sister Leanne is speaking before I can open my mouth.

'It's Dad,' she says. She's in tears. Her words come out in a rush. 'He and Mum wanted to wait until the end of the World Cup before telling you, but I have to tell you now.

He's been diagnosed with cancer. He's having more scans and going in for chemo and radiation.'

For what seems like a long time, I can't speak. My throat has gone tight and dry, and my eyes have welled up. I'm on my feet. My head is light. Leanne gives me more details: during dinner a few nights ago, Dad collapsed in so much pain that Mum and Leanne thought he was having a heart attack. He went to hospital for tests, and the diagnosis has come in today. I can only just hear her through the beating of blood in my ears. She says he has a number of cancers throughout his upper body.

Finally I can speak. 'I'm coming straight home.'

'No, no, please don't,' Leanne says. 'They really don't want you to come back. There's nothing you can do right now. Play the rest of the World Cup.'

The World Cup? A minute ago, it was all I was thinking about: my first World Cup. Now, it seems to have zoomed off, over the horizon. It's vanished. Everything, as it existed until a minute ago, has fallen out of my head. Dad has cancer. I have two lives: there is the life I lived up until today, and a different life that is about to begin.

2

THE LOVING OF LIVERPOOL

Will he ever come home?

I am six years old and sitting on the kerb outside our house in Leitz Street, Liverpool. My cricket bat is between my knees and I am spinning a tennis ball from hand to hand. There are so many places to set up a game – number-one pitch on the front yard, number-two pitch up the driveway and into the garage, number-three pitch in the cul-de-sac with the telegraph pole as the stumps – but I have no one to play with. Leanne is at after-school sport, so I can't nag her to throw balls to me. It feels like I've been sitting on this kerb forever.

My dad is a hard-working man. Even though I am only little, I have some sense of that. He works with his hands, and he believes in doing things himself. Soon after I was born, he gave up an opportunity to play grade cricket for Western Suburbs because he was converting the two-bedroom weatherboard house on this corner block into a more substantial brick dwelling with three bedrooms. With a wife and two young kids, cricket had to take a back seat. I was a toddler at the time, and would sit all day watching the workmen. At night, after they had left their gear, I would get on the job myself. Mum and Dad would be sitting in the kitchen unwinding, and from the next room there'd be a *Bang! Bang! Bang!* It was just me, hoeing into the walls with one of the workmen's hammers. They always say, 'Michael's a very, *very* active boy.' And roll their eyes.

Finally, Dad's truck swings around the corner and into the driveway. His business is to deliver bricks. His truck is a hand-wagon rather than a crane-wagon, which means he loads and unloads his capacity of two thousand bricks, by hand, on three delivery runs a day. That means he has shifted twelve thousand bricks with his bare hands since I last saw him this morning.

Doesn't matter: it's cricket time! I get up and run over, thrusting the ball at him. He says he wants to go inside and sit down with a cold drink, but I won't let him rest. Soon I have him under-arming the tennis ball. I'm whacking it everywhere. Dad has to troop off into the bushes or across the road to fetch it. He's feeling the effects of his day at work, but I'm at him to bowl more balls. More and more and more.

'I want to bat like you,' I say. I am a left-hander and, for a brief time, when I'm very young, I bat with my strong hand on the bottom. But I want to be like Dad, who's a right-handed batsman.

'Sure. All you have to do is stand on the other side of the bat.'

It's that simple. I become a right-handed batsman, with my strong hand on top. Little do I know it, but I've done the same switch as future team-mates and opponents such as Brian Lara, Adam Gilchrist, Mike Hussey, Marcus North, David Warner and a host of others who bat with their stronger hand on top. I don't know what their reasons are for holding the bat the way they do, but mine is the same that drives everything I do at this age: I want to be like my Dad.

'And you've got to stop hitting them everywhere,' he says. 'I can't keep playing if you're going to make me chase balls all over the place.'

'I can't stop hitting them,' I say. What's the point if you can't bash the ball as far as you can?

'You will,' Dad says quietly, with his usual don't-argue firmness. 'You have to block the first fifty balls before you begin belting them.'

Okay! That's fifty more balls he's committed to throwing at me! So I count them aloud. 'One ... two ... three ... four ...' It's like a countdown for Dad, having me block ball after ball before he has to start chasing. Once I get to fifty, I can swing hard again. Dad's off hunting in the bushes, his back stiff and his legs creaking from those twelve thousand bricks.

'All right,' he says a few sessions later. 'I can't take this. You have to block *one hundred* balls before you start belting them.'

'One . . . two . . . three . . . four . . .'

And on it goes, all the way to one hundred. By the time I'm ready to play real cricket, my batting is based on the defensive technique from all that blocking. Dad has shown me the fundamentals of forward and backward defence, the story of an innings: it always begins with a solid stint of defence. I learn from the earliest days to build an innings, like Dad built this house, from the ground up. For me, defence has a different purpose – it's the only way I can keep Dad bowling to me.

When I get on a real cricket field at last, this grounding comes in more than handy. I'm a slight and skinny seven-year-old when Dad and I wander down to Schell Park, a few short blocks from home. It's a typical western suburbs junior sports ground, big and dry and open with a fringe of gum trees and a low brick toilet block where you can get changed and watch from the shade. There's a synthetic pitch in the middle and a basic pair of cricket nets at one end where the under-10s for the local club, Woodlands Park, are practising. Leanne already plays netball and softball for the club. I've been playing tee-ball for a couple of years, but am desperate to get out and play on a real cricket pitch, facing real bowlers, just like Dad. He's not so sure I'm strong enough to play with ten-year-olds.

'Hey, Les!'

It's Jason Willmont, coach of the Woodlands Park under-10s. He's seen me looking longingly at the boys in the nets with my bat. At a recent presentation at Gunnamatta Park, he told Dad I should be given a go at real cricket.

'Why not let him have a hit with the boys?' Jason says now.

I look up at Dad. I'm begging him with my eyes.

'No, he's too young,' Dad says. 'He can't even bowl a ball the length of the pitch. He'll struggle against those boys.'

With the ball in my hand, I run over to the centre wicket. I sprint in as fast as I can and hurl the ball, left-arm quick, and it makes it all the way to the other end and stays on the pitch. Jason – with a lot of help from me – persuades Dad to give way. To my delight, I get to play the whole under-10s season. I score a total of 17 runs in a lot of innings, but the bigger boys only get me out once. Those defensive sessions to save Dad's back have set me up.

This is how competitive cricket starts for me, and I guess this is the time I set my eager foot on the path that will lead to playing for Australia. But in my world, there's not really a road or a link from Schell Park to the cricket I see on television. We don't have the money to go to watch a Test match at the Sydney Cricket Ground. What my world consists of is the enchanted circle around our house, encompassing Schell Park and Marsden Public School, and the people who dominate it, my heroes, are among my family and my friends. Anything that exists on the other side of Elizabeth Drive, the big main road cutting through our suburb, exists only on TV.

Our world gives us everything we'll ever need. Cricket is part of that world, but as a boy I never see myself leaving Liverpool. Where else would I want to be?

The centre of that world is our house, which has been converted and extended to the comfortable sandstock-brick three-bedroom structure that Mum and Dad envisaged around the time of my birth. Leanne and I are the type of kids who usually invite our friends to our place more than going to theirs; if a parent wants to find one of their kids, they only have to come over to the Clarkes'.

I'm a fidgety ball of nervous energy. I have the bedroom near the front door, and go to bed each night with the fear that if someone is going to break in, they'll come to my room first. I sleep with my cricket bat, partly because I love it but also to defend myself from an intruder. A lot of the time, I'll sneak into Leanne's room and sleep top-to-tail in her bed. When she goes away for a night or two on a school camp, I'll sleep in her room. I miss her, and I don't want to be near the front door. The cricket bat is with me night and day.

This has been Mum and Dad's house more or less since they married. They met, funnily enough, through cricket. Dad was born in Canberra, but after his father passed away when Dad was five, his mother remarried and they moved to Sydney, where Dad went to Ashfield Boys' High in the western suburbs. He didn't like the city and, desperate to get away from school, he decided, in year 8, to join the navy. He fudged his medical, concealing the fact that he had bad hearing, and signed the recruitment papers against his mother's wishes. As a 16-year-old, he was sent to the HMAS *Leeuwin* naval base in Western Australia. He wanted to get out into the world and have his own adventures.

Sport was a big part of Dad's life, and he got into cricket and rugby union teams on the base. As a young man he was shorter and stockier than me, and by all accounts he had a good mix of talent and positive intent in every sport he played. With his cricket, he says his downfall was over-aggression. In rugby, it was someone else's aggression. In a trial for the Combined Services team, playing for the Navy against the Army, he got kicked in the side of the head. A perforated eardrum spelt the end of Dad's navy career.

Discharged on medical grounds, he went back to Sydney, where he got a job as a process worker at Parsons Pumps in Enfield. When another company offered him a job, Parsons counter-offered with an apprenticeship as a fitter and turner. He ended up working there for nine years.

He played grade cricket for Western Suburbs, and his stepfather still had a connection with the Kingston-Narrabundah RSL cricket club in Canberra. Dad had an uncle, also called Les, who played for Smithfield RSL in Sydney, and the two clubs organised a social match each year, alternating the venue between Canberra and Sydney. Uncle Les encouraged Dad to play in the game, and that's where Dad met Ray Fox, one of the Smithfield players. At a barbecue when he was 19, Dad met Ray's daughter Debbie.

The Foxes were a Catholic western suburbs family. Ray, having grown up in Carlton, was a mad St George Dragons rugby league supporter and a cricket fanatic. The Foxes moved to Mount Pritchard, where Debbie grew up and went to school, and were living in the western suburbs when Ray met Les.

Dad, whose own childhood had been disrupted by his father's early death, got on extremely well with Ray from the start, and found a niche in the Foxes' family life. He and Mum married three years later, when she was 18, and after living briefly in Ashfield and in a flat in Liverpool they bought the house in Leitz Street. Leanne was born in 1979, and I came along in 1981. We were both healthy babies, but premature. I was never going to be good at waiting.

Dad had the notion that he wanted to call me John Michael, after his late father, but apparently, as soon as I came out he and Mum looked at each other and agreed that I was a Michael John. It just seemed natural, plus I had a cousin called John already and they didn't want to confuse things.

Mum worked as a teller at the local Commonwealth Bank for more than 20 years, but family was the centre of her world and she made sure, once Leanne and I were going to school, that she worked shifts that finished by 2.30 pm. From the start Mum was the organiser and disciplinarian in our house. When I created mischief, which was often, she would chase me around with the wooden spoon and rant and rave, whereas Dad would come home and, having heard Mum's reports, give me the silent treatment, which was far worse.

Leanne and I were very active kids. She was sporty, and I was just . . . active. My parents say I was fidgeting all the time and grabbing stuff I shouldn't, and a bit lippy as well. They took me to a doctor to test me for hyperactivity, but apparently I wouldn't sit still long enough for the tests to get done properly.

I just wanted to get on to the next game. Initially that involved Leanne or my cousin Phillip Gardner, my first two role models. Leanne was always playing games, running around with our Dalmatian, Zoe (succeeded by our second Dalmatian, Goss, both named after the cricketer Zoe Goss, who once famously got Brian Lara out in a charity match), or riding BMX bikes with me. If we weren't doing that, we were fighting: a huge fight and a huge make-up almost every day. Once, we were at home while Mum was out, and got arguing over something. Leanne picked up an orange and threw it at my head. I ducked, and it splattered all over the wall. That looked like fun, so I picked one up and threw it at her. Soon we were having a full-on orange fight inside the house. Only when we ran out of ammunition did we look around and survey the wreckage.

'Mum's going to be home soon,' Leanne said. We both knew what that meant, and without a word we knew what to do. Knowing what huge trouble we'd be in, we got together and cleaned it all up. That's how we were – fighting one minute, working together the next.

Mum didn't find out about the orange fight until much later, and the best conspiracies between Leanne and me were when we could put one over our parents. In the living room they had a painted plaster ornament, about two feet high, of Laurel and Hardy sitting together on a park bench. When we played soccer inside the house, we were always breaking one of Laurel or Hardy's fingers. Once we superglued a broken middle finger back on upside-down, so that Laurel was now flipping the bird. For as long as that went undiscovered, Leanne and I could look at it and have a giggle.

Most of all, I was extremely protective of Leanne – as she was of me. I have a scar on my hip, a lifelong reminder of how I wanted to look after her. One night, she had a blow-up with Mum and Dad at the dinner table. Food was occasionally a sore point. I hated all vegetables, especially peas, while Leanne didn't like meat. Mum gave us a standard meat-and-veg diet, and had a rule that I had to eat at least one green veggie per meal, while Leanne had to have some meat. She and I would engage in surreptitious meat-for-veg swaps beneath the table.

Anyway, this one time, an argument broke out and Leanne ran out of the house. My immediate thought was that I was worried about her walking around the streets on her own in the dark, so I ran out to chase her. I got on my bike, and as I was going around a corner I clipped a low brick wall and fell into a rose garden. I came up covered in scratches and had a nasty gouge in my hip from the brickwork.

I just wanted to look after her, and this has lasted to the present day. When Leanne moved into her first house, I moved in with her, for her safety and to help with the rent. Unsurprisingly, I was the toughest judge of her boyfriends. It was lucky that when she eventually met Craig, who she would marry and have kids with, I fully approved.

Leanne's friends became my friends, but my cousin Phillip, who was several years older than us, was the first of the 'big brothers' who would become a recurring presence in my life. Phillip came and watched me play cricket, and I would watch him play rugby league for Burwood United, where Dad played and coached for 16 years. Not having the money to go to Campbelltown or Sydney Olympic Park to watch my beloved Western Suburbs Magpies (later the Wests Tigers), the big rugby league event for me was to go and watch Phillip and Dad at Burwood United.

For a long time, rugby league was as big an obsession for me as cricket. I played league for Woodlands Park and then Macquarie Cobras. My hero was Allan Langer, the patron saint of all little boys who think big. This led me into some difficulties, such as on State of Origin nights when I wore a Queensland jersey. Alfie was my hero! As long as I was wearing that jersey, Dad wouldn't talk to me.

I was in awe of Burwood United, and loved hanging around the changing room. The smell of Deep Heat and the sound of footie studs on the concrete floor were intoxicating. I ran out a bucket of sand for the goal kickers and put my hand up for any job. Dad eventually had to draw the line, however, when I came home and began using the same language I'd heard him use with the boys at half-time. Swearing might be fine at the sports ground, but it was not tolerated at home. My Pop, Mum's father, would turn the television off if there was any swearing that Nan or Mum might hear. Dad had similar values, and he made it quite clear that I would not speak that way in front of my mother.

Years later, when a television microphone caught me warning James Anderson to 'Get ready for a broken f—ing arm' during the 2013–14 Ashes series, I was embarrassed that kids around the country might have heard it, but I was thoroughly ashamed that my mum would hear me speaking like that.

It was a happy day when my cousin Phillip would take me out on the back of his motorbike or down to the park or even just into the front yard for a kick or a hit. Dad was like a second father to him. My heart was broken when, some years later, Phillip was killed in a motorbike accident. I was at the Australian Cricket Academy at the time, and the head of the ACA, Rod Marsh, excused me from a game so that I could go to Phillip's funeral.

I felt that his spirit continued to watch over me. After his funeral, I went back to the Academy and scored a hundred in my first game. Dad, Phillip and I were huge Wests Magpies fans together, and magpies have had an uncanny way of turning up at certain moments in my life. During Phillip's burial, a magpie landed on his grave and stayed to watch. A year or two after Phillip died, I was walking out onto the Sydney Cricket Ground to bat in what was my tenth Pura Cup (as the Sheffield Shield was briefly called) appearance for New South Wales. A magpie flew down and walked beside me, on the turf, out to the middle, like it was Phillip's spirit keeping me safe. That same magpie hung around all day, and was sitting on the scoreboard when I brought up my hundredth run – my first century for my state. At that moment, the magpie flew away, as if it had done its job. Say what you like, but I couldn't help thinking Phillip was with me.

Our house was situated in what was known as the Orange Grove Estate, a Liverpool housing tract developed in the 1960s and 1970s mainly for young families. It is a working-class area in the south-west of Sydney, but to me it was rich in fun. Every street, every corner, nearly every house was an important landmark. The main frontier points were Schell Park, Marsden Public School where I went until grade six, and Elizabeth Drive, the four-lane main road that bordered our patch to the west.

Rather than walk the long way to school or the park, Leanne and I would jump the fences of neighbouring houses and cut through their back yards. There were some neighbours who didn't like these kids scooting past their kitchen windows, one scary man in particular who was always telling us off. Then one day, Leanne fell badly off this man's fence, hurt her ankle and couldn't get up. I was very concerned for her, but something must have softened in him when he came out and found us. Instead of barking at us, he drove us home.

Leanne says I had a knack for charming adults. At home, we alternated between our three cricket-playing areas. The drawback with the cul-de-sac was that Jim, the American man who lived at the end, didn't like children. But he made an exception for me, and tolerated our noise and our balls coming into his yard.

I don't remember having any special charm when it came to adults. The deputy principal at Marsden Public School thought I was an absolute villain, a reputation I fully deserved. In class, I was fairly good at maths, but in most other subjects I couldn't concentrate. I don't know if this was just because I was so fidgety that I needed the physical outlet of sports to burn up all my excess energy. Certainly, I lived for recess and lunch, which were, in my mind, the only reasons to be at school. But if you ask my mum, she says I was afraid of failing and unwilling to have a go at things I didn't think I was good at. Reading and English, for example – even though I had a reading tutor at home for a while, I couldn't put my mind to it. And when I was in that mood, I would back-chat the teachers, stir up my classmates and create havoc. Whether this was due to my inability to learn or I was covering up for my lack of confidence, I don't know. But I was not a model student, to say the least.

My patterns of misbehaviour would ebb and flow during my years at school. At the beginning of year 6, the other kids at Marsden Public voted me school captain. I wouldn't do it – there would be public speaking involved, and no way was I going to stand up in front of a crowd and make a speech. The deputy principal said to me, 'I hope you have lots of children, because I don't know what else you're going to do with your life.'

Although the deputy principal thought I was a rogue, others didn't. She warned my grade-six teacher about how bad I was, and at the parent–teacher night the teacher said to my parents, 'I have to apologise, because I went into this class expecting Michael to be a big problem, but he hasn't been bad at all.' As far as reports on my classroom performance went, this was as good as it got!

My sport coaches, on the other hand, tended to like me. Mr Wilson, the Marsden Public sports teacher, took me out of school to play cricket when I was in grade four, which was younger than the other boys, and I liked that. When I moved to Liverpool Boys' High School in year 7, I was picked in the cricket First XI to play with boys as old as 17 and 18. Mum told the sports master she didn't want me travelling on my own to matches, but he wanted me in the team, so he organised transport: two year-12 boys came in their car and taxied me around. As a 12-year-old, I thought it was very cool to be travelling with 18-year-olds.

Because Leanne's friends were my friends, and because of my cousin Phillip, I had an early affinity with kids who were older than me. When I began playing organised cricket, I was surrounded by boys who were two, three or more years older, and felt comfortable in their company. When Leanne had her 18th birthday party at our house, we made it a joint party with my 16th.

My local mates all tended to be a little older than me. Daniel Kent and David Fairclough were neighbours we could always round up for a game of some kind. They played cricket with me at Woodlands Park. My best mate, who I met through junior cricket and football, was

Dominic D'Bartolo, and his house, a few streets away, became another landmark in that magic circle.

The D'Bartolos were a big Italian Catholic family who lived in three adjoining houses – cousins, uncles, grandparents, the lot. Dom was the eldest of four kids, and theirs was the first two-storey house I'd ever been inside. I loved being there. Their food was grown in their yards: tomatoes, herbs, grapes for home-made wine. Dom's mother, Alfia, spent all day cooking amazing Italian meals. I fell over there once and split my head open, and she patched me up like the best nurse you could have. Dom's Nonno and Nonna became like second grandparents for me, and the family introduced me to their customs. When I stayed over on a Saturday night, we would all go to church on the Sunday morning. That was not unfamiliar to me – I did the full Catholic sacraments of confirmation and first communion with our family – but Dom's family followed their religion seriously. It was a terrible day when Dom's mother eventually died of breast cancer. He became a chef as an adult, which in its way has kept her legacy alive. I can still smell her cooking.

If I loved their place for the food, the bustling family atmosphere and the sound of spoken Italian, Dom enjoyed our place for the games. With other mates such as Daniel and David, as well as Leanne, we would play cricket on any of our three 'pitches' or Classic Catches in our pool. When the pool was still empty, waiting for water, we skateboarded in it. When it was full, we climbed onto the back fence and jumped in. I loved that house so much. When I was an adult and Mum and Dad were moving out, I considered buying it. That didn't come to pass, but it's a sign of how strongly I feel the bond to the place, the friends and the times I had there.

If home was where my heart was, at nine years old my heart was stolen by another place.

Until then, my cricket had revolved around home and Schell Park. At home, the front yard was my number one choice, and I was also the curator of that pitch. At one point, Dad said he had no time to mow it and might pay a guy to do it. I said, 'I'll do it, pay me instead.' Sure enough, when Mum and Dad came home after I'd done my 'job', I was playing cricket – on the pitch I'd mown. That's right: all I had mown was the strip, about ten metres long and two metres wide. The unmown remainder of the yard was 'outfield'. I thought it looked great!

Cricket in the front yard, usually with Leanne or local mates, was limited by how often we broke the bay window on the front of the house, which happened to be positioned at point to the right-handed batsman. When Mum rang John from Liverpool Glass, she would say, 'John, it's Debbie Clarke here. It's broken again. Yes, same one, you don't have to measure it.'

Dad had been self-employed for all of my life, owning his brick truck and also a milk run that he bought with Pop. In 1990, Dad was also playing A-grade indoor cricket at the Lurnea Indoor Sports Centre on Hoxton Park Road, about a 15-minute walk from our house. He also used the bowling machine there for batting practice.

The owner, Michael O'Brien, was stretched and asked Dad to come in and manage the centre for him. Eventually, Mum and Dad bought it, but he spent the next two years wondering if he'd made the right decision. The equipment was in such a state of disrepair that he spent hours and hours re-sewing damaged nets. When cricket was being played, the centre was a no-go zone for women and children, because it had a reputation for fights and all sorts of loose behaviour. In his typical no-nonsense way, Dad kicked out 15 of the 42 cricket teams, getting rid of the brawlers and the groups who routinely failed to show up for games or otherwise made life difficult for those who wanted to play. By doing so, he cut his own income, and for 18 months he and Mum didn't know if they were going to make it pay. But eventually, he improved and diversified the competitions so that they built up again to 90 cricket teams, 90 netball teams, and volleyball and soccer competitions too. Women and kids now felt welcome to come there too.

As a nine-year-old, my parents' business worries were none of my concern. To me, the indoor centre was heaven. Leanne and I would go there after school, picking up friends along the way like pied pipers travelling to Hoxton Park Road. I made a whole bunch of new mates playing at the centre, all of them older than me. There was Steve Phillips, an excellent cricketer I would play with at Western Suburbs, and also a group of guys who lived in and around the local area: Josh Pitt, Kane Landers, Tony Johnson, Mark Long, Chris and Michael Hampton.

Steve Phillips was my closest sporting mate for many years, a constant companion at the indoor centre, on the cricket field, or out and about. We always had fun together, and later on he would become a very good mate of Phillip Hughes's. Even though Steve was about ten years older than Hughesy, the pair of them were like soul brothers, with similar interests and a light-hearted outlook on life.

I will always be thankful to the people at the indoor centre who took me under their wing. There are too many of them to name, but they were both employees and participants in the sports there. They would stop what they were doing in order to bowl or throw balls to me, or face me when I wanted to bowl, or just be someone to talk to. Some of them treated me like a son. They helped Dad, and made it safe and secure for Leanne and me, creating a family-like atmosphere.

By my early teens, I had 'big brothers' all through the neighbourhood, friends I collected through school, cricket, football, the indoor centre. I got used to being looked after by older boys. We would go to Mr Ko's Chinese Takeaway every Sunday night – I still think it's the best Chinese in the world, and they even delivered to Liverpool Boys' High canteen. Mum and Dad wouldn't let me walk or ride home at night, so one of my 'big brothers' would ensure I got a lift. When there was trouble around, they would make sure that I, as the young kid, was not exposed to the worst of it. There was a bit of drug use, and once these older boys saw how serious I was about my cricket, they wouldn't let anyone smoke a joint near me – I was a drug-free zone.

Not that I was an innocent kid. Ask my parents, and they'll say how crazy I drove them. I was full of cheek. I remember getting into all sorts of trouble in a caravan park, on holidays, for ambushing Dad's stepfather and turning a hose on him full-bore.

Having said that, I was blessed to have two pairs of doting grandparents. Nan Conder, Dad's mother, never cared too much about cricket and wouldn't know if I was playing; all she cared about was that I was happy and healthy and safe. My cousin Phillip and I were her favourites. We would go to Dad's sister Aunty Anne's house for Christmas lunch, and the only people Nan would peel prawns for were Phillip and me. Nan Conder and Dad's stepfather, Jacky, lived a lot of their lives in caravan parks, which were like great playgrounds for us when we visited. I gave them cheek from time to time, but they were fantastic grandparents.

Mum's parents, Pop and Nan Fox, were more cricket-focused. Nan Fox wouldn't miss a game, even if it was because Pop would drag her along to everything. When we went to visit them at Bundeena, she cooked my favourite breakfast, bacon and eggs, and loved us to bits. This didn't mean I was perfectly behaved for them either. On one occasion, Pop, who indulged and encouraged me every day, got very cranky at me. He'd bought me a pushbike, and I rode it at Bundeena. There were two steep hills near the house, and I got it into my head that having brakes on a bike slowed it down. I cut the brake cables and removed the pads. Thinking I would stop the bike, if I needed to, with my shoe on the back tyre, I hurtled down the hill. Pop went off his head.

As I became a teenager, my smart-arse behaviour got worse. With my mates all being older than me, I figured I could do whatever they did. If they back-chatted adults, I copied them. We all got into trouble once for riding an unlicensed motorbike through Miller Technical High School. If the others were up to pranks, lighting fires or throwing eggs at houses, I was in there with them. We would rip out letter boxes and try to sell them at the indoor centre. On an indoor cricket tour to the Gold Coast, Steve Phillips and I, who were too young to go out with the boys to the pub, went out and bought a carton of eggs and waited on the balcony for our teammates to come home. We bought a heap of fruit, too. When they staggered back, we lobbed our projectiles at them, and we weren't bad throwers either.

But I wasn't smart enough to get away with much. It was a small world, and everyone knew whose son I was. Every whisper of trouble always found its way back to Mum and Dad. One time, Leanne and I got into all sorts of strife after a visit to the local Mobil service station. When Dad came home late that afternoon, he found Leanne and me with Daniel and Melanie Kent working our way through a big picnic of lollies on the pavement in front of our garage. We claimed that we were just with Daniel and Melanie when the lollies had migrated out of the servo, but Dad wouldn't have a bar of it. He dragged us all back to the Mobil to own up and repay the owner – who knew him, of course, and knew us. We never had any hope of getting away with it. Mum and Dad had two golden rules: Don't lie, and don't steal. Leanne and I maintained that we hadn't broken either; Mum and Dad considered that we'd broken both.

There had to be limits, but I was the type of kid who often chose to learn my lessons the hard way. When I was about 15 or 16 years old and getting more of a taste of independence, going away on cricket trips and spending more and more time with older boys who had looser ways, I was turning into a real smart-arse. One night in a game at the indoor centre, Dad noticed that our throws were having a suspicious tendency to hit opposition players in the back instead of hitting the stumps. Knowing that we were pretty good throwers, Dad guessed that we were doing it on purpose. Thinking I was an 18- or 19-year-old, I back-chatted, and it ended up in an ugly confrontation between Dad and me.

I'd definitely gone too far. For the next two weeks we didn't speak to each other, and the silence was agony. Dad wasn't one of my 'big brothers'; he was more important than that. The freeze between us brought home how much I loved Dad's company, and he was silently teaching me a lesson. I could lark around and act the dickhead as much as I liked, but I had bigger things at stake. A future in cricket was not just a possibility now, but close to becoming a reality.

My relationship with my family was everything. Dad had drawn a line in the sand to say, 'Carry on the way you're going and you'll give everything away.' After that incident, my attitude changed completely. I knuckled down at cricket training and took life more seriously. It certainly didn't cure the smart-arse in me forever, but it showed me at an impressionable age that if I thought I could skate along with the big boys and be one of the pack in Liverpool, that was where I would remain for my life.

It was a turning point. For my whole boyhood, to stay in that area was all that I dreamed of. To be the cheeky youngster following his mates in a circle bounded by home, school, Green Valley, Elizabeth Drive, Mr Ko's Chinese, Schell Park and the indoor centre – to be honest, there was a part of me that couldn't think of anything better. But there was another part of me that was getting a first glimpse of a bigger world, and my entry pass into that world was the game of cricket.

I had three posters on my bedroom wall: Michael Slater, Brian Lara and a 355 Ferrari. I dreamed of batting like Michael Slater, meeting Brian Lara, and owning that 355. Were they just fantasies, or things that I could actually make real? There was this little bubble I loved, and there was the world of my dreams. Maybe I could step out of the one into the other. If I could, I could do it through cricket. I was at a crossroads. Dad saw it, Mum saw it, and it took that big bust-up with Dad for me to see it too. I loved the world I was in. But cricket was beckoning me to a bigger world.

3

THE PUP

'No, Michael.'

'Please, Mum?'

'Not until you've done your homework.'

'*Mum?*'

'Homework first, and then you can go.'

'Mum, how come you *always* bribe me with cricket?'

'Because it's the only way I can get you to do your work, Michael.'

I don't know how many times we've had this conversation. I've raced home from school with one thing on my mind. My mum and dad are the best parents in the world. Every day is Christmas. They own an indoor sports centre, and I'm getting there *now*.

It even motivates me to finish that homework as quickly as possible. Maybe I rush it a little. Who cares? As soon as

I'm done, I hop on my pushbike and ride the couple of kilometres to the centre. Dad is always there working, but I don't need him to look after me. I love hanging around the place. There's often someone practising or wanting to play something: cricket, soccer, shoot some hoops. If there's nobody to play with, I'll take ten indoor cricket balls, seamed with leather over a cork interior, and practise throwing at the stumps.

I could stay here all night, but have to fit in with Dad's timetable. From the time I arrive, I train by myself, with a friend, or with Leanne. Then the indoor competitions start: games are at 6.15 pm, 7.45 pm and 9.15 pm. I'll umpire, or help out, or, best of all, get called in to fill a gap for one of the teams. For the 6.15 and 7.45 sessions, I'm hanging out for someone to not turn up so that I can get a game. I am a batsman and a fast bowler – left-armers, very fast in my opinion! – and can swing the responsive indoor ball. All of the sports played there are super-competitive, which is my introduction to the thrills of tough sporting combat. I live for these games, and would stay for the 9.15 pm game as well, but Mum has drawn the line there and I have to go home. I sleep with my cricket bat in my arms. I do not want it out of my sight. I don't even like going to school without it.

Dad is not quite as strict as Mum about getting my homework done. He's quietly pleased that I'm so enthusiastic about the indoor centre. When I'm old enough, he lets me earn some pocket money by umpiring or working behind the counter. I love going to work with him.

He's there for ten hours a day, vacuuming the playing surface, stitching nets together and doing maintenance, keeping the place running until the cricket competitions start in the evening. He makes sure the games start on time, and acts as policeman if there's any serious trouble. Usually, the players know better than to act up when he's watching. Even though he's cleared a lot of the worst trouble-makers out, he can't stop every competitive eruption. It's eye-opening to see some of the punch-ups that he has to step into to break up, but I'm proud of my dad when he shows his authority. People respect him.

My earliest memories of cricket are of going to watch him at his matches. As a very young boy, I was annoying the other men when he was on the field. It was 'Throw me the ball! Throw me the ball!' non-stop.

After taking his break from second grade at Western Suburbs to build our house, Dad played some more for Wests until he broke his jaw when he volunteered to open the batting at Petersham Oval in near-darkness. He stepped down to park cricket in the Southern Districts competition. Everyone at the Players club said Dad was the best batsman in the district comp.

When I'm old enough to play juniors for Woodlands Park, the moment my Saturday morning game is finished I rush off to watch Dad in the afternoon. They might want me to score, run out drinks or gloves, or best of all field, even if it's running from fine leg to fine leg.

Cricket's on both sides of the family. Mum, while she's pro-schoolwork, is definitely not anti-sport. Her father

Ray Fox, my Pop, is cricket mad. When I'm one year old, Pop pulls out a fence paling and shapes it into a bat – my first. Mum says I'm the son he never had. When we go to his place at Bundeena, a bushy village on the south side of Port Hacking south of Sydney, we play Classic Catches bouncing tennis balls off the rocks, or Pop takes me to the school nets next door. He wants to play cricket every time I see him, and I love every minute. He tells anyone who will listen that I am going to be better than Don Bradman, and luckily I'm too young to be embarrassed by that. Being such a mad St George rugby league fan, Pop is constantly singing their victory song, 'When the Saints Go Marching In'. That song becomes a seed he plants inside me that will sprout at the best moments through my career.

In summertime, it's all cricket. You can't imagine a kid being so in love with something as I am with this game. On Saturday mornings, I am up at 5 am, waiting for the sun to rise. When I see the first golden light on a blue sky, I'm yelping about and getting into my whites. *No rain! We're playing today!* Even when it looks gloomy or the leaves on the trees are drooping with raindrops, I feel confident that it's going to clear up. I'm an optimist. Every cricket day gives me the same feeling as Christmas. Saturday morning is like tearing off the wrapping to get a new bat or pads or gloves. I'm not a hard kid to please. Just let me play cricket all day.

Since that first year at Woodlands Park under-10s, when I made 17 runs all season, I've grown stronger and closer in size to the other boys. With more and more afternoons at the indoor centre to hone my skills, I've started to score some decent runs. I generally know that, if I stay in, our team will most likely win, so I've worked out how to be patient, how to control games and manage them so that we can get the job done.

One afternoon, a Western Suburbs grade batsman comes into the centre with a query for Dad. Neil D'Costa is a good player who has been doing some coaching in the district. Neil is full of energy and enthusiasm, a non-stop talker. Living nearby, he is always up for a hit and is a bottomless source of ideas and general cricket smarts. Dad knew Neil's father, who coached at the Fairfield club, and has known Neil for years.

'Are you okay if I do some one-on-one cricket coaching with kids here?' Neil asks Dad. 'How much will you charge for me to hire a net?'

Dad sees me lurking, as ever, in the background, like a puppy dog waiting for someone to throw him a ball. *Who's this guy with all the fancy gear? What's in it for me?*

'Tell you what,' Dad says to Neil. 'Instead of paying a hire fee, do you want to coach my son as well? He's only a youngster, but he loves his cricket.'

From there, Neil becomes the most influential of my big brothers. Every Wednesday, I am at the centre ready for practice. Because I am so small and have little power, Neil grooves my technique, especially my defence. Dad also keeps coaching me, and he and Neil complement each other. They never disagree on the science of batting. But I am not just a batsman, I consider myself a serious fast bowler. When I am 11, Neil breaks the news. 'Mate, you're never going to be big enough to be a real fast bowler, so let's start working on spin.' I start on left-arm wrist-spinners before switching to orthodox. I love bowling, because it keeps me in the game when I'm not batting or chasing every ball in the field.

The next year, Dad takes a year off from playing A-grade at the Players club and drops down to B-grade to play a year of district cricket with me. I remember my first senior game like it was yesterday. I get to bat in a long partnership with Dad. In the time I squeeze out 39 runs, mostly singles, he has smashed 150. It is the happiest day of my life so far. When I eventually retire from international cricket, nearly 25 years later, what I miss most is those days – that feeling I had being on a suburban pitch with my dad.

I am not the kid who goes out every match and takes 10 wickets before scoring a hundred runs. Dad plays a big part in that. He coaches at Woodlands Park, and when he is coaching my team, he retires me if I make 50 so as to give other kids a go. If I open the bowling and grab some wickets, he will take me off. He believes cricket is a team sport, about giving everyone else a turn, and this is years before participation rules become formalised in the junior game.

On Saturday mornings, Mum generally takes Leanne to her sport and Dad takes me to mine, but that's not to say Mum isn't keen on cricket. Whenever time permits, she comes along to watch my games. She remembers to sign me up for my club registration, makes sure my gear is in order and gets me to practices. Dad teaches me so much about the game, but I would never get on the field in the first place if it wasn't for Mum's tireless support and hard work.

Dad has an unshakeable sense of ethics in cricket. Although there are no rights and wrongs in how to bat, he believes firmly that there are rights and wrongs in how to treat kids. Sometimes that means things will go my way, sometimes not.

It's in a 40-overs-a-side under-13s game at Smithfield that I make my first hundred. When I come off, feeling pretty pleased with myself, Dad says, 'You'll be 12th man next week.'

I'm indignant. 'What? Nobody gets dropped after scoring a hundred!'

'Well, you are.'

I think I can call his bluff. 'Well, I'm not coming to the next game.'

'That's okay. If you are not ready in your gear at 7 am next Saturday, you have played your last game for the year.'

He's not bluffing. I am, and he's called me. Next Saturday, I'm awake at 5 am as usual, in my whites, hoping for a game, but I will be 12th man because of Dad's belief that everyone should have a go.

Dad will even step in when he is not the coach, if he thinks there's something unfair going on. One day, it's a rep trial against a struggling Canterbury team, and my partner and I have made a big stand. I'm about 80 and my partner has scored a century when Dad steps in, telling the coach that we should be retired. He can't see any point in any batsman, be it his son or anyone else, piling up runs while other kids don't get a bat.

Dad hates getting involved in cricket politics; he's almost allergic to it. When he and Pop come to my games, they sit away from the other parents, because they don't even want to hear the chatter. But Dad's sense of fairness sometimes overrides everything else. He never wants to step in on my side, but if the injustice is great enough, he will.

I am only eight years old when we have our first taste of cricket politics. Dad takes me to sign up for an under-10s trial at Smithfield and sends me to the club secretary, Sue. She tells me, 'Preference will be given to the older boys.' I promptly burst into tears. When I mope back to Dad and he asks what's wrong, I say, 'The lady said I was too young.'

Dad goes to her and says, 'Why not just let him try out and see how he goes?' She sends him on his way. Dad is prepared to accept that, until the coach comes running over.

'Michael, pad up and come and have a hit.'

I'm still wiping the tears from my eyes when I get my gear on. I have a bat and make the team. Dad doesn't think I should get any sympathy from crying, and he isn't one to step up and complain whenever I am upset. The opposite, in fact: he never seeks favourable treatment for me. But this time, he just thought it was unfair to not give a kid a chance.

Another time his sense of justice overrides his distaste for cricket politics is when I don't get chosen in an under-13s rep team. A meeting is called, but the coach maintains that my form isn't good enough. Dad is willing to accept that (even if I'm not!), but as we're walking away, the under-15s rep coach, Gary Stasson, comes over and says, 'I can't see why he's not in the under-13s, but we'd love to have him in the under-15s.'

Dad won't have that. It's nothing to do with me. His problem, he tells Gary, is that 'You've already picked the under-15s. It wouldn't be right for someone who's been picked to miss out now because of Michael coming in.'

Gary has an answer. 'Les, how about I get approval from the other players and parents?'

'Well, only if it's 100 per cent. If it's not, Michael won't play.'

It turns out that all the under-15s and their parents want me to play, so that's how I get a rep game that year.

Values mean everything to Dad, and that's the way he and Mum bring me up: values like honesty and fairness and treating people as they come. He and Mum don't play favourites between Leanne and me. As I grow up and begin to achieve promising things in cricket, there is never a sense in the family that I'm the golden child and get preferential treatment. The most lenient they'll get is that, say, in the middle of a cricket match, I won't get into serious trouble (they'll save that until later). Otherwise, I'm to be treated no differently from my sister.

Dad will take my side in an argument *only* when it's the right thing to do. When I'm nine, I fill in when a player hasn't turned up for an indoor cricket game at the centre. An opponent fronts up to Dad and complains about paying seven dollars to play against a kid.

'Just see how you go,' Dad says.

After the game, the man comes up and says, 'Bloody hell, where'd he come from? He's the best player out there.'

I don't really remember being the best player in most sides I was in, because I was among so many older kids, a lot of whom I looked up to as my superiors. Steve Phillips, Andrew Stasson, Trent Croft, Tony Johnson, Mark Long and Michael McNamara were all older than me and, I thought, more naturally talented.

I didn't have any feeling that Dad regarded my talent as putting me on a pedestal, but now and again something would slip out that showed he had a high opinion of me. In the summer when he came back and played B-grade with me, Dad and I were batting together and both copping some sledging. Dad had a shot back at them for sledging a 13-year-old. When he got out, he said to the opposition captain, 'I'm not your biggest worry – it's the 13-year-old who's caning you who's your big worry.'

After I scored about 90, the opposition captain came up and apologised and said to Dad, 'What a cricketer your boy is.'

What Dad did appreciate was how seriously I took my cricket. I dressed the part, took care of my gear, placed high expectations on myself and hated it when other kids mucked around at training. I whinged if I didn't get a bat in the nets, which Dad tried to stop me doing, even if it only confirmed in his mind how much I was putting into the game. But there were limits: it was only a game. After we won a D-grade game on first innings, I badgered the captain, Paul 'Uncle Chunk' Lulham, to send the opposition back in so we could go for the outright win. Uncle Chunk wanted to go and watch Dad's game and have a beer. I lost that one, and was not happy about it. I was 12!

I became more disciplined in my late teens, after that extreme smart-arse period. I still hung out with my older mates, but began to realise that if I wanted to achieve my goals, I had to put cricket first. The boys would be all set to go out in Cronulla on a Saturday night. I'd say, 'Dad, can you come pick me up and take me home by 8 pm?'

'It's 7 pm now and you haven't even gone out yet.'

'Oh, okay. I won't go then.'

When Dad saw me prove my commitment, he responded by putting more time into my development. He taught me so much about batting. A problem for me, when I was little, was when spinners would lob the ball up and I would charge out to hit it. The ball would bounce on the synthetic pitch and go clean over my head, and I'd be stumped. So Dad drilled me with lobs, saying I had to run down the wicket and get to them on the full. We did hour after hour of that. If I became a good player of spin, it was due to those drills with Dad. The next season, I went down the wicket to the spinners all the time, and didn't get stumped once.

He had great ideas on how to teach young kids about playing fast bowling. The faster they bowled, the more I liked it, but I was no different from any kid in that I hated getting hit by a short-pitched cricket ball. So that it wouldn't affect my technique, Dad took me to the nets with a tennis ball and sent down bouncer after bouncer so that I could learn to play them without the fear of hurting myself. Then he stepped it up to indoor cricket balls, which hurt a little more than a tennis ball, but not as much as a cricket ball. By the end, I was as ready for short-pitched bowling as I was ever going to be.

At the end of each day at Liverpool Boys' High School, I am itching to get home. If the bus isn't going to come soon enough, I will run. I never want to wait for anything. I'll do my homework and then race off to the indoor centre, or to Schell Park for practice. On winter weekends I play rugby league. All sports have my interest, but cricket is steadily asserting itself as my number one.

The best thing about advancing in junior cricket is the gear. When I make the Metropolitan South West Regional Sydney team, I am awarded a green hoodie. It is the first hoodie I've owned and I live in it. Even in 30-degree heat, I am so proud of that hoodie I won't take it off. Selected for the NSWPSSA (New South Wales Public Schools Sports Association) team, I get a whole tracksuit. We don't have high-priced material possessions as a family, so I love any free gear: I even treasure the socks I get for being in a rep team.

One part of cricket I am not good at is losing. I sometimes cry when my team loses, and am absolutely shattered for days afterwards. But Dad instils in me that losing and failing are part of the game. Somebody has to succeed, so that means somebody else has to miss out. 'You try to win,' he says, 'but you're not always going to.' I can't come to terms with that at all. I think, *I've trained three times this week – how did I get a duck?* I've put the work in, I have the talent, and so I deserve a big score. Failure isn't just disappointing, it doesn't make sense to me (and somewhere deep down, it probably never will). I understand that there has to be a loser. I just don't understand why it ever has to be me.

What keeps my feet on the ground is playing so often among boys and men who are bigger and older and better than I am. Up to the age of 16, I play in junior teams as a batsman who also bowls medium pace; but I also play in men's teams as a spin bowler who bats down the order. I dream of being a swashbuckling batsman, like my hero Michael Slater, who bursts into the Australian team when I am 12 and captures my imagination with his positive, all-out attack on any bowling. But when I try to belt the ball against adult bowlers, it barely trickles to the edge of the square.

When I am 13, I get picked in Western Suburbs' A.W. Green Shield team, an under-16s competition that introduces me to turf wickets on first-grade grounds, getting changed in the first-graders' changing rooms, playing all-day limited-overs games against the other clubs, and being officiated by properly uniformed umpires, often first-grade level themselves. To me, the 16-year-olds are as big and tough as men, and I play as a left-arm orthodox spin bowler and number nine batsman. Again, the gear is foremost in my mind. In my first Green Shield season, Dad buys me a pair of Puma Sheffields – real cricket boots with spikes – making that Christmas a new contender for greatest day of my life.

My role is similar in first grade for Wests, which I make at age 16. My job as a batsman is to stick around at one end so my teammates can score runs at the other. I remember playing Sutherland at Caringbah Oval in my first season. Stuart Clark, not yet in the New South Wales and Australian teams but on his way up, is bowling, and he looms like a man mountain. He is bouncing me and sledging me and I am absolutely terrified. I think I make 20 off about 150 balls, but the defensive technique that Dad and Neil have taught me holds fast, and my partners are able to add some valuable runs.

Of all the major graduations of a career in cricket – club to state, state to international – I have no doubt that the most difficult is from boys to men: from under-12s to subdistrict, and from Green Shield and school cricket to grade. I was so short and lean, all of my scoring was through fine leg and third man, deflections behind the wicket. I was very determined not to get out, and to stand up to the verbal fire and belittling that sometimes came from the men.

Even with all my limitations, I was now determined to be a batsman, not a bowler. When I was 17, with Neil's advice and support, I asked the Western Suburbs first-grade captain to consider me only as a batsman. The selectors dropped me back to second grade, and I earned back my place in first grade with runs. I gained more strength and size as puberty kicked in, and the range of my strokeplay increased. My power was still on the off side, except for a pull shot to the short ball. I didn't hit much off my pads or through mid-on. Instead, I waited on the ball that gave me a bit of space outside the off stump and sliced it between cover and third man. If the bowlers pitched it fuller, I could cover-drive it, which was my most elegant shot.

I was still quite limited, and in fact remained that way right through until I was playing for Australia. I remember once, playing for New South Wales against Tasmania, carving my first two balls over backward point for six, just swinging hard through that area. It showed that my small-boy habits had never really left me. It's amazing to think that I had so much to learn when I began playing Test cricket for Australia, and was still coming to grips with how to play the game while I was in the international spotlight.

The dream to get there crystallises one day when I'm in the car with Dad. I'm 14 years old and have just played my first full day of grade cricket, for Western Suburbs fifths at Blick Oval in Ashfield. I am so tired I fall asleep in the car on the way home, but then I sit bolt upright and say, 'Dad, have you got a pen?'

I scratch away on a pad all the way home.

'What are you doing there?' Dad says as he pulls into the driveway.

'Writing down my goals.'

'So what have you written?'

'Play first grade by 16, New South Wales by 18, and then Australia by 20.'

It's the only formal goal-setting I ever do.

Mum and Dad would have noticed that 'Do my Higher School Certificate' and 'Get a good job' are not on my list. Mum is very strict about me doing my homework, not getting in trouble, and not missing school days because of cricket. Leanne is a better student, and Mum and Dad don't want either of us to leave school without a job. Leanne, who started high school at Liverpool Girls', will switch to Westfield Sports High School in year 11, study hard, get her Higher School Certificate and become a school teacher. My path isn't as studious.

I can't remember exactly the way it happened, but one of the kids at Liverpool Boys' High gets stabbed one day in the quadrangle. With everyone else, I am sent home that day. Only, I don't ever go back. I tell Mum that if a boy could get picked on like that, then I wouldn't feel safe. Mum and Dad decide that I would be better off at Westfield Sports High School, where I start halfway through year 8.

It's one of the most traumatic changes I've been through. For months, I am pining for my old life with my mates at Liverpool Boys' and regretting the decision to leave. Gang attacks aside, life was easy there, and a group of us had known each other since primary school. I really didn't want to leave a school where I was comfortably cruising through classes. I care a huge deal about my sport, and classes are like downtime. I was in a comfort zone at Liverpool Boys', and trusted my mates.

At Westfield, it is very different. I have to front up in long pants, a collared shirt and tie, which is strictly enforced compared with the more casual uniform of Liverpool Boys'. Westfield is a co-ed school, and maybe because standards are higher and there are girls, it's competitive in every aspect. I struggle to come to terms with that, and don't do well in my schoolwork. On the upside, cricket is a subject – I can have a double period of it during school hours, and it's treated as importantly as if it's maths or English. Or more importantly to me, anyway.

When Leanne transfers to Westfield from Liverpool Girls' High, netball is her main sport, though she's also excellent at swimming, softball, cycling and running. She's naturally gifted at pretty much any sport she tries. It's great to have her around, but she finishes her HSC when I'm in year 10, and goes to train to be a primary school teacher and involve herself in competitive triathlons. At 20, she is seriously injured when she's knocked off her bike by a car while training, and has to move back home. After she gets better, she leaves to travel to South Africa; it's the first lengthy period we will spend apart, and the separation is a wrench for both of us.

I get my first chance to go overseas on a New South Wales Schoolboys cricket trip to Britain. It's hugely enjoyable. As usual, I'm the youngster in a group of older boys, and am separated from them not only by age but by the fact that some of them are above the legal drinking age. When we go to Cupar in Scotland, some of us are billeted by the opposition captain, who is an adult. We all think he's the best bloke in the world for his warm and cheerful hospitality. Sure enough, he takes some of the boys out, gets them drunk, and they are terrible the next day as they try to play through their hangovers. Everyone still thinks he's the best bloke in the world.

My favourite part of that trip is the appearance of a surprise visitor. During the early games, I phone Dad every day, whether he's at home or at the indoor centre working, to tell him in breathless detail about the cricket. Dad has always driven around with me to schoolboy and rep games, wherever they are in New South Wales, and while I'm in Britain I miss him big-time. When we're out on the field at a game in Manchester, one of the other boys points to the edge of the field and says to me, 'That looks like your dad.'

'No,' I say. 'Dad's at work.' I'm thinking about where he was on our last phone call, and where he's likely to be on a Friday evening.

But when I come off the field, I can't believe my eyes: it *is* him. He got himself a passport, he joined the Youth Hostels Association, and he's going to backpack around England following the tour. I couldn't be happier. His presence even gives me a kind of false assurance when I get into trouble.

The problem begins when I go out one day and get my head shaved – completely. I don't know why, it just seems a good idea at the time. Before long, some of the other boys also shave their heads, and the hierarchy aren't happy with our new look. They identify me as the ringleader and talk about sending me home. Cheeky as ever, I say, 'That's okay; if you cut me from the tour, I'll just go on a backpacking holiday with my dad.' I'm fortunate not to be punished – for my back-chatting as much as my haircut – and the tour goes on.

Halfway through year 11, I leave Westfield to devote myself to cricket full-time. I have the confidence from doing well in representative teams, and playing cricket is all I want to do. There's a fair bit of angst in the family about my not doing my HSC, and Mum and Dad say, 'You can leave school, but you have to get a job. We're not going to have you do nothing.' I think of saying, *But being a cricketer is a job.* They mean a job where you get paid a wage. So Neil helps me get a position at Kingsgrove Sports Centre, a 45-minute drive from home, where I do mail order, sales, and other clerical tasks during work hours. From 6 am to 8 am, I do fitness or skills training with Neil, and then at 3.30 in the afternoon, I head off to Pratten Park to train with Western Suburbs. It's all I need. Education? After I leave school, my further education consists of enrolling in a course at Liverpool TAFE while I'm working at Kingsgrove. Just enrolling. I walk into the TAFE and can't find the classroom I'm meant to be in. I turn around and go home. That's it.

Not having the foundations of an HSC or a well-paying job doesn't worry me. I am determined to earn my own way in life through cricket. My nature is materialistic: I like *things*; I've known that about myself since I was a very young child sitting outside Payless Shoes refusing to let Mum buy me the cheapest ones.

What I also know is self-reliance. At Kingsgrove Sports Centre, I'm paid $168 a week. I pay my parents $50 in board. I get my driver's licence, not without some comical moments with Leanne, my first 'instructor'. We're in Dad's big white Ford Falcon driving down a wide straight road . . . at 15 km/h, because I'm petrified of hitting parked cars. Things soon change and I turn into a bit of a petrolhead. I save up $1800 to buy my first car, a dark-green 1981 Holden Gemini. It's as old as me, but I can't bear it being dirty, so I wash and vacuum it every week. I pay $30 a week for petrol.

When I get my first New South Wales contract, Mum uses her skills from the Commonwealth Bank to put me on a budget. She sets up my bank account and puts in $500 a week. I'm quite frugal, so some weeks I save $40 or $50. The next week, I look in my account and expect to see $540 or $550, my savings plus the next $500. But all Mum has done is top it up to $500. I complain to her, and when that comes to nothing I complain to Dad, but that's the way it is.

To this day, Mum still takes care of my bookkeeping. It's a nice way for us to have regular conversations. The good thing about it is, we've always been able to separate business from family. We'll talk about work, and then stop and agree that now we're talking as mother and son.

When I reached my thirties, I did wonder if it would have been a good thing to finish my HSC. I never needed that formal qualification to get where I got to in cricket, but once you're playing for Australia you need an education. To know how many runs you need in a tight one-dayer, for example, you need maths! When I was young, my mathematical talent went into memorising exactly how many runs I was on in games when there wasn't a scoreboard. But seriously, there is a great need for being educated, whether it's public speaking or writing or the thousand other things that you're required to do when you're an international cricketer.

When more commercial opportunities arose, at a time when personal management was becoming a bigger part of sport, everyone was telling me I needed a manager. I first went to the guy I trusted most, Neil, and eventually he said I was becoming too busy for someone of his experience, so he introduced me to Chris White of the management firm International Quarterback. My first management agreement, with Neil, kind of set the tone. Dad had wanted to follow Rod Marsh's advice, which was 'No one will look after your son better than you will.' But around the time I was in the Australian under-19s squad, I signed an agreement with Neil, who was mentoring me on and off the field. Neil was excellent with batting technique and also insulating me so I could concentrate: he was good at telling people, 'Don't talk to Michael now, his head's in his cricket, he won't hear you.' I trusted Neil with my life.

Eventually, he said that I needed more professional management, and I went to Chris, a great guy for whom I have great affection and respect. He was like a second father to me. I was with him for five years before I moved to SEL (Sports & Entertainment Limited), a firm with greater international reach, run by James Erskine, before eventually coming around to Rod Marsh's initial view, which was that nobody could ever be as protective of you as you are of yourself, and at 31 years old I became self-managed. This was all part of growing up, becoming an adult, while I was learning to play cricket and being captain of Australia.

I don't regret not doing my HSC, because I was chasing my dream. If I was reliving my life, I would do the same. But I hate failing to complete something I have started, and when I'm talking to youngsters now I encourage them to finish their education. Finishing secondary school may or may not change the direction of your life – it wouldn't have put me in a different place – but a formal education is something you appreciate more and more when you don't have one.

Instead of school, I spend what would have been year 11 at the Australian Cricket Academy in Adelaide.

My initial entry into the academy is, as so often happens, a matter of good fortune. I am playing an under-17s game in Adelaide when Rod Marsh and Wayne Phillips, the two top coaches at the academy, come to watch another batsman. It turns out that this other boy gets injured, and I'm moved up the order. The boy they wanted to see doesn't get to bat that day, but I play through until stumps. The next morning, Rod and Wayne come back for another chance to watch the other boy, who, having recovered from his injury, ends up batting but missing out. I bat on through the morning. Rod stays to watch me, and the outcome is an invitation to spend a two-week stint at the academy, which leads to my getting a full scholarship for the next year.

Leaving Liverpool is tough. I'm so gutted about leaving my family and friends, and anxious about flying. But I get used to travelling. The year I'm meant to do my HSC, I go with an Australian under-19s side to England. My teammates include Adam Voges, Mitchell Johnson, Nathan Hauritz and Michael Klinger, and at Chester-le-Street I get into a big partnership with the future Tasmanian Sheffield Shield player Sean Clingeleffer.

It's the lead-in to a breakthrough season back home when I'm 18 years old. I score three hundreds in a row against state Second XI sides, and get picked for New South Wales. My first game is against the touring Indian team, and I manage to put on nearly 50 as the junior partner in the first innings with Brad Haddin. A week later, my first Sheffield Shield innings is a disappointment – bowled by Damien Wright for six against Tasmania at the SCG – but I atone with a half-century in the second innings, the first of four fifties in that season, batting at number six or seven.

I shuttle back and forward to the Australian under-19s, going to Sri Lanka for the under-19s World Cup (along with future Test teammates Mitch Johnson, Shane Watson, Shaun Marsh, Nathan Hauritz, Andrew McDonald and Ed Cowan), but I'm itching to get back into Shield cricket.

Throughout my first years at New South Wales, my family are always behind me. Leanne, though she doesn't have much patience for sitting and watching cricket, tries to come and watch when she can, and every game, whether she's there or not, she sends a message with her love and support. That will continue without fail until the end of my career. Mum and Dad attend as often as their work will allow. Dad, of course, loves all cricket, but it's more of a challenge for Mum and Leanne. At one of my early Shield games, they're sitting in the SCG Members Stand waiting for me to bat. Michael Bevan is playing a customary big innings, and one of my family says, a little too loudly, 'I wish Bevan would get out so that we can see Michael.' Someone hears, the comment gets back to me, and I have to come out to the family and tell them that it's not the right thing to hope our most productive batsman gets out just so they can see me. They might think it, but they can't say it!

My heart is in my mouth to be playing alongside international representatives such as Bevo, Steve and Mark Waugh, Brett and Shane Lee, Stuart MacGill, Glenn McGrath and Gavin Robertson. My idol growing up was always Michael Slater, and it's amazing to be in a team with him. Graciously, he doesn't mind having this 18-year-old following him around watching everything he does, and he is always brilliant to me. Steve 'Stumper' Rixon is a hard but fair head coach, a terrific old-school mentor who gives my skills a great boost. I always like being around Stumper, even when he's showing his tough side. One day, I'm doing slips catching practice with Steve and Mark Waugh. Stumper nicks 20 or 30 balls and the twins wander off, happy with the way they're catching it. I, of course, tag along after them.

'Eh! Where do you think you're going?' Stumper's still there with his bat in hand, glowering at me.

'Um, I thought we were finished?'

'Those two are finished. You're staying on for more.'

In those circumstances, you gravitate towards other players who are your age and experience. My closest friends in the team initially are Mark Higgs and the new wicket-keeper from Queanbeyan, Brad Haddin, who is stepping into the big shoes left by former state captain and 11-year New South Wales incumbent Phil Emery.

Hadds, a couple of years older than me, is my next 'big brother' figure in cricket. We train together in our fitness work, our families get on well, with his father being as much of a cricket nut as my dad, and when the team goes out at night, Hadds looks after me by making sure I can come home to the house in Abbotsford, in the inner west, that he shares with Higgsy and opening batsman Greg Mail, rather than me going all the way to Liverpool or Chipping Norton late at night. Where I really click with Hadds is in how serious and ambitious we both are about our cricket. He is meticulous about planning the steps in his career. He has moved from the Australian Capital Territory to New South Wales to capitalise on Emery's retirement, and, being a wicketkeeper, competing with a lot of other class players for one spot in a team, he knows he has to be strategic. Adam Gilchrist has just stepped up into the Australian Test team this season, replacing Ian Healy, so Hadds knows that he might have a long wait to get to the top. But he has a clear plan to entrench himself for New South Wales and be the next cab off the rank when Gilly gets hurt or retires.

Compared with Hadds, I'm pretty simple. I don't strategise or analyse it. I want to play for Australia, and I want to do it yesterday.

4

THE BAGGY GREEN

While I still think that the toughest transition in my cricket life was from playing against boys to playing against men, that's not to say that any step up was easy. In my first two seasons for New South Wales, I averaged less than 30 and made one hundred in 22 innings. I was lucky to be a teenager; the selectors wouldn't have been so patient with that kind of output from an older player. I grew more comfortable at that level over the next two seasons, and my 2004 winter with Hampshire was a great finishing school for my technique and professionalism.

But I was not a dominant first-class cricketer when I was selected for the Australian tour of India in 2004. My batting average was still in the 30s. It was commented, probably correctly, that I was a beneficiary of the fact that the Test team had a lot of mature and veteran players heading towards the last phase of their careers, and there was not a glut of batsmen in their early twenties making big scores in the Sheffield Shield. I was picked not on weight of runs, but because I was young enough to offer scope for long-term development.

Ever since I had made under-age rep teams and seen others, more talented than me, fall by the wayside, I had often wondered what the main difference was between those who made it to higher levels and those who didn't. Sometimes the latter group didn't really want to, sometimes they found it hard to cope with the travel, sometimes the psychological toughness of serious cricket got too much, sometimes there were family reasons.

In fact, there was a different set of reasons for every person, but if I had to boil down what made me different, I would say it was my all-consuming love of the game. I loved it more than the guy who wanted to have coffee with his girlfriend. I loved it more than the guy who had a late night out and backed himself to be right by the morning. I always put cricket first. If I could have played cricket 24/7, I would have. I just wanted to win, score runs, take wickets, get a run-out.

I loved the social side of being in a cricket team. Whenever I joined a new team going up through the levels, my team-mates became my best mates, and whoever was on a tour with me, they were my best mates at that time. Nothing – *nothing* – was as much fun as playing cricket.

From the time of my first tour with Australia, to the West Indies in 2003, I came into that group with the same attitude as if it was a schoolboys tour, an under-19s tour, or a New South Wales tour. As an excited kid, I was a sponge to all the influences around me. I got my chance to go to the Caribbean in early 2003 because Damien Martyn had broken his thumb in the World Cup in South Africa, which the boys won. The Test component would be Steve Waugh's last overseas tour as captain, and it was an honour to be part of that.

As the spare batsman for the first-class and Test segment, I was hoping to be picked in the one-dayers that would follow. Accordingly, I wasn't at my fittest when we flew into Guyana for the lead-up to the first Test match; the Blues had won the Pura Milk Cup (the Sheffield Shield), and my preparation had consisted of two weeks of celebrating. I wasn't expecting to play more than one tour game for my first three weeks or so in the Caribbean.

Having just landed from Australia, I was walking with a driver towards the car waiting at the terminal in George-town. As I got in, a familiar face came up. 'Are you heading to the team hotel? Can I have a lift?'

I was tongue-tied. Here, talking to me, was one of the two heroes I'd had on the posters on my bedroom wall growing up: it was Brian Lara.

It turned out that Brian thought I was a journalist trav-elling with the Australian team. I told him I was a player, and that was the start of our friendship.

Brian had always been my favourite player. He could perform in any conditions, any country, and he led by example in West Indies cricket when they were struggling.

When I was 18, he had almost single-handedly taken the Frank Worrell Trophy from Australia, winning Test matches with his 213 in Jamaica and 153 not out in Barbados before blitzing another hundred in Antigua. If I had a choice as a cricket fan, I would have liked to see Australia win but Brian make runs. I loved his one-of-a-kind style and his ability to find success anywhere in the world, no matter how difficult the conditions.

He was so friendly to me in that taxi, talking to me candidly, as if we were equals. Before we left Guyana, he invited me to come to his house when the tour moved on to his home country of Trinidad. I don't know why he was so welcoming to this excitable kid, but we just hit it off.

It was a tour I really enjoyed. After being a spectator during our team's exciting Test series win, I got my chance in 50-over cricket and remained not out in my first three games, all of which we won. My first dismissal in one-day international cricket was in Port-of-Spain, off Merv Dillon – caught by Brian Lara. Off the field, I went to Brian's home and met his young daughter Sydney, named after the ground where he made his first Test century, his epic 277 which I had watched on TV when I was 11 years old.

The nightlife was fun at a time before the routines of recovery took over cricket. It was a culture of post-game celebration: drink at the ground, go to the hotel and change, go out to a bar or restaurant. Every one-dayer, the grounds were packed. There were blow-up pools, and crowds drinking all day and making it very clear they wanted and expected the West Indies to win. I liked the West Indies people, got on with their players, and learnt how to accept that things would happen in their own time and there was no point getting stressed. The older guys told me that if I let my natural impatience get the best of me, I would have a bad tour, so their example helped me settle down.

The education I was getting from the senior players was as diverse as their personalities. With Damien Martyn, the West Australian number four batsman who was as laconic off the field as he was stylish on it, one of my first deep cricket conversations was about how nervous I got while waiting to bat. I got so worried about it, I said to Marto, 'Will it get better?' Always one to defuse the tension with his unique dry humour, Marto said, 'No, it'll get worse and worse. When you're past 30, the media will be onto you every time you fail, saying you're under pressure and will get dropped. So don't look forward to it getting any better.'

Fast bowler Jason Gillespie was another with humorous advice. In India, as we battled the routine outbreaks of 'Delhi belly', Dizzy stated with complete assurance that the only medication that worked was six 'Sters' (cans of Fosters) a night. Nothing else worked, according to him. But Dizzy had his own approach to cricket, and the centre of which was not to get too worked up about anything.

Others gave me most through their example. Justin Langer and Ricky Ponting were batting nerds and workaholics. No detail was too small for either of them. Whenever Justin wanted to work on a mental problem, he would attack it with a boxing or other kind of fitness session.

Lang showed me how physical fitness really mattered for batting. Ricky showed me more on the skills side. He hit more balls than any other player, and after his net sessions would go to have dozens of throwdowns to iron out a particular bug in his batting system.

These top-order batting greats were all at their peak when I came into the Australian team, and I wanted to soak up everything I could learn from them. In their own ways, they were all obsessive technicians of the game.

Matthew Hayden taught me about playing straight at the Gabba and WACA where it was so hard to drive early. 'Play straight or horizontal,' he said, 'nothing in between.'

While Lang and Ricky responded to any challenge with the mantra of 'work harder', the Queenslander Haydos was more cerebral. When things got tough for me, he pulled me aside and said, 'If you keep telling yourself you get the bad decisions or the good ball, it's not going to change. You've got to be more positive. What you say out loud generally happens, it becomes self-fulfilling.' It was great advice.

Adam Gilchrist was the best vice-captain I've ever played with, teaching me that you don't have to be a captain to be a leader around the group. When he got the opportunity to be captain, as he was in my first one-day international and my first Test match, he was also top-class. I enjoyed batting with him, he was so positive, and put on a lot of runs with him. At this stage of his career, he was a legend of the game already, having changed the role of wicketkeeper into a dynamic all-rounder who could win matches with his bat.

The bowlers were all great mentors in their different ways. I got on extremely well with Brett Lee, being a fellow New South Wales boy, and we spent a fair bit of time together off the field. Also Andrew Bichel, who was often twelfth man, but was the ultimate team player, putting aside his disappointment to go the extra mile for the other guys. Glenn McGrath was amazing. I said to Pigeon in those early days, 'If I can face you, Dizzy and Binga in the nets, then I can face any bowler in the world. Can you do me a favour and bowl to me in the nets exactly as you would in a game?' Not only did Pigeon do that, but he would talk me through his thought processes of how he was trying to get me out. Funnily enough, his first ball to me was always a bouncer. Sometimes I wouldn't be in the mood, or I'd be rusty, and he'd send one whistling past my ears. When I looked up, Pigeon would be grinning away.

I was absorbed into the Australian set-up via one-day cricket. Aside from its intrinsic benefits, the one-day game provided a great pathway for someone like me, who was not yet seasoned enough for Test cricket, to become more comfortable in a changing room stacked with superstars of the game. We went on tours to India in the spring of 2003 and Sri Lanka in autumn 2004, on either side of the home summer, when I was a regular in the triangular series against India and Zimbabwe.

I batted down the order, with a brief to chip in some handy runs late in the innings and supply energy with my fielding and occasional bowling. It was a blast to train with such outstanding fielders as Andrew Symonds and Ricky

Ponting. Leaving aside their obvious skills as batsmen, Symmo and Punter were the two best fieldsmen of their generation. We competed against each other in drills, each of us trying to win our little contests, and thanks to fielding coach Mike Young, always raising our standards through those internal battles.

In May 2004, we had a three-match one-day tour to Zimbabwe. The planned Tests had been called off for security reasons, and we spent the entire time in the capital, Harare, where we weren't allowed to leave our hotel. The dry, wisecracking Queenslander Jimmy Maher made a typically funny quip when our bus was driving down a street called Robert Mugabe Way in Harare. 'That'd have to be a one-way street, wouldn't it?' said Mahbo.

After a year in the middle order, I got my chance to open the batting when Matthew Hayden was rested for the final game. I made my first hundred for Australia, opening with Adam Gilchrist, putting on a big partnership with Symmo, and bringing home the win in a partnership with my Australian under-19s teammate Shane Watson.

The great thing about being in the Australian one-day team was that, even though it was a separate entity from the Test team, who were just about unbeatable at that time, it also had a winning culture. We took a lot of pride in our performance and set out to win every series and produce consistent performances. I couldn't think of a better apprenticeship before my entry into Test cricket.

THE INNINGS

151 versus India, Bangalore, 2004

I've been too busy to think about the magnitude of what's happening to me. As soon as I found out this week that I am playing my first Test match for Australia, I've been organising how to get Mum and Dad, Nan and Pop, and Neil to Bangalore from Sydney. There have been flights, ground transport and hotels to book from here; I've been too busy to get overwhelmed by nerves.

I'm loving India this time. It's my third trip here. When I came on a youth tour, I actually didn't learn much, to be honest, facing spin on crumbling, badly-prepared wickets with surfaces like crusts of bread. I learnt more by facing throwdowns on grass at the SCG – where you got spin, bounce and pace – than on those dustbowls. But the first-class and Test wickets are a different matter: much firmer and more consistent. Compared with the youth tour, in fact, nothing is the same – we stay in different hotels, eat different food, and play in front of big, joyful crowds. Most days I'm thinking,

This is nice, I'm not eating hot chips on bread for lunch and dinner like I did on my first tour!

Once I know I've been picked for this Test match, I am focused on repaying the selectors' faith. I know I'm lucky to be here. Punter has a broken thumb, which is going to rule him out of at least the First Test. Brad Hodge and I both batted for the vacancy in the tour match at Mumbai, and I got run out for 10 in the first innings before making a fifty in the second. My career first-class average is under 40. Hodgy's record is much more substantial than mine. I know I haven't produced a compelling case for selection and they've taken a bit of a punt on me. Talk about big shoes to fill: I'm only replacing our captain, the best Australian batsman I have ever seen, a guy everyone looks up to when he's here and misses when he's not, and who is devastated at being kept out of this, his first big series as Test captain. No pressure.

There is massive hype and expectation around this series. Australia hasn't won a Test series in India since 1969–70. Even the great teams led by Mark Taylor and Steve Waugh couldn't win here. For the senior players around me – most of the team were here in 2001 when they had their hearts broken by V.V.S. Laxman, Rahul Dravid and Harbhajan Singh – this tour feels like a mission, one last chance to conquer that final frontier. The preparations have been thorough, the stage is set.

On match morning, it's sunny and warm. Mum, Dad, Nan, Pop and Neil are safely in the stand. During the warm-ups, Dad has to fight his way to the fence to talk to me, battling to persuade security that he is my father.

Shane Warne presents me with my Test cap. It's an incredible buzz to get the cap off him, and not only because he is the greatest bowler in the game. Since I have joined the team, I have felt that while I am mates with everybody, I'm best mates with Warney. He has really singled me out. Whether it's for a chat about cricket or life advice, Warney's door is always open for me. I will go out with any of the guys, but when it comes to him, there is a special connection.

Presenting me with my cap, he says a few words encouraging me to continue playing the way I have played to get here. It all passes in a blur. I actually want to play a lot better than I have played to get here.

After Gilly wins the toss, we have a steady morning before wickets begin to fall in the afternoon session. I am so pumped about getting my baggy green, so excited about the opportunity, that as I sit in the grandstand I'm almost wanting someone to get out, so that I can have my turn. It's not that I really do want a wicket to fall, but I want to bat so much that I'm jumping out of my skin.

Justin Langer, Damien Martyn and Darren Lehmann all lose their wickets in a clump around the middle of the day, and in the 48th over I'm walking out to bat, replacing Boof. Simon Katich, the West Australian left-hander who has slotted into the retired Steve Waugh's number five position, is at the other end. I can't hear what he says to me. The bowler is Anil Kumble. Boof's wicket was Anil's 399th in Test cricket, and there's a lot of noise: the crowd is winding up for a celebration. I have only ever faced Kumble once before – five years ago, in my first ever first-class match at the SCG, when he got me out for not many.

It's impossible to prepare adequately for Kumble. He is not only a great bowler, but he has a unique kind of delivery, high and looping and fast for a leg-spinner, using a lot of topspin. I've been looking at footage and getting fast leg-cutters thrown at me, but he's so unusual, there's a lot I will have to learn in the middle.

First ball, everything in my head has gone quiet. I lunge forward and almost smother the ball, I'm so anxious. It's a wrong'un which bounces up past my inside edge onto my pad and gets jumbled up amid my glove and thigh. The umpire signals a no-ball.

Next ball is another wrong'un, and again I'm nervously throwing my weight forward. It hits my glove and bounces off toward gully.

'YES!'

I can't get a word out, but Kato is calling and tearing down the pitch, and I'm off the mark, second ball, not a convincing first run in Test cricket, but I'll take it.

The weather is hot, and I soon swap the helmet for my baggy green. The crowd noise in India is intense. Whereas in Australia people only tend to make a huge roar when a wicket falls or a big shot is played, here in Bangalore the noise is full-bore all the time. People are just screaming and whistling non-stop. But it stays at that background level, and I get used to it. Spinners are operating from both ends: Kumble and Harbhajan, and then the part-timer Yuvraj Singh. I get a couple of boundaries away off Kumble, and begin to breathe again. My heart rate comes down below about 150. I know Kato well from Sheffield Shield encounters, so it's comforting batting with him. It's a good wicket, with consistent bounce, and although it's turning a lot for a first day, that doesn't worry me.

As the afternoon develops, Kato and I build a partnership. Even with my nerves and excitement, I have a crystal clarity to my batting. I'm just watching the ball and reacting, and when I get a loose one I'm launching myself into it. Anything short, I'm back for the pull shot. If they're flighting it, I'm scampering down the wicket as if Dad is lobbing me a tennis ball back at Leitz Street. I hit a lot of drives in the air, backing myself to clear the fielders. By the evening session, my nerves and determination to repay the selectors have gone into the back of my head: I am batting without any fear of getting out. It's so much fun.

Sourav Ganguly, India's captain, is switching his bowlers around. The left-arm quicks, Zaheer Khan and Irfan Pathan, are on and then off. Virender Sehwag comes on for a few overs of part-time spin. I get him away for a six, and then loft another, straight down the ground, off Kumble.

Life couldn't be better than this. If I close my eyes, I'm a boy having a dream, and this is exactly what it's like. I open my eyes and see my family sitting in the grandstand. Their being here makes it real. I'm not dreaming.

Kato is bowled by Kumble for 81 an hour before stumps, and Gilly and I make it through to the end of play. The team is five for 316, and everyone in the changing room is upbeat. I am walking on air. I know I've been a bit lucky – my bad shots were either play-and-misses, or the edges flew away from the fieldsmen – but I'm as happy as can be, 76 not out and a contributor to our strong position.

With Gilly urging me to make the most of it, the second morning has a different feel. I didn't sleep much last night with the excitement of it all, and I've lost the fluency of the first afternoon. Against Zaheer and Pathan with the second ball, I play and miss and edge two fours through the slips cordon. Gilly is in great touch, however, hitting freely down the ground, which takes the pressure off.

When I'm on 92, I think I'm gone. Kumble gets one through and hits me on the pad. I look up at umpire

Billy Bowden, my throat dry. Please, please, please ... And he shakes his head, indicating that the ball was going over the top. I'm not so sure. It felt plumb.

Thirteen overs into the day, I'm on 98. Even though the paceman Pathan is bowling, I call for my baggy green cap. This is for Dad. I've promised him that if I ever played for Australia and was lucky enough to make a hundred, I would be wearing my cap when I passed the milestone. It all works out. Pathan bowls one on my pads, and I get it away for two wide of mid-on. I carry on like a dick, kissing my cap and my shirt and pointing to everyone I can see in the stands. It all pours out. I guess this doesn't happen to you every day.

Gilly gets to his hundred by crashing a couple of fours off Kumble, but after he and Warney both get out within minutes, I go on the attack and race to 150. The team score passes 450, and by now I'm mentally and physically cooked. I'm lashing at almost everything, and it's a tired drive I play at a wide ball from Zaheer that gets me out. When I feel the nick, I turn and walk off without looking at the umpire. What a day! I'm done. The innings is over ten minutes later, before McGrath rips into the Indian top order and we have an irresistible momentum. The fairytale is under way. I am having the time of my life.

The support in the Chinnaswamy Stadium is one of my favourite memories from that innings. From the middle, I can see Mum's tearful face as she stands up to cheer my hundred. My family also have some fun with the Fanatics, the Australian supporters group who occupy almost the whole of one of the stands. After I pass the hundred, the Fanatics unroll a huge banner made of thin cotton, coloured Australian gold, with the words: 'Congratulations, Pup, 100 on debut!' As they leave the ground at the end of the day, they lose the banner to a group of Indian fans who hold it up outside the gate. They retrieve the banner, and Dad ends up with it. When I get home after the tour, we have a barbecue at the D'Bartolos' house in Liverpool, and Dad pulls out the banner. It goes around the whole of their back yard and still has some metres to spare.

In Bangalore, my family are staying in the same hotel as the match officials, as it turns out, and Dad and Pop bump into Billy Bowden in the lift that night. Referring to the not-out lbw decision Billy gave me, Dad says, 'That would have been a close call.'

Billy replies, with a big smirk on his face to make clear that he is joking, 'You tell that son of yours he owes me a case of beer!'

Dad says, 'Yeah, he'd have been walking if I'd been the umpire.'

This is enough to rile up Pop, who never thinks I'm out, and he still argues long and hard to this day that the ball was missing.

THE INNINGS

141 versus New Zealand, Brisbane, 2004

During that first year in the Test team, my batting doesn't change. I am always positive, attacking, trying to take every opportunity to score. Until I get dropped in late 2005, I don't question my game. I trust everything about it.

One thing that won't change throughout my career is how I love batting on the Gabba. The extra pace and bounce of the wicket suit my game, especially in my early years when I am more of a back-foot player, with my first movement back and across rather than forward. That will change when my hamstring and back problems erode the strength in my right leg. But for now, in my first Test match on home soil, I am riding the wave of confidence that started in India.

We have only 14 days and no cricket between the end of our victorious Indian series and the beginning of the three-Test Trans-Tasman Trophy series with New Zealand. It goes without saying that I'm as excited as a puppy dog, and I arrange for Mum, Leanne and my aunt to come and watch. Dad is busy with work, but we're texting and speaking on the phone several times a day.

New Zealand make 350 over the first four sessions. The second day is beautiful and sunny and I get my chance just before stumps, joining Damien Martyn at four for 128. Parts of the Gabba are under construction, so the crowd is not big, but there's no lack of atmosphere in my head. To be representing Australia on home soil is something that I've always set myself to achieve, but it's also a complete surprise, as I know that I haven't proved myself over many years of run-making in first-class cricket, like other contenders have. I just got a fortunate opportunity in India, due to Punter's broken thumb, and I am grasping it and running with it as far as I can.

Marto and I bat for the last 20 overs of day two, and I'm 31 not out overnight. It's always a thrill to bat with him. He is a batsman I've always been in awe of, so perfectly balanced, such a crisp timer. He carried the burden of being the next big thing and was picked for Australia as a 21-year-old before spending half a decade out of the team, learning his game in Shield cricket. For the four years leading up to my debut, he has been a fixture in the Test and one-day teams and has fully realised his potential. When I came into the team, I gravitated towards him because I admired him so much, and found him to be generous in his encouragement and an easy, relaxed guy to sit and talk cricket with.

Overnight, my phone fills up with text messages from mates and family members wishing me well for tomorrow. I love being not out at the beginning of a new day, with enough runs on the board to know I can't get a duck.

On the third day, Marto and I push on until he's out for 70, so I'm again lucky enough to partner Gilly when the bowlers are getting tired. Gilly plays his cricket much as I would have expected from a distance. In just five years he has changed the game of cricket, hitting hundred after hundred in the lower middle order and winning Test matches off his own bat. As a team leader he is a perfect big brother, asking me what I'm thinking and looking out for my welfare. In the middle, he is very composed and always ready with a smile, as if it's only a back yard game. He's telling me to stay calm and focus on the next ball, but I'm in a very aggressive mood and he lets me roll, like *Okay, fine, have it your way and have some fun*. Early in the innings, most of my scoring was square of the wicket, but as I gain confidence I drive the ball more. It's a carry-over from childhood. The cover drive was always my favourite shot and my first way of scoring. I was never scared of nicking. More worried about getting out lbw, I used to stay leg-side of the ball and make my runs between cover and third man. I still bat with vestiges of that little boy's game.

I've always wanted to be like my hero Michael Slater, a swashbuckler, who once made a hundred in a session of Test cricket. I'm absolutely on top of my game at the Gabba, where it's such a great feeling when the ball hits the middle of the bat and pierces the field with an audible buzzing. I have real fearlessness in knowing what my strengths are, and also a bit of youthful confidence to see the bowler thinking, *How did he do that? That wasn't a bad ball.* Getting on top of each bowler mentally is what I love.

Having started on 31, I don't score a hundred runs in the session, but it turns into a race to get to the century mark before lunch. I'm 89 at the start of Chris Martin's final over before the break, and seven runs off the first two balls take me to 96 and off strike. I'm happy to wait until the break, but Gilly takes a single off the second-last ball. He comes down the pitch and says, 'How are you feeling?' I know what he's meaning. Am I prepared to take a risk and try to hit a boundary off the last ball before lunch? 'I'll tell you after this ball,' is all I can say.

Martin drops it short, and I get in behind it. Fortunately my pull shot comes off, and I'm able to carry on like a bit of a goose again, kissing all the parts of my equipment I can get to my mouth. Gilly's laughing. After lunch we take our partnership to 216 at about five runs an over, before I play around a flighted ball from Daniel Vettori. To ice the cake, Glenn McGrath and Jason Gillespie both make fifties, and we're on a team high as we close out the match by an innings.

It's unbelievable to do this after what happened in Bangalore. I'm told that, after Kepler Wessels in the early 1980s and Harry Graham in the 19th century, I am the third Australian to make Test hundreds on debut overseas and at home. I try to keep my head on my shoulders. I tell the press, 'Unfortunately in life some things don't go to plan. At the moment for me in Test cricket they have gone to plan, but there are going to be down times and I know that and expect that.'

I say the words, but not until I really experience those down times will I know how they really feel. The truth is that, with two hundreds in five Test matches and a series win in India under my belt, I'm flying, totally fearless, and know very little.

5

DROPPED

On the one-year anniversary of my century in my first home Test match against New Zealand, I'm sitting in the changing room at Bellerive Oval in Hobart with my face in my hands. Up to this point, it is the worst day of my life. The boys are celebrating a Test match win over the West Indies, and I want to crawl into a corner and disappear. I've been told I have lost my position for the next match.

I'm given the news by Punter. I have felt it coming, and a couple of days ago, after I missed out for the fourth time in the series, I said to Ricky, 'If I'm going to get dropped, can *you* please tell me, you are my captain and I play for you, not the selectors.'

When it happens, I say, 'Thanks for being the one to say that.'

It's not that I don't think I deserve it. Since that amazing day in Brisbane 12 months ago, I have not made another hundred for Australia. In a home Test series against Pakistan, a three-Test tour to New Zealand, an Ashes tour, a one-off Test match against an ICC XI, and the first two Tests of this Frank Worrell Trophy series, my best score was 91 at Lord's and I've only made two other fifties. That's 15 Test matches, and my time has run out.

In the middle of the changing room celebrations, I pull Punter aside.

'I don't want to dampen anyone else's night,' I say. 'Can I fly home separately tonight?'

He understands. It's happened to him too, at a similar age.

Being dropped from the Australian team feels like a public humiliation. I'm ashamed of myself.

On the flight out of Hobart, I pull my cap down low over my eyes and jam in my headphones. The TV news on the screen in the plane shows the announcement that I've been dropped. I hunch down lower. I'm so embarrassed, I don't want to show my face.

It's devastating, far worse than anyone says it's going to be. For weeks, I've been feeling that the axe was about to fall, but now that it has, there's no relief and no upside. It's not just that I haven't scored enough runs. It's that I've been my own worst enemy. For the past year, since I made the Australian team and scored those hundreds on debut in India and Brisbane, I've been inundated with sponsorship offers, media attention, all the perks that come with the tag of rising new talent. In a team full of familiar faces, the public has grown complacent with success, and I became the fresh new face to fill the vacuum. I didn't ask for it, but I haven't said no to anything either. If a sponsor has wanted me to turn up for a photo shoot, I've said yes and put off my training to another time. If a magazine wants an interview, I've said yes and reshuffled my cricket commitments around it. The 'trappings of fame' – they're called trappings for a reason.

I haven't been hardened by a lot of setbacks through my cricket life. My early seasons with New South Wales weren't easy, but I always felt I was on the up and up. I didn't have much self-doubt. When was the last time I missed out on selection? When the rep under-13s didn't pick me, and I burst into tears? I know I've been extremely fortunate, down the years, to have selectors reward me for my effort and potential. It's left me weak when finally that tap of approval is turned off. My goal has always been to strive to keep going forward, not go backwards. Getting dropped, I'm heartbroken; I am going backwards for the first time. Never having experienced such a setback before, I don't have any resistance; I haven't built up any scar tissue.

Instead of going home, when I fly in from Hobart I go to Mum and Dad's house in Caringbah. They're the two people I feel I can turn to.

'I know you're upset and I'm here to support you,' Dad says. 'You can let this go one of two ways. You can stay here and cry on our shoulder, or we can go to the nets tomorrow and start working to get you back in the Australian team.'

It happens just like that. I know I have to get out of the spotlight in order to clear my mind, reassess my priorities, and really ask myself if I want to be an Australian cricketer. For the last six to 12 months, I think I have wanted it, but I haven't acted like it's the be-all and end-all. I haven't put cricket first.

For the next four days, Dad and I practise together, just like old times. I have the option to stand aside from New South Wales's next game, against Queensland at the SCG. It's a risk: Queensland's pace bowling attack is all internationals, present and future: Michael Kasprowicz, Andy Bichel, Mitchell Johnson and Ashley Noffke. It's a better bowling attack than the West Indians against whom I couldn't get a run in the Test matches.

But I make myself available, following Dad's advice that playing is better than sitting around feeling sorry for myself. The first day we field, and the second day is washed out. It's not until lunch on the third day that I finally get in the middle with a bat in my hands, and I can't believe how natural everything feels. I end up batting six and a half hours and making 201 not out, my first double-hundred in first-class cricket. It shows me that my skills haven't disappeared. My problem has been that my mind has been caught up in so much rubbish that I've been getting in my own way.

For the rest of the 2005–06 summer, I know I won't get back in the Test team, so I set my heart on selection for the autumn tour of South Africa. The innings against Queensland and another hundred against South Australia get me in as the spare batsman. I'm also playing well enough in the shorter formats to be retained in the Australian one-day and Twenty20 teams, going on a tour of New Zealand and playing in the home triangular series, so I'm still in good form and don't feel like I've been completely cast out into the wilderness.

The big change is in my attitude. I don't break with my sponsors, but I become ruthless about putting training first, other commitments second. It's been the other way around for too long.

My road back into the Test team is full of potholes. In South Africa, the boys win the series brilliantly. They only use eleven players for the three matches, and the batting order of Langer, Hayden, Ponting, Martyn, Hussey, Symonds and Gilchrist looks set in stone – to the South African bowlers, and to someone hoping to get back in.

We go to Bangladesh on the way home, and I get a recall due to the concussion 'Alfie' Langer suffers in his 100th Test match in South Africa when he's hit on the head by Makhaya Ntini.

The Bangladesh leg is a strange tour, with the team exhausted after a long campaign, and some individuals struggling for motivation. When Warney goes wicketless for 112 runs off 20 overs in Bangladesh's first innings in the First Test at Fatullah, his body language looks like the selectors would have been better sending him straight home. Typically, though, when the match is on the line and a surprise defeat is staring us in the face, he lifts himself to take the last three wickets of Bangladesh's second innings, and Gilly and Punter get us across the line with an innings that teach me a lot about their determination and professionalism.

With scores of 19 and 9, I haven't taken my chance.

In the Second Test at Chittagong, I don't get an opportunity at all, in the most bizarre circumstances. We bowl Bangladesh out on the first day, and when Haydos gets out just before stumps, Punter sends in Jason Gillespie, our regular number ten, as night watchman. I'm so keen, I say, 'Skipper, let me be the night watchman, I'll go in!' Dizzy not only lasts till stumps on day one, but is still there at lunch on day four. He puts on 53 with Phil Jaques, 90 with Ricky, and then 320 with Mike Hussey. I'm going absolutely stir-crazy. I'm not a good waiter at the best of times, but this can't be happening. Surely Dizzy is going to get out ... No, he's not. When he finally passes his double-hundred after nearly ten hours in the middle and does his celebration routine of galloping on his bat like it's his horse, I'm the guy at the other end, getting half an hour of batting practice.

I haven't done enough to hold my place in a full-strength Test team, but my performances in one-day cricket have been consistent enough for me to be included in one-day tours to Malaysia and India and inviting me to the 'boot camp' that coach John Buchanan organises with some army personnel in bushland outside Brisbane. It's one of John's ideas to take us out of our comfort zone and bring us closer together before the 2006–07 Ashes series.

Due to Stuart MacGill suffering a knee injury and Warney's need for his 'medication' in the form of packets of cigarettes, the boot camp will become somewhat infamous in the team folklore. I have to admit that I really enjoy it. The minimalistic approach of having to turn up with nothing but two pairs of runners, three pairs of socks and three pairs of undies fits in with the way I am trying to strip all unnecessary distractions out of my life and making cricket my single priority. The pre-dawn starts suit me fine.

In attendance are the 25 players with Cricket Australia contracts and about ten support staff, and we are broken up into groups for several days of physical and mental exercises in the bush. Our group, 'Foxtrot', comprises Adam Gilchrist, Mike Hussey, Brett Lee, the IT analyst Richard McInness, and me. Due to the uneven numbers, Foxtrot has one fewer member than all the other groups, but we forge a good team spirit as we march up and down mountains, carry 20-kilo water drums, push cars uphill, overcome obstacles, sleep rough, and take a lot of punishment from the instructors. I think I surprise some of my teammates by going through five days without a shower and not complaining about being dirty.

We finish with a group heart-to-heart session about a lot of issues, including leadership, and I tell everyone that I have learnt a big lesson about the need to insulate the captain from every little worry that's going on. In the past I have had a habit of taking my cares to Ricky at every opportunity, and some of the leadership training at the camp has shown me that there is a chain of command, a group of leaders, and not everything has to go up to the captain. That structure is very much a reflection of Ricky's style. Mine, in years to come, will be different. As a captain, I will prefer everything to come through me.

I feel I get on well with John Buchanan. He is a nice guy who brings a left-field approach. He doesn't coach me in batting: I still rely on conversations with Neil and Dad, and regularly talk with Punter, Marto, Justin Langer and Matthew Hayden, the senior batsmen I admire. Within the team during that period, it's mostly the players who coach each other. I'll admit that I hate writing poems or making speeches to the boys about myself, as Buck sometimes demands of us. I wouldn't draw a firm conclusion about whether he is a good coach or a bad coach. The legends in the team are coaching and guiding me, and John sets up training while helping Ricky set a general tone.

I rely a lot on Tim Nielsen, Buck's assistant coach. An ex-South Australian wicketkeeper, he is a hard-working, positive, energetic presence around the team. Nothing is ever too much for him. If I have a net session where I get out 15 times and need something else, 'Vinnie' is the one I generally ask for help. He will give me throwdowns all day if I want. He responds to exactly what I need. For my first year in the team, I was saying, 'I'll have what Ricky has. If he hits 50 balls, I'll do the same.' I copied Marto and Haydos as well. As I mature, Vinnie helps me adapt their methods to my own requirements, so that I develop as myself, not as a would-be Ricky Ponting.

At the end of that summer, when we win the World Cup and Buck retires, Vinnie will become head coach. He enjoys an amazing bond with Ricky. Very often the coaching job is a matter of complementing the captain – as Buck had done with Steve Waugh. When my time comes to be captain, I will also search for a coach who will complement my style.

As the campaign begins to regain the Ashes in 2006–07, which has been obsessing the group ever since we lost the urn in England in 2005, I am outside the team. My return in Bangladesh was only as a fill-in for Justin Langer, and I didn't make enough runs there to press my case. When the team is picked for the first Ashes Test match in Brisbane, my name isn't there. But Shane Watson injures himself a week or so before the match, and I get a reprieve again. This time I am not going to let go of my chance.

THE INNINGS

124 versus England, Adelaide, 2006

My whole game straightens up once I start playing for Australia. Watching people like Damien Martyn, Justin Langer, Matthew Hayden and Ricky Ponting at training, talking and listening to them, their whole talk is, 'Play as straight as you can early. That gives you the best chance of survival. If you can't play straight early in your innings, let the ball go.' My Pop always told me that Don Bradman said, 'Play in the V and keep it along the ground and you won't get out.'

I feel that I only learnt how to play cricket properly once I was in the Australian team. On my debut in 2004, I played fearless cricket and backed myself, but I didn't really understand how I was doing it. All that was in my head was, *See the ball, hit the ball, score runs.* I didn't know my strengths and weaknesses properly until I got dropped.

During that dark time at the end of 2005 and the beginning of 2006, Dad was the one who helped most with my batting, particularly when my self-confidence had evaporated. At the time I got dropped, he helped me to look deeper into my own game and work out my strengths and weaknesses. If something was off, he could remember how I looked when I was batting well.

By the time I get my chance in the Australian team again, only thanks to Shane Watson's injury before the 2006–07 Ashes series, I have worked on the hardest shot for me to play ever since I was a kid: the on-drive. I used to love watching elegant, superbly balanced right-handers like Michael Slater and Sachin Tendulkar play through mid-on, but I had never been able to do it. At the time I was dropped, I was so anxious to get across to cover the ball around my off stump, my balance was falling over to that side, so that when the ball was on my pads, I was playing across my front leg and either missing it or hitting it too square. I remember a lot of drills in 2006 where I was hitting ball after ball back past the bowler, between him and mid-on, instead of turning them to square leg.

I also focus on eliminating risk early in my innings. I will never play like I did in 2004 again. Being dropped was so traumatising, that fearless youngster has gone. I've sent him away. I'm going to be a more careful and selective batsman now, more focused on playing straight. I'm going to be more professional.

The Adelaide Test match in the 2006–07 Ashes series is my real return to the team. I didn't make runs in Bangladesh and wasn't central to our efforts in Brisbane, and this is a moment when my team needs me. England score six for 551 before declaring their first innings, and we are still 256 runs behind when Punter is out, after a fighting 142, in the first over with the second new ball.

I love facing the second new ball: it's always a great time to be aggressive. My first ball, Andrew Flintoff fires it in at my leg stump. Does he know my weakness? Does he know how much I've been practising? I play straight, just like I've been doing in the drills, and the ball races off to the on-side boundary. If one ball can give you a complete injection of confidence, that does it: an on-drive off one of the toughest bowlers I've ever faced.

By the end of the day, we're still a long way behind, but the ingredients are all there: I've made it to 30 for the start of a new day and I'm batting with Gilly. He goes on a bit of a tear before holing out in the 60s, and I get a rare chance to put on a partnership with Warney. He has a fine time chatting with Paul Collingwood and Kevin Pietersen, among others, and that helps me focus on my own game. It's like he's shielding me, stirring up the Englishmen so he can deflect the heat away from the youngster. I would love Warney to make that first Test hundred he's been waiting for all his career, and would give anything to be with him when he does.

As it turns out, not long after I get to my hundred Warney, on 43, is lbw to Matthew Hoggard, who also gets me a few overs later. But we've got our team score up past 500, which will enable a famous win, set up by Warney's four wickets in England's second innings. I'm there with Mike Hussey when he hits the winning runs just before stumps on the fifth day.

For me, that innings is a turning point: my first real contribution since before I was dropped, my first Test hundred since Brisbane two years ago. It's been a long time and I'm a different player now, two years older and, I hope, many years wiser.

6

LOOK AT THE SUN, NOT THE RAIN

That beautiful morning in St Lucia during the 2007 World Cup has turned dark. After my phone call from Leanne, I sit on my bed, both deflated and agitated. Questions are racing through my head about Dad. Cancer – what kind? Chemo and radiation – when will they start, and what will they do to him? How long has he got? Is this one of those cancers that can be fought, or is he going to be taken from us?

My mind is racing, but I have to find a way to parcel up all those thoughts and send them to a back storeroom of my head. I have to be thinking about cricket, cricket, just cricket, for the next few hours.

Minutes ago, the World Cup was all I was thinking about. We have been on a dream run. We whitewashed England in the Ashes, before farewelling Warney, Glenn McGrath and Justin Langer from Test cricket in emotional style at the Sydney Cricket Ground. We had a few problems with form and injuries during the home one-day series, but since arriving in the West Indies we have been like a machine, with McGrath and Matthew Hayden leading the way. It's my first World Cup, and I am very confident.

Or, I *was*. Now it's vanished. Gone.

I'll admit that I'm one of those people who, when they see a car accident or some other tragedy on the television news, think *It can't happen to me*. I don't know why, maybe it's that self-confidence I take onto the cricket field. The worst things that have happened in my life so far were the death of my cousin Phillip and getting dropped from the Australian team last year. Both of them seemed like the end of the world. Compared to this news about Dad, getting dropped was nothing.

I walk in circles around my hotel room. I want to slide straight back into life as it was before Leanne called, and start my preparations for the game. I look at my gear, but can't focus on it. I try not to think about Dad, or else it'll make me cry. But I can't go back to normal life. I ring him up.

'I'm coming home,' I say.

'Look, don't do that, stay there,' he says.

'What's happening? How are you? What can I do?'

'There's nothing you can do,' he says, sounding calm but emotional. 'I'll start my treatment, and you'll be back soon.'

The cricket distracts me: we have a great morning, with McGrath and Shaun Tait ripping out the South Africans for 149, before I score an unbeaten 60 in the afternoon, getting us past the target with my mate Symmo. I'm too emotionally drained to be very nervous for batting. The hour or so of my innings feels like a holiday from real life.

In the three days before the final, which will be in Barbados against Sri Lanka, I can think of little else but Dad. I try to stay in the moment and concentrate on the logistics of travelling and practising, but every day I'm calling home to get regular updates. Dad is making out that everything's okay, playing it down. I find out that his diagnosis is Hodgkin's Disease, about which I know precisely nothing. My World Cup final preparation involves spending hour after hour on Google. Hodgkin's Disease is a form of lymphoma, starting in the lymph glands, but it can spread throughout the body rapidly. Every night, I think about the scans he's having. I don't know a thing about chemotherapy, radiotherapy, everything he's going to have to go through. I look it all up and there's plenty of general information, but nothing clarifies what will happen to my dad.

I'm petrified. My life has changed instantly. I'm thinking, *No way can this be happening*, but it is. Is Dad going to die? I can't accept that possibility. How will it affect Mum and Leanne? What am I going to do? Can I do anything to help from here? It feels like the skies have opened up and a voice has told me that life has now got serious. But at the same time, I'm so far from home, I feel totally useless.

The final itself goes well, between a chaotic beginning and ending. Before the game, we're sure that it's going to be postponed due to rain, but then it gets going in a rush and Gilly smashes 149 off 104 balls to put the result almost beyond doubt. Sri Lanka have some dangerous hitters, but Gilly convinces a sceptical Punter to use me as a bowler on the low, slow pitch. I manage to get two wickets, including the danger man Sanath Jayasuriya.

On the field, my mind is strangely clear. Cricket has been my whole life, but now, when I am playing in a World Cup final, cricket means absolutely zero. I'm thinking that if I have to retire now to look after Dad, this might be my last match. So what? No more cricket. I might as well enjoy this game. Something in my head has switched off 90 per cent of the thoughts that usually spool out during a game. In this state of fear and fatalism, with so many parts of me numb, I play the final like a character in someone else's video game. I'm there, but not there. Funnily, as it did in the semi-final, this detached mental state sort of helps my cricket.

At the end of the afternoon, there are some fun and games with the umpires trying to get the match finished while the darkness is closing in, and we conclude it by celebrating on the field in the worst light I've ever known for a cricket game. It's so bad that Symmo has to bowl some gentle lobs in the last over for the Sri Lankans to knock it about like pat-ball.

None of that dulls our celebrations, but while I throw myself into it with the usual outward enthusiasm, half my mind is on getting home. Earlier in the World Cup, James Packer organised a boat to assist Cricket Australia, and after the final the team goes out on it to enjoy the moment and have a great time. It's a World Cup, and we've won it. I get involved, on the surface anyway. I don't want to dampen anyone else's celebrations, so the only teammate I confide in is Andrew Symonds, who is also close to Dad.

I can't get home soon enough. From Sydney airport, I catch a taxi to my home in Lilli Pilli, in the southern suburbs. When I get there, Mum and Dad are in the driveway waiting for me. He looks his normal self, not sick at all.

We hug. At first, we are too choked up to say anything.

Mum goes into the house, leaving Dad and me to speak in the driveway. We spend about 30 minutes there. We have to talk before going through the normal motions of walking down the drive, opening the door, putting bags down, getting a glass of water. We just talk. He tells me that his specialist, Professor Harry Iland, has told him that they can't guarantee he'll still be around in 12 months' time.

Dad explains how he found out. He owns a tyre shop in Brookvale, and while he was working on the first floor he fell through some rotten floorboards. Thinking he'd broken a rib, he decided to just tough it out. Mum said to go to the doctor, but Dad, typically, refused. A week and a half later, he was still having trouble breathing, and when he collapsed in pain during dinner with Mum and Leanne, he finally gave in and went for X-rays. His rib wasn't broken but they found two tumours in his chest and two more in his throat.

'The luckiest thing was falling through that floor,' he says. 'Otherwise they mightn't have found out.'

I'm glad Leanne told me, even on the morning of a World Cup semi-final. That's how close we are: family comes first. I wouldn't have had her do it any other way.

'Listen,' Dad says, to put it into proportion. 'I lost my dad to bowel cancer when I was five years old. You and I have had a lot of good years together. You're 26. If my time is up, my time's up.'

Dad's treatment takes place over a 12-month period. Leanne moves back in with him and Mum as the drugs and radiation begin to knock him around badly. He's in and out of hospital for seven months of chemotherapy and then, after a month off, 30 consecutive days of radiation therapy. He's always stoical and cares less about his own fate than he does about seeing young children as patients in the cancer ward, which hits him hard.

During this period he loses a lot of muscle as well as his hair. It breaks my heart to see. His moustache, which he's cultivated ever since he was in the navy, is gone too. In his old-school way, he says that losing his mo is the only thing he really cares about. He grew it as a sign of resistance against naval logic: the guards wouldn't let him through the gate if he was unshaven, but would if he was growing a moustache. He was always tickled by that story, and the origin of the mo said a lot about who he is and his attitude to authority. I wonder where I get it from?

Some months later, he comes to ask if he can borrow my shoes. He usually wears smaller shoes than I do, size 8s to my size 10s, but the pins and needles and swelling in his feet are so bad his normal shoes are compressing his toes.

I happily give him as many pairs of shoes from my sponsors as he needs. 'At least there's an upside,' he says. 'Free shoes for life!'

Dad's cancer changes all of our lives. I've always loved spending time with him, but now I value every second in his company. He watches all of my cricket, and is typically crusty in his responses. It's not often he will crow about anything I've achieved, and more likely he'll say, 'You should have made 200; what a shit shot to get out on when you've made 100!' He won't pump my tyres within earshot, but his mates tell me how proud he is of the effort I have put into my cricket for all these years. He's proud of the results, but more than anything he feels a strong sense of justice when I am rewarded for all that hard work.

Our relationship goes through a transition from father–son to mates. I start to go out with him for a beer with his friends, even when he says he's too old for it or feeling too unwell, and I become part of that group. We have more in common as buddies as I get older, and in 2012, at my wedding, Dad will be my best man.

By then, his cancer will have gone into remission. Or, I should say, his cancers. His lymphoma responds well to the chemo and radiotherapy in 2007 and 2008, and the tumours steadily shrink. On 21 May 2008, a day Dad regards as his 'second' birthday, Professor Iland calls to tell him the lymphoma is in remission. Even when it's in remission, he still needs regular scans, and in 2011 he is diagnosed with cancer of the prostate. Fortunately, due to how frequently he's getting scanned, they catch that early and he fights it off. But it's an ever-present threat, and I know that I share that cancer gene with him.

My first skin cancer is cut out in the early 2000s. I keep it quiet publicly, but it's a matter of constant vigilance. Cricket is such a bad game to play if you have a susceptibility to skin cancer or any other skin condition. After Dad's diagnosis, I decide to become more active in cancer prevention campaigns. I come out publicly about what I've been through, and do a lot of promotional work for the Cancer Council.

As a cricketer, I can set some kind of example. I always wear long sleeves while fielding and often while batting, and never play without my collar turned up to protect my neck. I lather myself in sunblock, and wear a broad-brimmed floppy hat when I'm out in the field. The only exception to this is for a period after 2004, when I am so proud of my baggy green I can't resist wearing it all the time. But by 2007, when I'm getting pre-cancerous lesions on my skin zapped off every few months, and when I meet so many old cricketers fighting serious sun damage, I go to the floppy hat whenever I'm fielding in the sun, other than for our team ritual of first session of an innings in the baggy green.

Hard as it is to say it, Dad having cancer changes my outlook on life for the better. His condition also brings me closer to Leanne and Mum. Whenever I cop public criticism for my personality, I fall back on thoughts of my family; at those moments I think, *I'm proud of the way my family brought me up, I'm proud of the values they taught me as a young boy*. I cop plenty of smacks in the mouth, and deservedly sometimes, but thanks to the way my family raised me I know I'm not a bad person. Their love is my protection.

Dad's second cancer diagnosis kicks off a wretched year for the family's health. In 2011, Leanne's first baby, Byron, is born five weeks premature, and in the hours after his birth she starts to bleed internally. Her life is saved, but while she's in hospital Dad also has to go in, to have a benign tumour cut out of his head. His Hodgkin's lymphoma seems to be under control, but it's a reminder of the risk that hovers over him. That same year, my Nan passes away, and my Pop has a heart attack and a stroke. And one day, I get another of those calls from Leanne.

'It's Mum. There's something wrong with her head.'

I rush to Sutherland Hospital, where Mum has been taken. She has had a cerebral haemorrhage and has to be rushed to the bigger and better equipped hospital at St George, 15 minutes away. I sit in the ambulance with her. I struggle to believe, on top of everything else, that this is happening to Mum. She is such a physically fit and busy person, I can't imagine her being stopped in her tracks. Having been a hockey and netball player through her life and a regular at the Gymea gym, she is, in my eyes, a ball of athletic energy. But here she is, in the care of paramedics, and we don't know what's coming next. Like any son, I grew up thinking my mother is always there for me and expect her strength to be my foundation. Mum was the core of our family: making sure I was organised, fed, clothed and taken where I needed to be every day. If fees needed to be paid for my cricket, she took care of it. No matter what, she had my back. Things have changed since Dad's cancer, and I cherish and appreciate her more, but this event knocks the stuffing out of me.

One thing I am determined to do is protect her privacy while she recovers. In the period of Leanne almost dying in childbirth, Dad getting another tumour cut out, Nan dying, Pop having a heart attack, and now Mum having a brain haemorrhage, I have just been made Australian Test cricket captain. I'm constantly in the spotlight and dealing with the pressures of this new role, but don't go public about this sequence of events at the centre of my life. The world doesn't know that I am preoccupied by one body-blow after another to the people I love most.

Nor have we revealed publicly that, while Dad was at the lowest point of his cancer treatment, he decided that he needed to prepare himself for what he would do if things didn't go to plan. During and after his cancer treatment, he kind of retreated into himself, so that he was in a shell where he could minimise the hurt to everyone else. He detached himself emotionally from Mum and, after more than 25 years, they split up. They still got on fine together, but he closed in around himself and his condition and wanted to be alone. When his cancer went into remission, he kept this determination to live his life differently.

Their break-up affected me to the core. When I split up with my then fiancée Lara Bingle in 2010, part of the undercurrent in my thinking is that if a couple like Mum and Dad can't make it, what hope have I got? I don't even want to start a serious relationship if it's going to end in separation. Mum and Dad are my heroes, and their marriage has always been a kind of gold standard for Leanne and me. I can't imagine myself measuring up to my parents' partnership. How can I do it, if they can't?

It takes me a long time to get over that fear. When Kyly Boldy and I start dating, I open up with her about it. There is a strength of love between us that helps me get over my self-doubt.

The road to happiness with Kyly is a long one. We were in the same year at Westfield Sports High, where she was specialising in dance, but didn't have much to do with each other. In 2007, before I began dating Lara, I introduced myself to Kyly at a bar in Cronulla. We reconnected over a drink, and as we left, I sent my best mate Steve Phillips to ask for her number. She declined, saying I could come and ask myself. Now I was so embarrassed, I decided to leave it to chance, hoping we would bump into each other at another stage.

That was it for Kyly and me for the next three years. In 2010, when she got onto Twitter, Kyly thought, as she didn't really know anyone on Twitter, she would try getting in touch with me again. She sent a message along the lines of, 'Hey stranger, how are you going?' I was in the West Indies at the time for the World Twenty20 and we caught up when I returned home.

By that stage I was going through a rough time, and Kyly's warmth and compassion touched me. She had been brought up in a very close and loving family, and encouraged me to let my vulnerability show rather than seeking ways to cover it up. She and I shared fundamental values – she knew that when things were at their most difficult, the people you turned to were your family and close friends. She could see that I was needing the comfort of family, and I fell in love with her family too. That strong bond of unity provided an extra reinforcement for me at a time when my self-confidence was being shaken. She convinced me that I could hope for the kind of home life I wanted, that I shouldn't give up on myself.

While all of those events are overtaking our family life between 2007 and 2011, I am still trying my best to improve my cricket and contribute to Australia winning matches. But this is also when a section of the public mood has taken a turn against me. While I'm trying to support my family, I wake up one day to find that *The Daily Telegraph* in Sydney is on a mission to tell the world what a dickhead I am. My friendship with Andrew Symonds breaks down, I have a changing room altercation with Simon Katich, and finally, to ice the cake, when I break up with Lara, these separate episodes are all linked as a sequence of black marks against my name.

I say nothing in public about these clashes and, until the end of my Test career, I never will. Throughout, I feel like my family is my anchor, my most basic connection to things like love and loyalty. What do my troubles matter compared with what's been happening to Mum, Dad, Leanne and my grandparents? I cherish them more and more during this period, and they and Kyly will become the platform for the second half of my international career, when I will be determined to be a better person, a better batsman and a better leader.

When I think things are tough in my world, a friend tells me to go and take a walk through a cemetery. Nothing like death can put your issues into their proper proportion. Feel what you feel when you lose someone close. Walk through a children's hospital and imagine that's your own child in the ward. Look up, and see the sun rather than the rain. Then you'll live life the way you should. After those horrible years for my family, this becomes my new direction. But, as with every resolution, it's easier said than done.

7

DEPUTY

I found it very difficult to be Australian vice-captain. Ricky was by far the best batsman I ever played with, he was one of my heroes and I loved playing with him, but his style of leadership was very different from mine, and being so close to him as vice-captain, it was hard for me to be a yes-man when I disagreed with what was happening around me. Vice-captaincy wasn't a role that suited me well. In his autobiography, Ricky wrote that he was 'disappointed with some of the things' I did as vice-captain. He didn't accuse me of being treacherous or disruptive, but said that I was reluctant to get involved in planning meetings and daily debriefs or take on a leadership role. When my private life was turbulent, he said, I would go into my shell.

He was right. I was not a good vice-captain to him.

This might surprise a few people, but I never set out on my journey in cricket with any desire at all to be vice-captain, let alone captain, of Australia. My dream was simply to *play* for Australia. When I went to bed, cradling my cricket bat, I would literally dream that I was walking out to bat for my country. In my dream, I was wearing the same helmet as Michael Slater. When I made a hundred, I take the helmet off and kiss it on the crest like Michael Slater did.

But I never dreamed of being captain of Australia. In junior teams when Dad was coach, he wouldn't make me captain for more than one game. He swapped the job around so that someone different got a go every week. That was part of Dad's basic principle of team participation. Although I argued against it at the time, I loved that sense of fairness he had and it taught me to celebrate the team over the individual achievement. Dad taught me that, whatever game I was playing, the team came first.

I was captain in some junior representative teams, which was my first taste of the conventions that apply in Australian cricket. The batsman who is first picked, who can lead by example, is usually captain. People expect it. It doesn't mean you've got the best cricket brain in the team, but it was the way things were done, and I did like it. As a captain of junior teams, I was pretty aggressive. One of the things I loved about captaincy was that it gave you the chance to express yourself and have an impact throughout your team. But from the under-19s level onwards, I had no captaincy experience.

This often happens to batsmen who play up an age group: they are often the youngest and smallest batsman in their team, so their experience of captaincy is via exposure to their elders. Don Bradman didn't lead teams until he was captain of Australia, because until then he had been the youngest in every team he played in. I was in year 7 when I played in the Liverpool Boys' High First XI, and was 16 when I played first grade for Western Suburbs; there was no way I was going to be captain when I was a boy playing among men. This pattern was repeated when I made the New South Wales and Australian teams.

My exposure to my elders left a deep impression on me. One of my early first grade captains at Western Suburbs was Michael Swan, who was in his mid-thirties at the time. He was big on wanting us to be the best fielding team in the comp. We may not have won premierships, but we got close and often beat more talented sides because we were the best fielding team. Michael was very positive and aggressive in his bowling and fielding tactics, always driving hard to win games. This was also Dad's philosophy of cricket. You are out there to win, and sometimes to achieve that you need to risk losing. It made cricket a much more exciting game if you were always trying to think up a way to get a result, one way or the other.

As an observer coming up through the ranks, I loved Mark Taylor's creative instincts. If he won the toss on a greentop, he had the courage to open the batting on it, knowing he had Shane Warne and Glenn McGrath to bowl on the last day. Due to their success rate, he believed that batting first and bowling last gave them their best chance of winning. That self-sacrifice showed how Tubby put the team first.

I also loved Steve Waugh's ability to fight hardest when his team needed him most. He would stamp his authority on matches by trying to score more than 300 runs a day and then unleashing Brett Lee bowling 150 km/h. It was all action in those teams Steve led.

By far the biggest influences on my captaincy ideas were Ricky Ponting and Shane Warne, in completely different ways.

Punter's trademark was how he led by example with the bat. He was always the best batsman in any team he captained. He performed day in, day out at training and in games – he really was the ultimate professional. When you played with him, he inspired you to be better. You wanted to put on a big partnership with him, and you wanted to impress him. My cricket was lifted merely by being in Ricky's team, and I don't think you can say more of a captain than that.

There's a lot that comes with captaincy besides tactics on the field. Warney was the best tactician who never captained Australia. I think, having played under him at Hampshire and later watched him with the Rajasthan Royals, that he would have been an unbelievably good Test captain. He was a peerless reader of the game on the field. Off the field, he built friendships with individual players like no one else I've ever seen. He could man-manage players and do all the parts of the job successfully.

When he became a commentator and I was captain, I would ask him nightly what he'd seen. We've always had an honest relationship, so he would say, 'You should have used Mitchell Johnson a bit more', or 'I thought you brought Lyono on a bit late'. He saw things nobody else could see, and put it together for me with insight and candour.

Warney's style of captaincy was to take wickets, score runs, move the game forward. I grew up watching all sports and loving the contest, with the anticipation that somebody would win and somebody lose. The fear of losing was never in my system because of that. Warney, at the highest level, had similar thoughts. He wanted to see the game always progressing towards a result.

From my Australian debut until my retirement, the greatest gift he gave me was letting me learn from his experiences. There's no better way to learn than to sit side by side with an Australian cricketing legend who is such a good mentor. I would never have been the player and captain I was without Shane Warne's help. I see him and my Dad as my two biggest cricket influences.

Unlike Punter, who was my Australian captain for seven years, Warney never held that position, but what he showed was how a senior player could contribute ideas and creative leadership, whether he had the *(c)* beside his name or not.

And this was the nub of the matter when it came to me. I would probably have been better, between 2008 and 2011, as a senior player tossing ideas Ricky's way than I was as the vice-captain.

By 2008, four years after my Test debut, I was asking New South Wales if I could be captain to get some experience, but because I wasn't playing enough games for them, they said they wanted to stick with the one captain – which I certainly understood. But I was feeling pressure externally to gain captaincy experience. Everyone seemed to be saying I was the heir apparent to the Australian captaincy. I came onto the Test scene and scored a century on debut in India, in a series where we won in that country for the first time since 1969. Then I came home and scored another hundred in my first Test match. It was a charmed run. After I came back from being dropped, I felt that there was a growing expectation from outside that I would be the next captain. I was much younger than the generation of leaders in the team, seven years younger than Ricky Ponting, Adam Gilchrist and Mike Hussey, and it seemed that I would fit the timetable. I didn't ask for that designation, but once it was placed upon me, I felt that I had to deal with it.

The best Australian batsman is almost always the captain – Greg Chappell, Allan Border, Steve Waugh, Ricky Ponting, and so on – and it seemed that I was marked out at an age when I wasn't even aware of it. I was trying to help us win games and hold onto my place in the team, never mind becoming the best batsman. I wasn't a natural captain as a young man. What Ricky said was right: I didn't have that instinctive Mark Taylor ability to forget about my own performances and put the team's needs first. I did get preoccupied with my own performances and go into my shell when I wasn't doing well. When I was dropped, I couldn't just put it to one side and party with the boys in Hobart. When my family and personal life were weighing on me, I couldn't just put them into the too-hard basket.

Nor was I the standard type of character for the Australian cricket captaincy. I was a western suburbs boy with my own style. From a young age, I was too keen on having a good time to be the textbook head-prefect type. As a kid, I never wanted to be seen as a goody-goody and, as my parents and teachers can tell you, I was often an argumentative little pest. There were lots and lots of reasons why I shouldn't have been captain, but from 2006, when I got back into the team after being dropped, it seemed that I was being 'groomed'.

When I became aware of the plans being shaped for me from higher up, I was humbled. But it was the worst thing for me to be anointed as the heir apparent. Somehow, the perception became that *I* was telling the world I was going to be the next captain, and that *I* had sought it out. The truth was the opposite. Whenever anyone asked me about it, I tried to talk it down. Would I like to captain Australia? Of course. It would be an honour. But it had never been a goal.

I could honestly and literally deny that the captaincy would be 'a dream come true'. It wasn't my dream at all. But once you read it enough in the papers and see it in the news, everyone believes it and there's a sneaky part of you that begins to adapt to it. Your mind starts a transition. I began to think, *If this is going to happen, I have to perform well and learn as much as I can.* I was never seeking the job, but I began adjusting to the reality that was developing around me.

As I had never sought the vice-captaincy, when I took over the job from Gilly in 2008, I was walking on eggshells. Gilly was a hard act to follow, because he was the ideal vice-captain to Ricky. He formed a valuable bridge between Ricky and the boys, taking the load off the skipper's shoulders and providing counsel to the younger players. Brad Haddin, late in my captaincy career, was a perfect deputy for the same reasons.

I entered the vice-captaincy torn between two opposite forces. One was that I wanted to help Punter by offering suggestions and coming up with ways to win games. The other was that I was self-conscious about people thinking I was pushing myself forward, so I would go out of my way to *not* look like the heir apparent. Often, when I thought I had a good idea, I would bite my lip. But I've always been a bad actor and, as Punter wrote in his book, sometimes when I was trying to say nothing, my feelings were written all over my face.

When I disagreed with things Ricky was doing, I got in trouble for saying nothing. It wasn't that he wasn't trying to win the game or help us have success, but my ideas were different from his, on and off the field. If I thought we could have got a key batsman out, declared at a different time, scored more runs, or played a different style, I was too scared to say what I thought, because I didn't want to offend Ricky or undermine the captain's authority, but teammates and support staff could see straight through me. I couldn't mask it. They knew I was pissed off with Ricky's decisions or didn't agree with something that was happening, even if I was acting – very unconvincingly – as if I was backing his decision.

There were also times when I couldn't understand why Ricky was going along with decisions that *he* disagreed with. He delegated a great deal to others, but then griped about it later. It might be something like the manager, Steve Bernard, announcing that the team bus would be leaving the hotel the next morning at 6 am, when play wasn't starting until 11. Ricky would be grumbling with the rest of the boys about going so early. My view was, 'If you're the captain, you should be stepping in and we should leave when you want us to leave. Isn't that what the captain does?'

Another example that sticks out clearly in my memory is when a consultant, Martin West, was brought in to help us with our team culture. Martin is a champion guy I grew to respect. He was the third consultant to be asked in to present to the team in two years. He asked us to write our 'Values' on a whiteboard and then sign the piece of paper saying we would live up to these values.

Martin came on the 2008 tour to India with us. We were sitting in a room going through the 'values' discussion. A lot of the guys were thinking, *What are we doing here? We don't need this shit. Yep, yep, yep – can we get out of here now?* Few guys had any interest in it. Because of my age, I was close to those restless younger players and shared their thoughts. Ricky and Tim Nielsen said the group needed a values statement, but the guys weren't buying in. I was so frustrated, thinking, *How much more shit are we going to talk before someone has the balls to come out and be honest?*

So I stood up and said to Martin, 'You're the third guy who's come in to do this with us. You can write whatever you want on the board. But when it's day five, we're playing here in India, our arses are hanging out, it's 40 degrees, we've got Delhi belly, and we're getting flogged, we're not going to be thinking, "We have to uphold some values we've written down on a piece of paper".'

I thought we were wasting everyone's time – again. It wasn't that I didn't agree with what Martin was saying, but it was the wrong time and place, the boys weren't receptive, and we were being told to write down a list of words that had no meaning there and then. 'If we win, we win, that's good,' I said, 'but if we lose, everyone's going to go back to looking out for himself, they're not going to be thinking about "team values".'

(I have to add that Martin West would become one of my closest confidants and was always someone I could pick up the phone and call and discuss anything with, particularly in the back half of my career. He gave me perspective: urged me to see things the way others saw them. And that relationship had a firm foundation because it had begun with me being so honest. When we came back to Australia after that 2008 tour, he said he'd rather me be upfront like that because if you sit there silently, you contribute nothing.)

Back in 2008, we were, in my view, holding some meetings for the sake of holding a meeting. We had lost a lot of senior players, and the younger guys weren't up for that kind of thing. Nobody else had the balls to say it. But that was the explosion for me. I didn't want to disrespect Punter, but this was bullshit.

Anyway, my objections were noted and we carried on. I have no doubt that this is one of the things Punter was writing about in his book. And the difficult truth is, he was right. A vice-captain has to back the leader; there's no room for anything else. He might sit on the fence, but he can't disagree and, if he does, he should neither voice those opinions nor bite his tongue on them. Vice-captaincy just wasn't a role I was cut out for.

I went to Ricky a number of times and told him, behind closed doors, that I disagreed with something, but by then that wasn't the right approach either. Through those years, we had some bad results – losing heavily in India, losing to South Africa and England at home, losing to England away, getting knocked out of the World Cup in the quarter-finals – and lost a raft of senior players to retirement. Ricky didn't need a Warne-style deputy, who was throwing up alternative ideas all the time. He needed someone to say, 'Yes, sir, you're right, sir.' That wasn't me, and I couldn't adapt.

It would have been better if I hadn't been made vice-captain. If the selectors thought I might be the right guy to captain Australia in the future, they might have been well advised to keep Gilly or someone like him as vice-captain and let me learn, as a senior player, from Ricky.

What seemed to aggravate the tension between public expectation and my private ambivalence was when Ricky missed matches and I became captain. I couldn't help myself – of course I wanted to do a good job and enjoy it on those one-off occasions, so I ran the tactics and the style of play my way. But then, when people said positive things about my captaincy, I felt terrible, because I thought Ricky would be offended. I hated anyone saying I was tactically better than Ricky, because to him it would look like I was angling to take his place. It was not healthy for our relationship.

I had to work hard, during the last year or so of his captaincy, to reassure him. He was coming under increasing pressure as our results went up and down, and whenever a commentator praised my captaincy as a stand-in, I would go to Ricky and tell him I had nothing to do with it and didn't want that praise.

The trickiest times were when it was Warney, who was now working as a TV commentator and newspaper columnist, saying positive things about me. Ricky knew how close I was to Warney, and the pair of them had also had their differences over tactics while Warney was still playing. Each time Warney said or wrote something praising my stand-in captaincy, I had to contact Ricky and say, 'I can't control what Warney says, and I haven't been putting my case to him.' I hoped Ricky would believe me, but looking back, I'm not sure if he did.

Whether or not I had the ambition to be captain, I didn't enjoy being vice-captain. If I had said to Ricky, 'I don't care if I never captain Australia', would he have believed me? I don't know, but it was the truth. I never saw the captaincy as something that would make me a more successful player or person. I was doing fine. But the world was telling me that I was the next captain. It was all being set up around me. When it becomes a public designation, the more I was put up there, the more I believed it was going to happen.

I don't think I needed the vice-captaincy to be prepared as the next Australian captain, but I guess I only realised this after I had it. I accepted that the vice-captaincy was part of the transition to being captain, so okay, I plugged away. I think it ate away at my friendship with Ricky who, I always felt, I liked a lot more than he liked me.

But the most painful toll of the vice-captaincy was upon my closest friendship in the team.

8

SYMMO

It's 2003 and I'm a brand-new member of the Australian one-day cricket team. It's obvious to all and sundry that I am not your typical Aussie man. I only ever open a can of Victoria Bitter to spray it on a teammate during a celebration – I can't stand the taste of beer. I don't have a ute or a cattle dog. I experiment with different hairstyles and I have an earring.

But opposites attract, and somehow Andrew Symonds – who loves beer or Bundy, drives a ute, goes fishing and shooting in his spare time, and is the archetypal Queenslander – and I find our way to each other. We share a sense of humour and, after play, are like heat-seeking missiles looking for fun.

Symmo, six years older than me, is the next in my succession of 'big brothers'. One of the things I absolutely loved when I first came into the Australian team was that all of a sudden I had about a dozen new big brothers. They were all good to me, Warney first and foremost. When Warney retires in 2007, my closest big brother in the team is Symmo.

On and off the field, Symmo protects me. He has played a lot of international cricket by the time I break into the Australian team. He is an electrifying cricketer in all formats of the game – one of the best fielders I've seen, an explosive batsman when most players are still risk-averse, and a more than handy spin and medium-pace bowler (who got me out nicking for a golden duck in my first Shield match at the Gabba). He has been a fixture in the one-day international team from the time he scored 143 against Pakistan in the 2003 World Cup.

Over the course of several overseas tours, we bond as mates. He is always very funny, sometimes unintentionally – such as when he buys a ticket in a lottery and, hearing that the winner will be drawn on the 31st of the month, says sternly to the ticket seller, 'I will be contacting you on the 32nd'. Sometimes his humour is intentional, such as during the 2007 World Cup when Shane Watson lights an incense candle to mask a nasty smell in the dressing room, and Symmo says deadpan to team manager Steve Bernard, 'If it's come to this, I don't want to play for Australia anymore.'

It amuses both of us to surprise people by our closeness, the country boy and the city slicker. But we're both very close to our families and talk about them a lot, and we play cricket with the same go-forward spirit. At training, we're always competing against each other to go harder.

For Symmo, by his own admission, the problem is knowing when the fun has to stop. In England and Wales for the one-day series leading up to the 2005 Ashes, we are preparing for a match against Bangladesh in Cardiff. The night before, it's Shane Watson's 24th birthday. I'm in bed early, but Symmo comes knocking at my door.

'Come on, mate, what are you doing? We're going out! It's Saturday night!'

He throws open my curtains, and the streets outside are packed. I put my jeans and shirt on and go with him, joining a group of teammates at a bar.

At about midnight, I say to Symmo, 'I'm cooked, mate, I'm going back to the hotel. Are you coming?'

Symmo looks at me. 'Nah, mate, I'm going to stay.'

After trying about five times, I can't get him out, so I go back to the hotel on my own. Others who are staying on with Symmo, such as Brad Haddin, Brett Lee and Watto, are not in tomorrow's team.

Next morning, I'm on the bus with everyone else, waiting to leave for Sophia Gardens. Someone says, 'Where's Symmo?'

Nobody knows. I try his phone. It rings out. Brett Lee, Shane Watson and Brad Haddin get on the bus.

'What happened to Symmo?' I ask quietly.

'Oh, we left him.'

'What time?'

'About 4.30.'

I rush back into the hotel and grab a key from reception. In his room, I find Symmo passed out on his bed, still in his going-out clothes.

'Mate! Symmo, wake up!'

He just grunts. I open the mini-bar, grab two bottles of water and pour them over him, slapping and pinching him and eventually getting him awake. He showers and climbs into his gear.

Unknown to me, he's already in trouble. Three hours ago, at about 7 am, he waltzed in from the street to the hotel dining room and ate some breakfast in front of John Buchanan – before coming up and passing out.

By getting Symmo out of bed, I don't know if I've done him a favour or not. Maybe if I'd left him sleeping, a doctor could have come in and said he had the 'flu'. Instead, I hustle him onto the bus, saying, 'Just keep a low profile, don't say anything, and stay away from everyone else.'

That's no good either. He's raucous on the bus, slapping Brad Hogg full-strength on the face as he walks past him. Hoggy directs a remark at Symmo, who can't reply coherently. Some of us call him 'Barry Bronco' when he's like this, and he's in full Barry Bronco mode now. Then, during warm-ups at Sophia Gardens, he leans against a wheelie bin to do his leg-swings and brings it tumbling down. Punter comes to me and says, 'What the f— is going on with Symmo?'

'What are you talking about?' I say, playing dumb.

'You know exactly what I'm talking about. Is he pissed?'

'Um, I think he's just tired.'

All hell breaks loose, with Punter and John Buchanan asking him straight-up what time he got in last night and if he's still drunk. Symmo buries himself deeper by saying he's played in this condition plenty of times before. He is ruled out with a 'mystery illness' before the start of play, which turns into a second disaster when the management is caught out fudging the truth. And then, as if it's not bad enough already, we lose to Bangladesh, then ranked 11th in the world in ODIs.

Over the next day, it looks like Symmo will be sent home. The day after the match, everyone has a meeting and the team is split down the middle. The leaders, Punter and Gilly, are furious, while the younger blokes reckon a fine, administered in-house, should be enough. Symmo is pretty sheepish by now. What I know about him is that he has done this before, and once he's settled down he understands how much he's let everybody down, and will gather himself up and produce incredible performances on the field.

He's not the only one who's stayed out too late. He's looked after me as often as I've looked after him. In the meeting, I stand up and say, 'It's my fault. I could see what was going to happen and I came back to the hotel. I should have dragged Symmo with me. I think he's had a harsh enough penalty being left out of the team. If you send him home, you might as well send me home too.'

I am too young to know whether what I've done is right or wrong, stupid or courageous. It is simply that he's my mate and if he is going down, I'll go down with him.

He would do the same for me. Symmo comes up later and thanks me, though he admits that it wasn't my fault. There was no stopping him that night.

I don't know if my speaking up for him has had any effect, but the hierarchy settles on a fine and a two-match ban. Symmo comes back with a blast, predictably, scoring 73 and 74 against England and taking five for 18 against Bangladesh. He goes off to county cricket while the Test team, which he is not in, gets together for the Ashes tour. We stay in contact for the whole time in England, and our friendship is secure. He knows I have his back.

Between the two of us, this is how things continue over the next two years. We go to South Africa in early 2006, and amid some enjoyable one-day cricket together I have to save Symmo's skin again, when, in a Cape Town nightclub, he begins eyeballing the Springbok rugby prop Ollie le Roux and asks him to settle the matter in the old-fashioned way.

'Come on outside,' Symmo says.

'No problem, let's go,' says big Ollie.

They actually lock arms. Ollie is going to eat Symmo alive. Seeing the trouble building, I rush in, jump up and literally sit myself on their locked arms.

'Come on, you two, you're not going anywhere,' I squeak, feeling like either of them could pick me up and crush me in his fist. But I convince Symmo that a late-night punch-up on tour may not be the best way to follow up what happened in Cardiff, and before we know it he and Ollie are having a beer and swapping stories like old mates.

During that tour, Symmo and I cook up a plan for an off-season trip: we're going to hire a Winnebago to drive from Sydney to Brisbane, and then fly to Rockhampton, where he's going to take me out bush for some fishing and hunting. I'm not a rough-camping type, so I organise the best Winnebago you've ever seen, big enough to sleep eight people and with all the mod cons. We drive up the coast slowly, getting lost more often than not, and drop in on my dad's mother and stepfather in Coffs Harbour. We stay in caravan parks and use their amenities blocks. People say, 'There's Michael Clarke and Andrew Symonds!' Others say, 'No it's not, they wouldn't be in a caravan park.'

Symmo teaches me how to fish, and he has indoctrinated me in country-boy ways by the time we fly up to Ingham in north Queensland to stay with his mate Yogi and his family. We fly in a helicopter from there to Esmeralda Station in the Gulf of Carpentaria, where Symmo's friend Mick is the manager. We go out chasing bulls, and although Symmo's pig-hunting plans are spoilt by rain, I manage to catch my first barramundi. There are crocodiles everywhere. I've fished in the bay around Cronulla, but that's no preparation for this. When the helicopter lands on the riverbank, crocodiles scatter everywhere. I say, 'No way, boys, we're not going here.' But off we go. Symmo fixes my line, puts the lures on, and I don't have to do anything. I cast away, get a barramundi on, and I'm winding it in when Yogi jumps into the water to get my fish in. Thinking of the crocodiles, I yell: 'I don't need the fish that bad!'

It's one of the best things I've done in my life, a special trip that cements our friendship, which goes well beyond the boundaries of the cricket field.

Some of our best moments in that period are on the field – the 2006–07 Ashes whitewash, the 2007 World Cup in the West Indies, and winning the Border–Gavaskar Trophy in Australia. When I find out about Dad's cancer, Symmo is the one teammate I confide in. My friendship with him is also part of the controversy in the Test match in Sydney in that Border–Gavaskar series.

Having won the first Test match in Melbourne, we go to Sydney with the opportunity to win the trophy. We are also on the brink of a record-equalling 16 Test match wins in a row, quite a comeback after losing the Ashes two years ago. On the first morning, our top order collapses, but Symmo saves the innings with a fantastic unbeaten 162. Assisted by Brad Hogg and Brett Lee, Symmo gets the Australian score from six for 134 to all out 463, an addition of 329 runs for the last four wickets. That would be demoralising enough for the Indians, even if they weren't sure that Symmo had been out nicking early in his innings.

Hundreds by V.V.S. Laxman and Sachin Tendulkar get India past our total, but Matty Hayden and Mike Hussey reply with big scores to enable Punter to declare just before lunch on the last day. We have 72 overs to bowl India out and they need to score 333 runs to win.

In many ways, it's one of my favourite Test matches. All through the last day, I'm standing beside Ricky in slips, bugging him. 'Give me a bowl, give me a bowl!' Out of the side of his mouth, he's saying, 'Shut up, shut up.'

I give credit to Ricky for sticking to his guns. In his view, bowlers are paid to bowl and batsmen are paid to bat. He places faith in the bowlers who he thinks will win us the game.

But I also give him credit for his flexibility. He could just say, *You're not bowling, piss off*, but when there are only four overs to go, it looks like we're not going to win. India are seven wickets down, with Anil Kumble and Harbhajan Singh, both capable lower-order batsmen, digging in for the past ten overs. Our main pace bowlers, Brett Lee, Mitchell Johnson and Stuart Clark, are spent. Symmo has bowled more than anyone, and Brad Hogg hasn't taken a wicket.

As the shadows lengthen, Punter thinks, *I've got to shut this kid up*. He turns to me and says, 'Okay, go and have a bowl.'

My self-confidence as a young man, with bat and ball, is a big part of why I made it to the highest level. I believe I can have an impact on any game I am playing in. I love to field where the ball is going most, I love to open the batting in one-dayers and be in for all the overs, and whenever I have the ball in hand, I believe I can get these guys out.

I bowl one over to Kumble without any result, but at the other end Symmo manages to keep Kumble on strike, so I'm going to get a chance at Harbhajan. He's a bit of a slogger, but in the last hour or so he's been tempering his instincts. I toss up the first ball of my second over, and it bites in the crumbly wicket. Harbhajan pushes forward, and the ball clips the shoulder of his bat before carrying to Huss at slip.

Next ball, I push it in a bit faster to RP Singh. He's caught on the crease, and when it hits him on the pad we all go up. A clear lbw.

Now, with the last man in, we are suddenly favourites to win. Ten balls to go, and I'll get to bowl four of them. Punter brings everyone in around the bat. Ishant Sharma, who's playing in his first Test match, is the unfortunate batsman. We can't get going at first, because he's brought out two right-hand gloves. The SCG crowd boos him, but I can understand. You can be so nervous in this situation that you could forget to bring out any gloves at all.

Finally he's ready. I push through the first two balls, going for the lbw again, but they're both down the leg side. I have two left. I float the next one a little slower. Ishant has no option but to defend and, in a carbon copy of the Harbhajan dismissal, edges it to Huss.

We go off our heads with delight and surprise, probably so elated that we don't notice the Indian batsmen trudging off. Kumble will be unhappy that we didn't immediately shake hands with him, and in his press conference later, he'll accuse us of not playing in the spirit of the game.

From a personal point of view, I'm excited beyond belief, thrilled to have been able to come through in the dying moments. I love my bowling and think back to all those days as a kid when I was picked in teams for my pace, first, and then my spinners. For a batsman, sometimes there's no greater delight than taking key wickets with the ball.

But within minutes of the match ending, the fun comes to a shuddering halt.

My role in 'Monkeygate' is only on the fringe, but it still sours what should have been a great memory. On the fifth night of the match, several of us have to attend a tribunal hearing until the early hours.

Punter has made a racial abuse complaint against Harbhajan, on account of words he spoke to Symmo on day three of the match. I had heard in Sydney what I believed to be a racial sledge. In a seven-hour hearing before ICC match referee Mike Procter, I am one of the witnesses, along with Punter, Symmo, Matty Hayden, Gilly, the umpires, Harbhajan, and his batting partner at the time of the incident, Sachin Tendulkar.

At the end, Procter gives Harbhajan a three-match ban for racial abuse, which sets off an uproar from India and also from sections of the Australian cricket community.

The Board of Control for Cricket in India (BCCI) threaten to call off the tour, and Cricket Australia is more keen to broker a compromise than to defend their players' integrity. Harbhajan ends up with a reduced punishment for 'verbal abuse', and we are all left with the feeling that our own board is more interested in appeasing India than in any principles or loyalty.

I probably don't hold as strident a view as others. I know Ricky is filthy about being let down by Cricket Australia, and many in the team feel a sense of betrayal by our employers. I thought CA should have had the courage to say to Ricky and Symmo, 'We're sorry, but we're not going to fight India. We can't win. So let it go.' That's what should have happened. There was no great principle of racism at stake. I was never sure that Symmo felt deeply offended by what Harbhajan said, and he said as much in his autobiography. If he had been offended? Different story. But he wasn't, so he was pursuing it for different reasons than the racial abuse law was set up for.

After the first hearing, I go to Symmo and say, 'Mate, you haven't been offended by this at all. This doesn't bother you.'

He says, 'But I'm sick and tired of them getting away with it. We never get away with anything, but they do.'

I say, 'If you push this, it's going to be massive.'

Whether my involvement helps or not, I don't know. I support him and tell the truth under oath about what I heard. But it's never been about racism. Symmo was frustrated with a situation where we are always portrayed as the bad guys. I agree with that, but taking it up in this manner is never going to win us any satisfaction. When it comes to suffering from racism in historic terms, we're not going to be able to grab the high ground from India. So it would have been best to cop it and move on, rather than stage a fight we were never going to win.

The whole business changes Symmo. Ricky has written that Symmo was 'gone from this moment' as a committed

Test cricketer. Maybe he was. I didn't realise it yet, and wanted our relationship to stay as it always had been. But in the next 12 months, Symmo would turn on me.

Four months after that Sydney Test match, we are in the West Indies for a three-Test series followed by five one-dayers. I miss the First Test, as I stay in Sydney to grieve with Lara, whose father has just died of cancer. My dad is also having further cancer treatment. When I get to the Caribbean, the boys welcome me back warmly, and I put my head down in the Second Test match with 110 in the first innings, motivated in part to thank the team for their loyalty.

Throughout my career, I prioritise my family. Sometimes I cop some stick for putting my personal issues first, but I do what I believe is the right thing. The culture of the Australian cricket team changes during the span of my career. By the end of my playing days, if a cricketer's child is being born, 99 per cent of them will have permission to leave the team, and will want to leave the team, to be with their wife or partner. In past generations, it was the opposite: 99 per cent of cricketers would not have left their team to be at home for the birth of their child. This cultural change is progress. Your family are with you for life, and it is right for them to be placed ahead of cricket at these important moments – especially when, in most of our cases, our families have made so many sacrifices so that we can place cricket first.

My decision to miss that Test match in the West Indies wasn't an emotional reaction. If I had my time again, in the calm of hindsight, I would make exactly the same decision.

We win the Third Test in Barbados to seal the series 2–0. Before that match, we get a few days off, and one night I get together with Brian Lara for a quiet drink. Brian has always been generous with his time and advice for me, and we have enjoyed each other's company whenever we've had the chance since that first meeting in Georgetown airport in 2003.

I know that Symmo has been a bit down since the Australian summer. He was the main victim of 'Monkeygate'; he was the guy, even more than Punter, who felt he was hung out to dry by Cricket Australia. During the West Indies trip, Symmo has said something that surprises me: that he would like, one day, to be considered for the Australian captaincy. That is the first I knew of it, but I can understand. He has great leadership qualities and a cricket brain as good as anyone's. He doesn't like always being portrayed as the larrikin but he can't seem to appreciate that it's his own actions that have led to that portrayal. I sense that the issue is driving a bit of a wedge between him and me.

From Symmo's point of view, his knockabout mate, his drinking and fishing buddy, is being groomed for the captaincy and getting all the royal treatment from the hierarchy, whereas he is being dealt a rough hand. We're soul brothers, and it doesn't seem fair to him that I am the golden boy while he is the outcast.

When he tells me about his ambition to lead, I do everything I can to stop him being pissed off with me. 'I wasn't made vice-captain by my dad,' I say. 'It's not something I've gone after. They've given it to me. You'd make a great captain, Symmo, but what do you want me to do about it? You should go and talk to the selectors about it, throw your hat in the ring. I wouldn't mind at all.'

In the lead-up to the Barbados Test match, when I'm sitting in the restaurant with Brian Lara, Symmo comes in with his girlfriend. They have been out for lunch, which turns into dinner, which turns into after-dinner drinks. Symmo and his girlfriend join Brian and me, and although it's obvious that Symmo has had more than a few, it's all quite friendly at first. Brian mentions a funny incident in a game against Sri Lanka a few years ago, when Symmo hit the ball down the wicket, it smacked into my leg and rebounded in the air, and he was caught. As he walked off, he laughingly said to me, 'You owe me a beer.'

We are laughing about it, but then suddenly something in Symmo's brain snaps and he decides he'll give me that drink now: he pours a glass of wine over my head. It's a stunning moment. He's frothing with anger, and Brian has to get between us before Symmo storms out.

I can't figure out exactly what I've done. Maybe it's all the circumstances around Symmo losing his love for playing cricket for Australia. I'm quite at home with the increased intensity and professional focus of the team environment now, and so it's quite understandable that, as his mate for so long, Symmo should see me as a sell-out, someone who personifies all that he dislikes in the set-up.

But I don't know for sure what he thinks. Despite my efforts to reconcile, he won't talk to me again on the tour.

Brian Lara has told Ricky that if a player poured a drink over a West Indies vice-captain, he would not play for the team again. Ricky doesn't do anything about it. It's a month and a half after the West Indies tour when we gather again, for a mid-year series of one-day internationals in Darwin against Bangladesh. I've been trying to patch things up with Symmo, but he's having none of it.

By the mid-year series, Ricky is recuperating from surgery on his wrist and I am captain. We have a lot of new young players, such as Shaun Marsh, James Hopes, David Hussey, Brett Geeves and Cameron White, and I make it clear that, as captain, I have to put the responsibilities of the job ahead of personal friendships.

The day after a warm-up game against an academy side at Marrara Cricket Ground in Darwin, we hold a team meeting. Symmo isn't there. He'd gone fishing earlier in the morning, having organised a mate to bring his boat all the way from Queensland, and hasn't come back. When he does return, he's not exactly apologetic. His mood is challenging, he reeks of alcohol, and he says he didn't know the meeting was on. His attitude is that missing the meeting would have no effect on his cricket.

In a hotel room, we convene a disciplinary meeting: Tim Nielsen, Steve Bernard, myself and Symmo, with Ricky on speaker phone. My gut is screaming, *I want nothing*

MICHAEL CLARKE

Me as a bub. Dad wanted to name me John Michael, after his late father, but my parents took one look and knew I was a Michael John.

MICHAEL CLARKE

A bat and ball, my favourite toys. I would sleep with the bat for protection. I'm a natural leftie but switched to right-handed to be like Dad.

MICHAEL CLARKE

Holidays with my older sister Leanne. We were active kids and both loved the beach.

MICHAEL CLARKE

A family camping trip. Mum was the organiser and disciplinarian of our house. She always looked after me. She still does!

MICHAEL CLARKE

Above: My first cricket team. I'm the skinny seven-year-old (middle row, right) in the Woodlands Park under-10s. I scored 17 runs in my first season, but the bigger boys only got me out once.

MICHAEL CLARKE

Above: Dad (far left) was my coach from the moment I could hold a bat. When he bought an indoor cricket centre it was heaven on earth for a cricket-crazy kid like me (bottom row, middle).

MICHAEL CLARKE

MICHAEL CLARKE

Above: My selection in the NSW under-17s squad was a major stepping stone on the path to first-class cricket. Not long afterwards, Australian Cricket Academy coaches Rod Marsh and Wayne Phillips offered me (front row, middle) an academy scholarship.

Above: My prize for making the Metropolitan South West Regional Sydney team was a green hoodie. I lived in it.

MICHAEL CLARKE

Right: Beer and skittles with the Australian under-19s side in England.

MICHAEL CLARKE

Right: I saved up my $168 weekly pay packets from Kingsgrove Sports Store and bought this old Holden Gemini, then proudly parked it on the nature strip outside our home.

AAP IMAGE/DAVE HUNT

Below: Dad and Neil D'Costa look over my first Slazenger bat contract. I had a bigger deal than any other Australian Test player except Ricky Ponting. The money was embarrassing given I hadn't even earned my baggy green yet.

MICHAEL CLARKE

Below: I was only 21 when I first put on the Australian one-day international shirt. I'd never felt so hyped in my life. I even forgot about my bad haircut.

HAMISH BLAIR/GETTY IMAGES

Above and below: The transition from playing boys to playing men is the toughest of a cricketer's life. In my first season for NSW I found myself batting alongside stars such as Steve Waugh (below left).

NICK LAHAM/GETTY IMAGES

Below and right: My 2004 winter with Hampshire was a great finishing school for my technique. Shane Warne took me under his wing and became a great friend and mentor.

MIKE HEWITT/GETTY IMAGES

AAP IMAGE/PA

Below: Some of my favourite cricket memories are of English summers. Here I'm batting for the Hampshire Hawks against the Middlesex Crusaders, July 2004.

JULIAN HERBERT/GETTY IMAGES

WAYNE LUDBEY/NEWSPIX

HAMISH BLAIR/GETTY IMAGES

My Test debut against India at Bangalore in 2004 was a dream come true. I was nervous and excited but my batting had crystal clarity as I made my way to 151.

HAMISH BLAIR/GETTY IMAGES

HAMISH BLAIR/GETTY IMAGES

HAMISH BLAIR/GETTY IMAGES

As a boy I promised Dad that if I ever scored a Test ton I'd do it in a baggy green. When the moment came, I kissed my cap and all my emotions poured out. As I celebrated the ton, I looked to the stands and saw Mum crying tears of joy. Dad was proud too – even if he did tell umpire Billy Bowden I should've been out!

HAMISH BLAIR/GETTY IMAGES

HAMISH BLAIR/GETTY IMAGES

HAMISH BLAIR/GETTY IMAGES

Above: Having my parents, grandparents and coach Neil D'Costa (far left) at Bangalore meant everything to me. They'd shared the journey. The glory was theirs too.

Below: A century on debut and a win in India. I think Warney was as pumped as I was!

HAMISH BLAIR/GETTY IMAGES

ROB ELLIOTT/AFP/GETTY IMAGES

WAYNE LUDBEY/NEWSPIX

Everything I touched on that first Test tour turned to gold. In Mumbai, I tidied up the Indians' second dig by taking six wickets for nine runs.

ROB ELLIOTT/AFP/GETTY IMAGES

Right: In 2004 I became only the third Australian to make Test centuries on debut both overseas and at home. I was flying, totally fearless, yet knew very little.

ADAM PRETTY/GETTY IMAGES

HAMISH BLAIR/GETTY IMAGES

It's such a great feeling when the ball hits the middle of the bat and pierces the field with an audible buzzing. I have real fearlessness in knowing what my strengths are . . .

Against New Zealand at the Gabba in 2004, I got to be a swashbuckling batsman like my boyhood hero Michael Slater.

HAMISH BLAIR/GETTY IMAGES

Simon Katich was my partner when I first walked out to bat for Australia in a Test. It's a far more important memory than what flared between us five years later.

HAMISH BLAIR/GETTY IMAGES

With the great AB for my first Allan Border Medal in 2005. I was on a high but the crash was coming. I was dropped from the Test side ten months later.

HAMISH BLAIR/GETTY IMAGES

Growing up, Brian Lara was a poster on my bedroom wall. He was a champion cricketer and is a champion bloke, and has always been generous with his time and advice since we first met in 2003.

AAP IMAGE/ROBERT CIANFLONE

Above: We spent the night after the 2008 Sydney Test in a tribunal investigating a racial sledge Indian spinner Harbhajan Singh had allegedly made against Andrew Symonds. The 'not guilty' verdict changed Symmo and our friendship suffered afterwards.

Below: Dating Lara Bingle, I was chased by the paparazzi and gossiped about 24/7. Our life became a media circus.

AAP IMAGE/DEAN LEWINS

GREGG PORTEOUS/NEWS...

Above: The Adelaide Test in the 2006–07 Ashes marked my real return to the team. I played the new ball straight, and hit 124 to get my career back on track.

AAP IMAGE/SERGIO DIONISIO

By 2009, the tide of public opinion was turning against me. I was earning big money. I did photo shoots in my undies. I drove flash cars. I lived in Bondi. I had a model fiancée. For many people, that was all they needed to know about me.

at all to do with this. I'm only the stand-in captain. I don't want to tread on Ricky's or anyone else's toes. And it's my mate. Is he expecting me to stand up and put my position on the line for him, like I did in Cardiff?

From the speaker phone, Ricky is blowing up at Symmo. 'Where do you want to be? With the Australian team? Or is doing your own thing more important?'

When the time comes to make a decision on disciplinary action, Ricky says, 'I'd send him home. It's the second or third time.'

Symmo turns to me. He looks at me and sees not the vice-captain or the stand-in skipper or a member of the hierarchy, but his mate.

'What do *you* think?' he says.

I'm pissed off at him too, but I've been biting my tongue. It's my first time as captain of Australia for a one-day series, and the guy I used to think was my best mate in the team has done this. He's let us all down. And now he appears to want me to put our friendship above the team, above the responsibilities of the captaincy. I'm trying not to be angry that he's put me in this position.

'I'm with Punter, one hundred per cent,' I say. 'If I was captain of this team, I'd have you on the next plane home.'

To Symmo, that's another sign that I haven't put my friend first. That I will sell out my mates for my personal ambition. And to him, I believe, that's the end of our friendship.

Maybe he thinks I've jumped onto CA's side. But when I accepted the offer to be vice-captain of Australia, I knew I had to put the team ahead of personal relationships.

When I was appointed, I said to Symmo and others, 'If I have to take tough decisions, I'm doing it in the interests of the team. Nothing is personal.' I hoped my teammates would understand that, and not put our friendships under unnecessary pressure.

Easier said than done.

Losing that friendship kills me. Ever since Warney's retirement in 2007, Symmo has been my best friend in the Australian team and my favourite cricketer to play with. After he is sent home from Darwin, I try to catch up with him and make amends and rebuild the friendship. I continue this effort on and off for years and we play together again, but it's never the same.

He is in and out of the team in 2009, until, during the World Twenty20 in England, he is sent home again for another alcohol-related transgression. I am in the 'leadership group', which we have brought in on the recommendation of AFL guru Ray McLean. So, once again, I'm on the opposite side from Symmo. Ever since 2008, he's seen authority as the other side, and he won't forgive me for joining them.

Some former teammates will take his side, and feed his conviction that I let him down and put ambition ahead of mateship. I would say that he let me down too – that if he had understood mateship as a two-way street, he would have seen that I had to do what was right for the whole team, and putting team above mateship was precisely what a leader had to do.

But by 2009 he will have lost the hunger to play cricket for Australia. He blames a culture of intense dedication and of striving to improve every day; it's a bigger issue than just me, but I feel that he accuses me of selling my soul to climb the corporate ladder. If I have changed, I make no apologies, because it's all been in aid of improving myself and my team as cricketers. I have a lot of flaws and am a poor vice-captain to Punter. But we sink to fifth in the world by 2011, an unacceptable place for Australia to be in Test cricket, and something has to be done.

When I become captain, I will be determined to do things a better way. It will cost me other friendships. None will leave as much pain as the one I lost with Andrew Symonds.

9

THE GENTLEMAN'S GAME

Australia versus India, Sydney Cricket Ground, January 2008. If we win the match, we regain the Border–Gavaskar Trophy. It's been five fraught days already overshadowed by controversy, but on the field it's another Test match that we are striving to win. I join Mike Hussey at three for 250 in our second innings. We lead by 181 runs.

I'm nervous, having failed in the first innings. Anil Kumble is especially dangerous on a crumbling fourth-day wicket, and first ball, he drops it short. Misjudging the topspin, I step back to cut it. The ball jumps and turns in at me, but I'm already committed to my cut shot. I nick it virtually out of the wicketkeeper's gloves and Rahul Dravid takes a good catch at slip.

The Indians are appealing, but initially the umpire, Steve Bucknor, takes his time to think about it. Eventually he raises his finger, and I'm off. But for those few seconds, I don't walk. I stand my ground. And that gets the Indians even more upset than they were already.

Am I a walker? Sometimes in my career, I have nicked the ball and walked. At other times, I haven't walked. It's very much guided by the emotions of the moment. I don't have a 'policy' on walking. Sometimes I go and sometimes I don't. I've always been taught that it's the umpire's job to give you out. Just because I saved the umpire from doing his job on occasion doesn't change my view that it remains the umpire's task, not the batsman's, to adjudicate on dismissals.

If a batsman walks, then good for him, but I never met a batsman who was a 'walker' – that is, someone who walks when he thinks he is out, regardless of the situation. I know Adam Gilchrist walked off against Sri Lanka in the 2003 World Cup semi-final, but by his own admission, Gilly didn't *always* walk when he knew he was out (and to this day, there are plenty in that Australian dressing room who didn't think Gilly was out that day!). The label of 'walker' got applied to Gilly, but he never asked for it.

Gilly will, like me, be among those accused of unfair play during that notorious Test match in Sydney. In his case, it is for claiming a catch that isn't out. I am similarly under fire on the last day. India's captain, Sourav Ganguly, has been batting well for an hour and a half with the aim of saving a draw. Brett Lee bowls outside Ganguly's off stump, and he nicks it to me at third slip. I get my hands under the ball as it drops, and in the split-second of action, I am certain

I take the catch. Ganguly doesn't want to walk, but goes off after the umpires, Bucknor and Mark Benson, confer.

To claim a catch unfairly is not in my blood. I would *never* claim a catch that I thought had bounced. And I never have. But I will claim a catch when I believe I have caught it. If I'm wrong? Then that's for the umpires to decide. There are insinuations that we Australians are going to do anything to win, including cheating, but that's not the case at all. To repeat: I would never claim a catch if I didn't think it was out. If I looked at a replay and it showed the ball had bounced, I would be the first to withdraw an appeal. But there's no such replay at the SCG.

Every cricketer appeals for catches and lbws that might not be out. Have you appealed for a caught behind where you are in doubt? One hundred per cent of cricketers have. You heard a noise, so you appealed. A replay might then show that the batsman hasn't hit it. Or in the ten seconds as you cool down for a DRS referral, you consult with others, and your view changes.

Gilly, whose name is a byword for fairness, acknowledges that he appealed for thousands of such decisions while playing for Australia, not just the one he is condemned for that day in Sydney. Very often, you are not 100 per cent sure of what's happened in the middle of a cricket match, whether you are a batsman or a bowler. You don't know if the ball carried? In the emotion of the moment, you appeal. You don't know if you nicked it? In the emotion of the moment, you stay. In both cases, you are leaving the decision to the umpire – because that's his job.

On the field, you're not in the same frame of mind as a viewer sitting watching in their lounge room, emotionally and physically distant, able to access slow-motion replays and other technology. When you're on the field, your whole being is desperately committed to winning, and events happen very, very quickly. If you're fielding, you appeal if there's a *one* per cent chance it may be out. An appeal is exactly that – a question you are asking of the umpire. If you're batting, and you're not 100 per cent sure you're out, you're going nowhere until the umpire puts his finger up. That's how the game is played.

In Sydney that week, the umpire decided I *had* nicked Kumble, and the umpire decided that Ganguly's edged shot *did* carry to me. I had no problem with either decision.

Labelling people as walkers or non-walkers is deceptive, because their actions are always going to be complicated by circumstances and emotions. In that Border–Gavaskar Test match, neither side was giving an inch. I went out to bat on the brink of a double-failure, with my team depending on me. It was the desperate match situation, both personally and for my team, that guided my emotional reactions. I've been in situations where I've made four straight low scores and am convinced that if I make no runs this time, my career is over. If I nick the ball, the only thoughts going through my head are, *Please God, please don't, please don't, please don't give me out. I've worked for this for 25 years.* If it's the end of your career, there is no way your emotions will allow you to give it up easily.

On the other hand, if you've made a hundred, your team is preparing to declare and you know you've nicked the ball, if you've played plenty of Test matches, if everything's going well, your emotions are different. It's a lot easier for the guy with a glittering record and a strong match situation to be in a contented mood. In my first Test innings, I nicked Zaheer Khan and walked without looking at the umpire. I'd made 151, and I was emotionally and physically spent. It's not that I made a *decision* to walk, but that emotion took over. Gilly and Brian Lara were both described as walkers. But did they walk when they were playing their first Test match and the result hinged on their success? I don't think so, because their emotional state wouldn't have let them. What can be hard for a viewer to understand is that for the player in the middle, walking or not walking is very often an unthinking, instinctive thing.

For me, I never planned to walk. Sometimes I just did it on impulse.

If there's one thing I wasn't, it was a cheat. Throughout my career, I always cared about the integrity of the game. So it was irritating, at Trent Bridge in 2013, when Kevin Pietersen accused me of being a hypocrite. That match had already had a fair bit of umpiring controversy, most notably when Stuart Broad hit the cover off an Ashton Agar delivery and I caught him at slip after a deflection off Brad Haddin's gloves. DRS was part of the game, but we had used our reviews up, and umpire Aleem Dar gave Broad a reprieve. We weren't happy, but those are the rules.

Broad didn't have to walk, and it was the umpire's job to give him out or not out. While I was furious at the time that we didn't have another review, I had no problem with Broad's refusal to walk.

The next day, chasing a target of 311, we are three for 161 and travelling well. On 23, I play and miss – I think – at Broad. The Englishmen appeal, and the umpire raises his finger. Now, I am certainly not sure I nicked that. I didn't feel or hear anything. So I refer the decision to the DRS.

Pietersen walks by and calls me a hypocrite. The previous day's events are fresh in everyone's mind. What's his reasoning? That because we had a bad decision go against us yesterday, I'll go to a video review to try to get a square-up today? That is too ridiculous for words. If I knew I'd nicked it, I wouldn't refer it. Simple as that, when you've only got two referrals. It turns out that I did nick it, and I wish I hadn't cost us a referral. But I wasn't sure, so I referred it. And that was another desperate match situation where you're not thinking as clearly as the viewer sitting at home on the couch, or the commentator in the air-conditioned booth with all the technology at his fingertips.

It's sometimes said that a batsman always knows when he's nicked the ball. That's not right. Sometimes he does, sometimes he doesn't and sometimes he's not sure. There was one decision in the Test series against Pakistan in the Emirates in 2014, where I inside-edged a ball onto my pad. I was given out lbw and didn't refer it. I walked off. The boys said, 'You should have referred it, you smashed it.'

They were right, I should have. But I didn't feel or hear a thing. You don't always know if you've nicked it.

If I nicked a ball and nobody appealed, I was never walking off! There's a lot of uncertainty. If it was black and white, you wouldn't need umpires. Sometimes, on the other hand, you are the only one who knows you have *not* hit it. In the 2009 Test match against Pakistan in Hobart, I went to cover-drive a ball when I was about 50. It made a huge woody noise and I was given out. I walked straight up the pitch to Punter and said, 'I haven't hit that.'

His eyes bulged. 'Mate, you smashed it!'

'I swear,' I said, 'it was the handle of my bat clicking. I'm going to refer it.'

'Mate, you're dreaming.'

I called for a referral. Snicko showed nothing, and Hot Spot showed nothing. What I knew was that I always used bats with broken handles or flexi handles. I liked that whippiness. When I received a new bat, I would break the handle to increase that flex. When the bat grew hot during an innings, it often gave off a creaky noise.

Given not out, I had a big grin when I next spoke to Punter.

The first thing he said was, 'Get rid of that bat! I was certain you smashed it.' But I kept the bat, stayed in, and scored 166. Punter made a double-hundred.

They say these decisions 'even out' over the course of a long career. Although this is not statistically true, I found that it was a good thing to believe in. I played my years in cricket feeling that good and bad decisions would eventually cancel each other out. Aside from the ethics of the matter, if you're not philosophical about it and let fate and luck have their hand, you'll drive yourself mad.

The context of all this is that you're trying to win a game of cricket, and you want to win it so badly, your emotions sometimes take over. Australian cricketers have worn some criticism for letting their competitive drives take over to the point where they act unethically or disreputably. I don't believe we deserve a poor reputation.

Personally, I learnt my lesson about on-field behaviour early in life. When I was about 11, I was given out, I thought wrongly. As I walked off the field, I threw my bat. Dad, who would never make a scene in front of other people if he could help it, drew the line here. He walked onto the field and intercepted me. He grabbed me by my shirt, dragged me into the changing room and made it clear that if I ever carried on like that again, it would be the end of my cricket career. I must respect the decision that the umpire has made and not carry on when I don't get my own way. That stuck with me until the end.

The way I was brought up as an Australian cricketer, we are competitive and we love winning, but we respect that there's a line you shouldn't cross. On occasions through my career I did cross this, and I was rightly criticised and punished. I took some fines from the ICC for breaching the code of behaviour, most notably for swearing at James Anderson at the Gabba in 2013. It was right that I was fined. The integrity of the game is more important than anything else. I was brought up thinking Australian cricketers played their best when competitive, but I knew not to cross the line, and for 95 per cent of my career I believe I upheld that. I wish it was 100 per cent, but sometimes the emotions of the game took over and I made mistakes. In my time in the Australian team, my teammates' occasional breaches of the ICC code of behaviour were, I believe, similar to mine. That is, they were not part of an intention to overstep the line, but simply mistakes we made when we got caught up in the emotions of the moment.

10

THE FEUD THAT WASN'T

It's January 2016. Four months into my retirement, I am at the Sydney Cricket Ground to commentate for Channel Nine on the New Year's Test match between Australia and the West Indies. The SCG media area is a buzzing hive of television, radio, press and internet reporters mixing and gathering. Simon Katich is doing commentary for ABC Radio.

This highly anticipated showdown – which I haven't even been aware of, as I didn't know Simon would be here – happens on the first morning.

'G'day, Kat.' I smile and offer him my hand.

'G'day, Pup.'

That didn't seem too hard. We have a brief and friendly chat. We are always like this when we bump into each other during the rest of the Test match. It might be news to those who think we're sworn enemies, but face to face we have nearly always been cordial. I can't speak for Simon, but to me it's absolutely natural. We were teammates for Australia for six years, and longer for New South Wales. We've played a lot of cricket together. Why shouldn't we be friendly?

The so-called Katich–Clarke incident took place several years ago. It's still around, and it seems destined to follow us around forever, like an unwelcome guest. Simon is, if not exactly dining out on it, still getting some airtime by telling the old story. Glad to know I could be of some help!

Only thing is, I've never told my side of it.

Sometimes I ask myself: *What happened back then? The Katich–Clarke feud, can it really be a thing? Or am I just imagining it?*

No, it must be a real thing, because so many people still talk about it. For it to become Kato's greatest claim to fame would be grossly unfair for a man who played 56 Test matches and scored more than 4000 runs for Australia, at an excellent average of 45. He's a substantial cricketer, not just the guy in an after-dinner story about what a dickhead Michael Clarke was.

Ever since 2009, I have tried to make it *not* a thing, because I was always told that, by responding to stories, you only give them more oxygen. I have never said a word in public to counter or correct the various versions of the story. My strategy hasn't worked, because so many others have put in their two cents' worth, and if fantasies are repeated enough in the age of the internet, they become truth.

It's not just that others, many of whom weren't there, have written about it. It's that it has acquired a life of its own through cricket followers who have opinions about me and Kato. My ideas about ignoring it to death were ideas from a previous generation. When the only public outlet for these stories was a newspaper article, or maybe a chapter in a book, the strategy of killing them by starvation was feasible. But these days, in the echo-chamber of social media, the story goes on and on and on. My strategy failed. The story didn't die. Instead, it got bigger and bigger, so now it's time to give my version.

Throw to February 2009, the Qantas Club at Sydney airport. Kato and I catch up for a coffee together. I've texted him since the incident a few weeks ago, assuring him that everything is sweet from my end and hoping he is the same. When we have a coffee, there are no problems at all. Kato is Kato: a tough, old-school cricketer from Western Australia who moved to New South Wales and fought for years to establish himself as an international batsman. By 2009, he is the first-choice opening batsman, and he appeals to what many believe are the foundation values of the opener: hard to get out, taciturn, highly respected. We're about to go on a momentous tour of South Africa, where Phillip Hughes will make his debut for Australia. Hughesy and I are as close as brothers, and Hughesy is also a huge fan of Kato, his opening partner. Through the tour, we all get on well, and this atmosphere continues for the next two years when Kato and I are in the Australian team together. We go to England, India, all around the world.

Not a shadow of a problem. The whole 'feud' could be a mirage.

So let's go back further: 7 January 2009, a month before that friendly coffee in the Qantas Club. Our team enjoys a redemptive Test match win over South Africa in Sydney after a tough series. I make some runs, and Kato is the next-highest scorer. Peter Siddle has an eight-wicket match, and Mitchell Johnson breaks Graeme Smith's hand as we storm to a 103-run victory. But our emotions are mixed because, while we have satisfied ourselves with our performance here, our defeats in the previous two Test matches in Perth and Melbourne mean that Australia has lost a Test series at home for the first time in 16 years. But a win is a win, and we are going to celebrate in style.

I'm excited, as always when we win. We come off the field late in the day, about five o'clock, jubilant after Mitch takes the final wicket. Sidds, one of a number of young players in our team, is man of the match. Doug Bollinger and Andrew 'Ronnie' McDonald have made their Test debuts, so it's a particularly special day for them.

Prior to the end of the match, a group of the younger players – Doug Bollinger, Andrew McDonald, Peter Siddle, Brad Haddin, Nathan Hauritz and Mitch Johnson – have let me arrange a group night out in Sydney. At 27 years of age, I am always keen to be the home-town boy and take them somewhere nice, maybe a bar where we can get in without lining up and be free to enjoy ourselves in a private space.

We know that we won't leave the changing rooms at the SCG until the team song, 'Underneath the Southern Cross

I Stand', is sung. For everyone, not least the debutants Bolly and Ronnie, that's going to be a moment to cherish.

The song master, since Justin Langer's retirement in 2007, is Mike Hussey. Huss is a close mate of Simon Katich from their days as juniors in Western Australia; Kato was even best man at Huss's wedding. After we come off the field, I say to Huss, 'What time do you think we'll do the team song by? The boys want me to organise something afterwards. If I make the arrangement for midnight, is that okay?'

'Sure,' Huss says, 'it'll be well and truly done by then.'

I make a call to organise the bar. The South Africans and numerous other people come in and join us in the historic changing rooms in the SCG Members Stand. We're all having fun, and it goes on for several hours. But towards the end of the night, there's a bit of a move, and not just from me, for Huss to get up and call the song. The team song is for about 30 participants including players and support staff, some of whom don't drink, have families and want to get home. In fact, I can't remember a team song where someone in the staff isn't eventually saying, 'You've been drinking long enough, can we do the song and go home?' For me, I don't usually care. I've always been happy to kick on. On occasion I will go to a bar still in my cricket whites and keep on celebrating.

I'm patient until about 11.30 pm, when I go up to Huss and say, 'Is everything still on track for the song at midnight?'

'Yeah, of course.'

I don't worry about it until an hour later. Midnight has been and gone, and we still haven't heard John Williamson's

'True Blue' on the stereo, the cue to join in a circle and start the song. I've had a word to Steve 'Brute' Bernard, the team manager, but according to tradition the timing of the song is solely in Huss's hands. In fact, Brute has been approaching Huss at regular intervals to get the song going, and Huss has said, mischievously, 'Brutus, every time you ask me I'm going to delay it another fifteen minutes.'

By now, a lot of the young guys have come up to me saying, 'What's the plan? How long is this going to take?' At about half-past midnight, everyone converges into the main changing room to hurry things along. Huss is sitting in a corner with Kato.

Whether it's the drink, or paranoia, or just my personality – I'm often impatient for the next activity to happen – I get the impression that Huss and Kato are enjoying seeing me grow agitated. I don't know if that's true, but it's the impression I have. I go up to Huss, and let my annoyance show.

'What the f—'s going on with the song?'

Huss says, 'Yep, yep, we'll do it,' and he can see that everyone is gathering in the room waiting for him. Three-quarters of the group have started to link arms, forming the circle. If this isn't a signal that a lot of people are getting antsy, nothing could be.

By this stage I have joined the circle, with a stubby of VB in each hand to throw over people as we do the song, as we always do by tradition. I have my arms around team-mates' shoulders. We're all ready.

But Huss and Kato seem to be enjoying the delay more and more, particularly at my expense. I think I hear them say something like, 'F— it, let's make him wait a bit longer.'

And then I lose it.

'Hang on, you're doing this out of spite, you f—ing dogs. Have the balls to say it to my face.'

Kato fires up. 'What did you say?'

'I said have the balls to say it to my face, you weak c—s.'

Kato marches across the room and grabs me by the shirt collar. For a few seconds, we glare at each other and mutter obscenities. If he ever wanted to hit me, now is his chance, with me having a beer in each hand and my arms around my teammates' shoulders. But he walks away. I stay in the circle.

Then Huss says, from the corner, 'Look, the moment's not right, we're not going to do the song right now.'

I put my beers down, grab my bag and walk out.

It's all over in seconds, and I don't think a whole lot about it. If you had told me at this moment that this is going to turn into a controversy that sits on my shoulder for the rest of my career, I would ask you what you had been smoking. It really doesn't seem like a big thing. I shouldn't have walked out before the song, but the provocation seemed to be aimed at me. Simple. I lost my head and, by leaving, reacted the wrong way. The next morning, once I've had a chance to reflect, I have strong regrets about missing the song. Huss contacts me to apologise for his part in it, and I text Kato to say something like, *That was out of control, hope everything's cool.*

Andrew McDonald puts it into perspective. After I leave the room, he says, 'No worries, this type of thing happens in the Victorian dressing room every week.' He's right. Momentary flare-ups are common in cricket changing rooms. For me, it's done and dusted. I see Huss throughout the one-day series and run into Kato at the Allan Border Medal dinner a few weeks later. We're absolutely sweet. No problem at all.

Then, on 6 February, a month after the night in question, the journalist Andrew Webster breaks the story in *The Daily Telegraph*: 'Clarke and Katich in SCG dressing room bust-up.' Kato and I both speak to the paper and say we've moved on, which is the truth from my end. The story, while over-dramatising the event, is basically accurate, though it makes the untrue suggestion that I wanted to go to the bar to meet my then fiancée. Lara wasn't even in Sydney at the time. My plans were all about going to the bar with those of the team who wanted to come along.

However, now that the media has got hold of it, it mutates like Godzilla. Initially, it was me overreacting to what I thought was teammates taking the piss, missing the song, and then talking with the boys and getting over it. A one-day wonder. Now that it's public, it turns into a monster, and it confirms the suspicions of all those who think I'm a dickhead. Simon's friendship with one of the cricket journalists, who hammers me during that period, probably doesn't help.

I don't seek to defend my actions publicly. I should not have organised the bar, as it aggravated any existing tension between guys wanting to stay in the rooms and drink into the early morning, and those wanting to leave. I'm no good at this party organising caper. Four years on, I will try it again after a Sydney Test match, and again it will end up as a mess. I should have learnt my lesson. If I wanted to go out later that night in 2009, I should have just stayed for the song, however late it was sung, and done my own thing.

My next mistake was the language I used towards Kato and Huss. I shouldn't have sworn at them. Using that language, and then walking out, made it into a bigger deal than it was, and I take responsibility for that.

I also didn't know that Matty Hayden was in the process of deciding that this would be his last Test match. He was a huge presence in the team, and had been in the five and a half years since I had come into it. I could have been more sensitive to what was going on, and picked up the signals he was giving off. I can see now that it looked disrespectful for me to be organising a night out for the young guys, and being keen to get going, when this was such a momentous occasion for Haydos. I didn't see it at the time – I didn't have an inkling – but I guess some of the senior players would say that that's an indicator of how self-absorbed I was, and they would be right.

There is a string of actions I took that night that I'm sorry for. That said, I tried to make it up immediately, and felt that I had. I've heard the accounts of the night given by Mike Hussey and others who were there, and they're substantially the same. The peripheral bit about Lara is wrong, but when it comes to remembering what happened in the dressing room, we're all on the same page. There is no major dispute on what happened.

How then did it blow up? I was slow to comprehend the nature of the fishbowl we were living in. I was still young and naive enough to think that these conflicts are the type of minor stoushes that happen between teammates in any club on any weekend, and they don't go any further. I didn't understand how social media culture works – how, because I was now viewed as a 'celebrity', it was all magnified.

And by 2009 many people in the public had decided that I wasn't their cup of tea. I was earning too much money, I was too brash and lairy in style, I had done photo shoots in my underwear, I drove flash cars, I lived in Bondi and I had a fiancée who was a model. For a lot of people, that ticks all the boxes for what they need to know about me.

I had no insight into that. I was just living my life and enjoying it to the max. I was an incredibly lucky 27-year-old from the western suburbs who was able to enjoy everything he had ever dreamed of getting. It was no more complicated than that.

Soon, it would grow a *lot* more complicated.

My relationship with Kato, as I've said, continued through 2009 and 2010 without missing a beat. We went to South Africa a day after the story broke in the paper, and were fine. If I had wanted to alienate Kato, I could have said to Phillip Hughes, 'Don't talk to him.' But that's not me. I loved the relationship that Kato and Hughesy had, and never said a single bad word about him. We were young men who'd had a disagreement. That's it. Even if we'd had a punch-up that night – and it never got to that – it would still have been something we could have smoothed over between the two of us. That's how I've been brought up: I've seen a lot of punch-ups where guys have been laughing over a beer ten minutes later. My way, which has never been afraid of confrontation, is to get it over with and move on.

Kato and I didn't catch up socially outside of cricket, but that was not unusual. Cricketers live in each other's pockets for several months of the year. When they get outside the game, most of them enjoy their non-cricketing friends. I had a few teammates in the Australian cricket team, such as Brad Haddin and Hughesy at that point, who I would also hang out with in the off-season. Kato would have been similar with his circle of friends.

He'd had a bit of a contest with Hadds over the captaincy of New South Wales, and it's possible Kato thought, because I was close to Hadds, that I was taking sides on the issue, but I wasn't part of that contest and never talked about it. My only connection with that story was that I would have liked to gain some captaincy experience with New South Wales myself, but once the decision was made to go with a regular state player, be it Kato or Hadds, I had nothing further to do with it.

I really think the way these stories snowball says more about the nature of fame than about us as individuals. Sections of the public characterised me in a certain way and Kato in another, and it gave them something to talk about. I was the metrosexual with the Bondi pad, and Kato was the plain-spoken Western Australian with enough body hair for a whole team. I was the flashy batsman, while Kato was the grinder who made the most of his talent. Never mind how much relation this bore to the truth. A lot of people had made their minds up because they weren't really talking about us, they were responding to celebrity caricatures and the society they lived in. They were expressing their feelings about money and Australian values, and pinning our names on those feelings.

The myth of the 'feud' came during a period when that negative perception of me began to solidify in parts of the media and in the public. I got mad when I read these stories, but I decided to cop it in silence. It's not worth the grief to respond to every single thing that is written about me. If I kicked every stone I'd come across, I would have no toes left.

The hardest part was Mum or Dad or Pop saying, 'Is this true? I've read it in the paper.' When I saw how hurt my family could get, every now and then I would confront an individual journalist to get my point across. Inside, I was wanting to punch their heads in. I was proud that I had the courage to say what I felt on those occasions, but as a strategy, confrontation never works. The journalists could feel my anger and were probably even less favourable towards me after we exchanged words. I never felt like I had won. At best, I got the impression that they would back away on a minor point, and let me have my say, but then just wait until the next chance to give me a smack in the mouth. I didn't feel that I gained their respect by confronting them, so for the most part I gave that up too.

So with my silence and the Kato thing taking on a life of its own, with only one side of the story being told, perception became reality. I did make a mistake in not publicly addressing the Kato story. I thought that the more I said, the more I would have given it legs. But it had legs anyway.

By 2010–11, I thought the Kato story had died a natural death. Then, during the Ashes series, which was a disaster for us as a team, Kato injured his Achilles tendon and was omitted after we lost the Second Test in Adelaide. I was having a disappointing series too, not making enough runs to help the team. Only Mike Hussey, Shane Watson and Brad Haddin were propping up our batting totals. Ricky and I, as captain and vice-captain, were not pulling our weight with the run-scoring that was expected of us, and in the Third Test in Perth, which we won to level the series, Ricky broke a finger.

He played in Melbourne, where we were trounced and England retained the Ashes. In Sydney, I was made captain while Ricky was injured, and we lost again. We didn't know it, but Kato had played his last Test match.

A few months later, after we are knocked out of the 2011 World Cup in the quarter-finals in India, Cricket Australia appoints me captain in Ricky's place. The Argus Review, as part of CA's revamp of Australian cricket, puts the captain on the National Selection Panel. During the winter, Cricket Australia announces its list of 25 contracted players, and Kato's name is missing. A squad to tour Sri Lanka is named, and he's not there either.

I can see how it looks to Kato. He has a fantastic Test record, with more than 4000 runs at an average of 45, and all he did was injure his Achilles. In the Ashes, I have an abysmal time, scoring 193 runs in nine innings, the worst series of my career. And yet, by the end of it, I'm Australian captain and he's on the outer. He's been reading the papers and hearing the gossip. Based on the perception of me that has been built up in the media, he joins the dots. Michael Clarke has taken the job of a national hero, Ricky Ponting, and now he's manoeuvred to get Kato off contract and out of the Australian team. Kato now hears all the people who say that I've acted out of revenge, paying him back for what happened at the SCG two years ago.

By now, in 2011, I'm much more aware of how the dark side of the fame game works. A persona has been created for me. Kato, who hasn't seen me in person for several months, might easily make inferences based on that persona. If I was in his position, I'm sure I would think the same.

While I regret and apologise for my actions in the SCG dressing room on 7 January 2009, I have nothing to apologise for on this occasion – because I have nothing, absolutely nothing, to do with the decisions the selectors make about Kato in 2011.

When it comes to Cricket Australia contracts, I was never consulted, even when I was captain. I was never once asked if a player should get a contract. I simply wasn't allowed to be in those meetings. We might have a team selection meeting, and then Andrew Hilditch or John Inverarity, whoever was the chairman of the panel, would say, 'Selection meeting's over, contract meeting is starting. Michael, you have to leave.' I was never part of any contract meeting.

I was part of team selections, and I remember the discussions in 2011. The only relevant part that I was consulted on was how I felt about Ricky Ponting continuing in the team as a batsman under my captaincy. During the Argus Review, before I had even been appointed captain, they had said to me, 'If you do become captain, if you want Ricky to stay, he can stay, but if you want him to go, he'll go.' It was an easy conversation. I had no doubt I wanted him to play. The group needed him around. We needed his runs and his experience, and the young guys could become better cricketers simply by watching him train and bat, by being with him in the field, and by chatting with him off it. There was no question at all in my mind, and if my input was needed, I was throwing it all behind keeping Punter in the team.

But I had no idea how that might impact on Kato's place. By the time I was appointed captain, the driving personality on the selection panel was Greg Chappell. Greg's view was that the champion batsmen had proved themselves in Test cricket at a young age, in their late teens or early twenties. He thought that the best young batsmen in the country in 2011 were Phillip Hughes and Usman Khawaja. If they were going to turn into the mainstays of the next generation, they needed a chance to grow into Test cricket now, when they were still 21 or 22 years old.

With the batting line-up we had in 2011, this left a numbers problem. If Hughesy and Uzzy were to be picked, and Shaun Marsh was getting his chance as well in the drive for renewal, that meant one of the senior men in their mid-thirties – Punter, Huss and Kato – had to miss out. Punter? No question. Huss? He'd been easily our best batsman in the losing Ashes series (and was about to be man of the match in all three Test matches in Sri Lanka). Kato? Outstanding batsman. So then the selectors looked at what else these players brought. Punter brought leadership and outstanding catching skills. Huss was a very good player of spin bowling, with our next tour being to Sri Lanka, and was one of the most popular players in that team. It was unfair for Kato to be put in a contest with those two, but that was the way the selectors were making their choice over the awarding of contracts for the next year. They decided that Kato would be the one to miss out. I had nothing to do with it.

But perception, as I say, is reality. The 'Katich–Clarke feud' story had bubbled away for so long, without me doing anything to refute it, that it became the default explanation for Kato's omission. Despite my best efforts to make the situation clear to him, he thought the driving personality in his omission had to be me. I felt like I was up against a brick wall, where nothing I could say would change his mind. It is one of the stories from my cricket career that makes me saddest.

There is one last twist to it. Two years later, in early 2013, the Australian team is in crisis again. Within weeks, Punter and Huss have both retired from international cricket. We go to India with an inexperienced line-up and get pounded 4–0.

In the two months between our return from India and the 2013 Ashes tour, I am part of a critical selection meeting. I actually volunteer to step down from the selection panel after India, for lots of reasons, but Cricket Australia have refused to accept my offer. So I'm on the panel with John Inverarity, Mickey Arthur, Rod Marsh and Andy Bichel.

I say that, without Punter and Huss, we were exposed for our lack of experience in India. If we go to England with this inexperience, we risk being slaughtered. I want Brad Haddin back as one of our two wicketkeepers, either to deputise for Matthew Wade or, if the selectors think he's playing well enough, to be our number one. Hadds has been to England on two previous Ashes tours, and I need his steadiness.

It's not just Hadds I need. There's another senior player, going very well in domestic cricket, who has also been on two Ashes tours and has scored a lot of runs in England. I say to John Inverarity, 'Give me Kato.' I plead with John over an extended period. I fight for Kato. I never wanted him out of the team, and I feel that I really need him back in it now that Punter and Huss are gone. He was sacrificed for them in 2011, and now that they are both gone, there is no rationale against bringing him back.

The other selectors consider my arguments but reject them. Instead, they pick Chris Rogers, the 36-year-old opener who played one Test match for Australia in 2007–08. I think Kato would have been brilliant on that 2013 Ashes tour, but Chris turns out to be an inspired choice, the highest run-scorer over the two Ashes series in 2013 and 2014, and our top-order mainstay until his retirement in 2015. I also wonder how many runs Kato would have made if he'd been given another chance. I wanted him there. But it's difficult for the world to believe that I fought to bring him back, because they think we're enemies.

I hope that, in the calm of retirement, Kato will understand it too, because he knows that we have no personal problems with each other and can look back on a lot of successful cricket as teammates over many years. We might be characters in a story that got built up into a fiction, but when we meet in person and look each other in the eye, we are just another pair of retired old teammates who can remember the same special games, and the privilege we shared for several years of playing for our country.

Kato was my partner when I first stepped out to bat for Australia in a Test match. That's a much more important memory for me than what happened in a changing room five years later.

11

ENGLAND

It's damp and cold, I'm struggling with the challenges of living on my own in a foreign country, and I'm embarrassed by my performance. Even though I'm only 21 years old, I am the professional cricketer at Ramsbottom in the Lancashire League and I am failing to contribute. The standard is probably the equivalent of first grade in Sydney club cricket – and that makes it even more annoying that I'm not pulling my weight. Mostly opening the batting, I've made 109 runs in my first six innings for the club.

I go to our captain, Mark Price, who has stepped into the role of big brother for me here. Pricey is 42 years old, a former Glamorgan first-class all-rounder who has played many years of league cricket. Today, I've scored 3 against Heywood playing at our home ground, Acre Bottom, in a one-day fixture. Tomorrow we're due to play the Church club, whose pro is my good mate from Sydney, Mark Higgs. But it's raining again.

In despair, I sit down with Pricey. 'I'm the overseas player,' I say, 'and I can't make a run.'

Pricey is completely unbothered. In fact, he's more interested in urging me to go to the pub with my other 'big brother' at the club, Kev Denton. 'There'll be no play tomorrow,' Pricey assures me, before sending me on my way.

One of my big weaknesses is my difficulty in switching off. I love cricket so much that I sometimes wish I didn't have to sleep. Ever since I was seven, I've got up at daybreak on match day and counted off the minutes until we can start. Since Ramsbottom approached my management during my third season in the New South Wales team, I've lapped up the idea of professional, six-day-a-week cricket. But the reality is that, when I'm not playing well and finding the springtime conditions a challenge, my wheels are spinning. Lots of energy but nowhere to go.

Pricey's is a valuable lesson, and it works – in an unanticipated way. My night out with Kev gets me well and truly off the subject of cricket. I get that mini-holiday for a few hours that Pricey has recommended.

The weather has cleared by morning. Mentally refreshed, I score 112 off 118 balls. Pricey's tactic has unlocked me. Two weeks later, the night before we play Enfield, I think I'll take his advice a little further. Again we think the game is going to be rained off, and I go out with Kev until 5 am. My only setback is when Pricey's phone call wakes me at 9 am.

'We're on, Michael.'

'Eh?'

'We're starting on time. The rain's cleared.'

'Please don't tell me that,' I croak.

He doesn't have to tell me that there's no option of asking for a day off. I'm the professional. I have to be setting some kind of example, and blaming the captain for sending me out for a big night is not part of my job description.

'Just promise me one thing,' I say. 'If you win the toss, field.'

'Sure. See you at the ground.'

Of course, Pricey does win the toss – and decides to bat. And I'm opening.

I piece myself together and walk to the wicket thinking, *It was a set-up. Pricey knew this was going to happen.*

Cramped and dehydrated, I score 200, breaking Ramsbottom's record for a one-day innings.

Pricey has taught me something about preparation. For me, alcohol is not a good idea before cricket, and never will be. His lesson wasn't to go out and get drunk, it was to allow myself to forget the pressure of being the overseas player, forget cricket; step back from my intense keenness and just go out and play the game I love.

Ramsbottom is my true introduction to English cricket. I toured there before, with the New South Wales Schoolboys when I was 16 and the Australian Cricket Academy at 18, but at Ramsbottom, and again at Hampshire two seasons later, I have to be an independent person. That's probably the most valuable part of the experience, though the cricket and the team environment provide a great schooling for me as well. I arrive not knowing anyone, and have to find a way to fit in. To my relief, I find the team atmosphere similar to how it is with my club and state back home, with the senior players holding a certain status and the youngsters watching and learning. I find it natural to attach myself to guys like Pricey and Kev at Ramsbottom and Shane Warne and Dimitri Mascarenhas at Hampshire, because that's what I've done ever since B-grade at Players with Dad. But it's different to be doing it so far from home, and the experience does a world of good for my self-confidence.

It's the start of what I regard as a happy personal relationship with English cricket. It might not seem so on the surface, because I will go on four Ashes tours from 2005 to 2015 and come away empty-handed each time. Winning the urn in England will become one of my burning ambitions in cricket, and it is one that will remain unachieved. I hate that, but on the other hand I always enjoy playing there. I love the people and the value they place on the game of cricket, and can honestly say that some of my favourite memories of cricket are in England.

English crowds make a lot of noise, belying the small-capacity grounds their Tests are staged in. I never feel that hostile crowds have any negative impact on my performance – I like to channel their energy – but when you're inexperienced, it's exciting and scary. For young players, an Ashes battle is built up as such a big series. Some people like and look forward to that stage, and others are a bit afraid of it. I love all the Ashes series I play in, but I never place that contest on a pedestal above others. My approach to cricket is increasingly methodical and systematic as I get older, and I prepare the same way for an Ashes Test at Lord's as I would for a Test match against Bangladesh in Fatullah. No difference at all. But when I get out into the middle, I find that I do love the English atmosphere and I set myself to rise to the challenge.

The 2005 Ashes tour is rightly fabled for the fantastic cricket that is played, the epic finishes to the Test matches at Edgbaston and Old Trafford, and the emotion that follows England's first Ashes win in 18 years. Both teams are stacked with big stars of the game, and for me the memory forms part of the dizzy ride from my Test debut in 2004 to getting dropped in late 2005. Although we lose the series 2–1, I confess that I am in a state of constant exhilaration. Having picked up some more English experience with a stint at Hampshire in 2004, I am primed to go and love *almost* every minute of it. I understand that the experience is not as fun for some of our senior players, who are struggling with distraction and disappointment, but for me, as a 24-year-old, that is all passing me by. Whether Ricky bats or bowls at Edgbaston, whether Pigeon is playing or not, I am jumping to it. Let me get my gear on, let's go!

That series opens my eyes to how hard-fought Test cricket can be. On the first morning of the series at Lord's, Justin Langer and Ricky are hit in the head and we are bowled out within 40 overs. Steve Harmison, who takes five wickets that day, is towering and fast and extremely awkward to face. Simon Jones traps me lbw for 11, and his fast reverse-swing is a handful throughout the series.

Andrew Flintoff, meanwhile, is the toughest fast bowler I ever face. He would never get me out in the three Test series I play against him, but he could have done so many times and I still rate him at the top of the heap. He is pacy and hostile, and every ball bounces surprisingly steeply. Unlike many fast bowlers, Flintoff never seems to flag in his second, third or fourth spells, even in hot conditions in Australia in 2006–07. He might not have got me out, but he is a nightmare to face, particularly in England.

I manage 91 in the second innings at Lord's, in a counter-attacking partnership with the ever-calm Damien Martyn. It will be my highest score in the 2005 series in the only Test match we win. I am pretty content with my performances, though I wish I could have done something more to lift the team in the games we lose at Edgbaston and Trent Bridge. I have a difficult Test match at Old Trafford. Second ball of the game, as I throw the ball in from point, I feel my back go. I am off the field for the remainder of the match and score 7 and 39 while enduring some pain; fortunately, Punter plays one of the great captain's knocks and helps us get away with a draw.

The cricket is hard and exciting to a degree I've never experienced, but at that age, when I walk out to bat, I have absolutely no fear of failing. Even with the crowd baying and an aggressive England side waiting for me, I am thinking, *Bring it on!* When I look back, it's poignant. That devil-may-care attitude I brought to my cricket in 2005 had been overshadowed by physical and mental fatigue by the time I went to England in 2015.

When we return to England in 2009, we hold the Ashes again thanks to our 5–0 whitewash at home, but we have lost decades' worth of experience. Since 2005, the retirements have piled up: Justin Langer, Matthew Hayden, Damien Martyn, Adam Gilchrist, Shane Warne, Glenn McGrath, Michael Kasprowicz and Jason Gillespie are all gone, and Brett Lee, while still playing, has finished his Test career. The only remaining players from the 2005 Ashes XI are Punter and myself.

With the added responsibility of the vice-captaincy, I take it upon myself to be like Ricky and lead from the front. Batting-wise, it is my best series in England, with hundreds at Lord's and Edgbaston, 93 at Headingley and 83 at Cardiff.

Statistically, we have most of the leading batsmen and bowlers in that series, but somehow our team effort doesn't add up to the sum of its parts. We dominate the First Test in Cardiff but can't close it out on a dead wicket in the face of some stubborn English last-day batting. I feel that if we'd won that match, we would have run away with the series.

Having enjoyed a massive series win in South Africa earlier in 2009, we arrive in England with a lot of confidence. The draw in the Cardiff Test seems to shatter that, and we fall victim to some well-timed bowling spells from Andrew Flintoff and Stuart Broad at Lord's and Edgbaston. England play very well in their conditions, and grab the momentum at critical times when they can convert it into victories. They deserve credit for seizing those 'big moments'.

THE INNINGS

136 versus England, Lord's, 2009

As shattering as losing the Ashes was, I again loved playing cricket in English conditions. The hundred I scored at Lord's in the 2009 series was arguably the best, technically, I ever made.

I am even more nervous than usual before my second innings. We got off to a bad start in the match, England racing away to 425 in their first innings before dismissing us for 215. I was out for 1, right in the middle of our collapse. England declare before lunch on the fourth day, setting us 522 runs to win, which we think, in six sessions, is not impossible. But Kato and Hughesy lose their wickets before lunch, and when Punter is out an over after the break, with Mike Hussey and Marcus North soon following, a draw seems our most realistic hope.

I'm conscious of Lord's being Australia's 'home away from home' down the years. We have not lost a Test match here since 1934. While I'm not a cricket history buff, I can't help but feel humbled by the stories here. When Ricky gets out, I leave the changing room and walk down the carpet they have rolled out through the Long Room. The Lord's members, on either side of the carpet, applaud me on my way out. I remember batting here in 2005 and blowing a hundred, getting out for 91. If I get the chance, I won't throw it away again.

As a batsman, I am a different player from that last Ashes tour. I have worked hard on holding my balance and committing later. During hours facing a bowling machine set on swinging the ball, I have drilled myself in waiting and waiting and moving only when I am certain. It takes courage and trust in my skills. I limit my backswing and rely on fast hands. My stance is lower as I keep my knees flexed, and wait . . .

First ball, I could be out. Stuart Broad is bowling down the slope, and I leave it. It darts in and I don't know how it's missed my off stump.

In my head, I have a song. I listen to music on my iPod before I bat, and usually I sing the last song I've heard before I leave the changing room. But sometimes the last song disappears, and my go-to is 'When The Saints Go Marching In', the song that Pop was always singing down at Bundeena. When I'm singing that in my head, it often feels like a good omen. At Lord's, I hit the ball, and mark my guard: twice middle, twice leg. Same every ball. The bowler turns at the top of his mark, and as he comes in, the song becomes clearer. It feels like an insulation – against the sledging, against the crowd noise, or, here at Lord's, against the pregnant silence around each ball. Singing Pop's song to myself, I could be at Pratten Park batting for Wests, I could be anywhere. It's the home of cricket but I'm in my own world.

The ball is swinging, and there's only one thing for it. As Warney always told me, the better the bowling, the harder the conditions, the more positive you have to be. But easier said than done. Andrew Flintoff is a nightmare, fast and steepling. But James Anderson pitches up, and I get away with a cover drive for four. That seems to confirm the theory: stay positive, score runs. I get three boundaries off one Anderson over, all between point and mid-off, and it just feels right.

Once Huss and Northy are out, I am joined by Brad Haddin. It feels great to be batting with Hadds, here at Lord's, and despite the desperate situation for our team the two of us can sense how special it is to be here, knowing where we've come from: all those years ago, training and playing together for New South Wales, spending nights out and dreaming that a day like this might one day arrive. Hadds is also great to bat with because, like Andrew Symonds and Mike Hussey, he is an aggressive runner between wickets. We want every single we can take, and when we punch it through the infield we want a two, maybe a three. I am fitter and leaner now than I was early in my career, and don't feel any fatigue.

I once didn't know how fit you really had to be for Test cricket, but I do now.

Even with the match situation being what it is, Hadds and I have a ball. We bat for 50 overs together and put on 185 runs, getting through to stumps at five for 313. There are even thoughts of an unlikely win. Flintoff gets Hadds for 80 in his first over on the last day, but Mitch Johnson and I set about building another partnership.

We have got the required runs down to 166 when Graeme Swann lobs up what looks like a juicy full toss. I can see this going for four through mid-off. Somehow I miss it, and am bowled. It's devastating, because I really thought we could win this.

They clap me off and through the Long Room, and the mixed emotions of cricket couldn't be more contrasting. To get your name on the honour board at Lord's for a century is a nice accolade in a batsman's career, and yet I've also let the team down with that shot. It turns out to be the story of that Ashes campaign: many individual highlights, but as a team we can't manage to convert them into Test match wins.

By the time we go to England in 2013, the world will have turned again. Punter will have stepped down as captain after we lose to England in 2010–11, Australia's first home Ashes loss since the mid-1980s. I am going to England as captain now, but we are a team in upheaval. Our Ashes planning anticipates both Punter and Mike Hussey going for a final England tour, but both retire in the 2012–13 summer. We will build up to this campaign for two years with Mickey Arthur as head coach, but our series loss in India in early 2013 puts paid to that. When we arrive at Trent Bridge for the first of five Ashes Test matches, we are rank outsiders.

Early 2013 will certainly be the most challenging period of my career so far: 'Homeworkgate', losing 4–0 in India, and having our coach replaced 18 days before the Ashes. It's a time when everything seems to be up in the air. My chronic back injury is getting worse and worse. By this stage of my career, the responsibilities of captaincy add a lot to my workload, while I am still trying to maintain my training and preparation to contribute as best I can as a batsman.

Over the previous two years, I have been scoring heavily while a lot of new batsmen were coming into our line-up, and in the lead-up to the 2013 Ashes this was adding to the expectation. I am happy, of course, to take on that responsibility, having admired the way Punter shouldered it for so many years, but in 2013 I am in almost constant discomfort with my back and hamstrings. My build-up in England is dictated as much by my need to be close to a MedX machine in London as it is by match practice.

With all this as background, I am as proud of that 2013 team as of any other I play in. We lose the series 3–0, but it is closer than that. At Trent Bridge, the amazing tenth-wicket world record partnership between Ashton Agar and Phillip Hughes keeps us in contention. In the changing room, as their stand builds, we count every single run and stick to our seats, superstitiously, like it's the last wicket on the last day. I love seeing the two lefties out there, both so talented, and now Hughesy, who has always been the youngster in teams he's been in, playing the part of elder statesman. Ashton idolises Hughesy and it's moving to see him in this role. Before the series, Hughesy and I have talked a lot about whether he should captain South Australia or the Adelaide Strikers if he gets the chance, and I've urged him to put his hand up for it. Now I see him in that leadership role. He has the gift of getting the most out of people, and he's doing it with Ashton. We knew Ashton was a good batsman, but his scoring 98 on debut catches us by pleasant surprise. As the runs pile up, there's a bit of joking in the changing room at the expense of Peter Siddle, Mitchell Starc and James Pattinson, all of whom have batted higher than Ashton in this innings. It won't be happening again!

It's a great Test match, right up to the final day, when all seems lost and Brad Haddin and James Pattinson build another stand at the end of the innings. It is heartbreaking to fall 14 runs short, a wafer-thin difference that means much, much more. For us, a win would have provided enormous self-belief after losing four straight matches in India. For England, the win reassures them that the plans they are pursuing under coach Andy Flower and captain Alastair Cook are working. They carry that momentum to Lord's, where they take a 2–0 advantage.

We still believe we can win the series, and the wheel seems to be turning our way in the Third Test at Old Trafford. I win the toss and we bat on yet another dry pitch that heavily favours the side batting first. I make 187 in our score of seven for 527, the first time in the series we have been able to establish a stronghold. We remain well ahead in the game and are very confident we can finish England off on the last day, but a steady downpour puts an end to that and enables our hosts to celebrate retaining the Ashes.

A loss in Durham and a draw at The Oval mean we go down in the series without winning a Test match, but we are sticking to our bowling plans, which we will bring to full fruition in Australia three months later. Unusually, two Ashes series are being played back-to-back in 2013. We play full-on to win in England, but we also keep an eye on the return series in Australia. Through the England Test matches, our bowling unit of Ryan Harris, Peter Siddle, Nathan Lyon, Mitchell Starc, Jackson Bird, James Pattinson and James Faulkner chisel away at the England top order with tight lines and specific plans for different players. Ian Bell gets away from us a few times, but Alastair Cook, Jonathan Trott and Kevin Pietersen don't contribute as many runs as previously against us.

On that tour, coming off the back of our disaster in India, you would normally expect a team to fracture. We undergo a lot of personnel changes, we are dealing with a new coach, and we don't win a Test match, all prime ingredients for faltering morale and performance. Instead, we hold firm throughout, fired up by our eagerness to get England in our back yard later in the year. Harris, Siddle and Lyon come into their own on that tour, and Mitchell Johnson, after a lay-off from the game, is about to come back to provide us with our X-factor.

All up, I suppose you could look at that 2013 Ashes tour as an excellent build-up to the series that followed it. We grow more and more sick of losing, until we won't take it any more. We are not happy with our results, but in a good way. We gain clear sight of what we need to do to fix it, and the back-to-back schedule is giving us the chance to do it straight away, rather than wait two years.

For me personally, it is a different kind of tour. My cricket now is my profession as much as my love, and my back injury means I have to put more and more time into off-field preparation. Evenings are spent quietly with Kyly and my other closest companion, physio Alex Kountouris. The job of captaincy runs 24/7, while the adjustment to a new coaching structure means we have a lot of meetings. I do enjoy it – don't get me wrong – but in a different kind of way from the more carefree tours of England in the past.

The 2015 tour will be another animal yet again. We go to England with a strong sense of destiny. A lot of things feel so right: we have beaten England 5–0 at home and then defeated South Africa and India. We have won the 2015 World Cup. I have never been on an Ashes trip when we've been better prepared. En route to England, we win a Test series in the West Indies in poor conditions on very slow wickets, a tough tour marked by an absence of any whingeing from the boys.

Once we are in England, we win all of our practice games. That is our goal: to win everything. When I have spoken to Allan Border, Mark Taylor and Steve Waugh about how to succeed in England, the first thing AB says is, 'Get more first-class games, and don't muck around with them. Play them to win.' That suits us fine. We have plenty of cricket and training before the First Test and prepare with new Duke balls that swing and seam.

The first domino to fall is Ryan Harris. Rhino is the cornerstone of our bowling plans after his comeback to Test cricket during the 2013 Ashes tour. His knee gives him grief every time he plays, but there are times, such as when he picks himself up off the canvas to deliver the final match-winning spell at Cape Town in 2014, when he is truly heroic – there's no other word for it. Through the second part of the Australian 2014–15 summer, Rhino has been cotton-woolled by selectors, and then he stays at home while we go to the West Indies to be with his wife Cherie for the birth of their first child and to get himself fully fit for the Ashes. The strength and conditioning coaches tell me regularly that he's in as good nick as he's ever been.

Rhino is a champion bloke, a real team leader, and everyone looks forward to his return, which gives us a huge boost on the eve of the Ashes series. Will this be it, finally? Everything feels perfect to me, until, three days before the First Test in Cardiff, Rhino's knee flares up and the X-rays show a fracture. The medical staff quickly ascertain that this is not something that will mend during the tour. For Rhino, at 35 years of age with a long history of knee injuries behind him, it means retirement. For me, as his captain, it's devastating. I feel that the effect of losing Rhino is as critical as losing Glenn McGrath in 2005, but I keep those thoughts to myself.

I try to force it to the back of my mind, but I can't let go of my regret about Rhino's absence. In the conditions we get through the series, he would have been unplayable. We are expecting dry wickets, in line with what England served up in 2013, and we do get a barren, thatchy pitch in Cardiff, where England outplay us in all departments. However, after another dry pitch at Lord's, where we turn the tables, the pitch preparation does a U-turn.

It is no secret that English curators are participants in the game plan, and a decision appears to have been made. Against the pattern of the previous seven Test matches over two series, the Third and Fourth Tests of 2015 take place on underprepared green seamers at Edgbaston and Trent Bridge, the latter being the worst pitch I ever see in my 115 Test matches.

Throughout, as the series develops this way, I can't shake off how much we are missing Rhino. These are seaming conditions, and he is our one authentic seam bowler. Mitchell Johnson and Mitchell Starc swing the ball, but don't seam it.

Josh Hazlewood can seam the ball, but still lacks experience. I stand at slip, watching things unravel, thinking, *If Ryan Harris is in our attack, it's a completely different series. I don't even think they'd have prepared these wickets if he was fit.*

That's not a good way to think, but it's indicative of my mindset. Knowing that I will most likely retire at the end of the series, win or lose, might have caused a subtle change in my psychological approach. Through my career, I have seen cricketers get clouded over by a sense of 'Here's another thing not going my way', and before they know it they feel that the whole world is against them. That has never been me. I don't pity myself, but there's no doubt things are adding up.

Fatigue from a big summer starts to catch up with a few of the guys. We thought we were still up for the challenge, but deep down some of us are burnt out from a long Australian summer, followed by the World Cup, the IPL, the West Indies and England: almost a year of uninterrupted cricket. It is one of the times when, if we were winning, none of those distractions would be visible. But because we lose at Edgbaston and Trent Bridge, five or six different factors continue to niggle.

The team, I have to say, are awesome throughout. Their attitude at training has been unbelievable. I get a lift from them. I wish I could give more back. Becoming desperate about my need to contribute runs, I set myself to work harder. I never knew anyone in cricket who got better from doing less. Even Warney wouldn't leave the nets until he was bowling the way he wanted. He wouldn't run laps, but he prepared really thoroughly.

I look at each individual at training and think, *This guy's ready*. Everything I want as a captain, they give me 10 out of 10.

Now it is up to me. Why am I feeling so slow on my feet? I've faced faster than Broad, Anderson and the rest, in tougher conditions, and had no problems. Am I over-practising, hitting balls for the sake of hitting balls at training? Something's not right. My body is fine, but my mind has moved on. Maybe I need someone like Pricey to step in and say, 'Forget about cricket, have a night out with Kev.'

That would have happened when I was 21. There is no such option when I am 34, nearing the end, and battling with my demons and confusions.

A win at The Oval in my farewell Test match, and a 3–2 scoreline, hardly allays the disappointment. It still eats away at me. I feel that it was the only thing I didn't achieve in my career, winning a Test series in England. It's hard to swallow, considering how much I loved playing there.

12

CHASING THE MIRAGE

On 18 January 2003, I get off the plane in Coffs Harbour with my New South Wales teammates, super-excited about a one-day ING Cup match tomorrow. Here's an illustration of the strength of domestic cricket: stepping into the terminal with me are Steve and Mark Waugh, Michael Slater, Stuart MacGill, Brad Haddin, Simon Katich and several other top-line players. Our opponents, Western Australia, have Justin Langer, Mike Hussey, Chris Rogers and Shaun Marsh. None of these players, on either side, is a current member of the Australian one-day team.

We go through the terminal and pick up our cricket bags. I am in the bus waiting to leave for the hotel when our team manager comes up with a flustered look, his mobile phone in his hand.

'Michael, you've got to turn around.'

My stomach sinks. *What have I done wrong?*

'You've got to fly back to Sydney,' he says. 'They've picked you in the one-dayer.'

I'm confused. 'I'm *here* for the one-dayer.'

He shakes his head, caught up with the logistical complications.

'No, Australia. You're in the one-dayer in Adelaide.'

My first thought is, *Oh no*. My hand goes up to my head, as if to check that it's still there. It is – not my head, but my new hairstyle. I have just had my head shaved to a stubble and dyed white. It looks like a tennis ball. *No way, I can't play for Australia on television until it grows back. I'll look like an absolute idiot.*

Fixing my head doesn't seem to be an option. I fly back to Sydney and connect to Adelaide, and if I can do nothing about the outside of my head, I can try to get the inside in order. Australia are playing a triangular one-day series with England and Sri Lanka. With an eye to preparing for the World Cup in South Africa next month, two of the frontline batsmen – Matthew Hayden and Ricky Ponting – have been left out of the game in Adelaide, while Darren Lehmann is suspended on a racial vilification charge. I'm only 21 years old, and still the kid in the New South Wales team. It doesn't seem real that I'm playing for Australia.

When I get to my room in the Holiday Inn in Hindley Street, my heart skips a beat. A green Australian cricket coffin is on the floor, with my name on it. My clothes are laid out inside, and I try them on: every shirt, every pair of pants. On the back of the shirts is CLARKE. I don't think I have felt so hyped-up in my whole life. I even forget about my haircut.

My New South Wales teammates in the Australian team, Michael Bevan and Nathan Bracken, make me welcome and share a Thai meal with me across the road from the hotel. I don't sleep very soundly, unable to wait for the next day. I've fallen asleep at night dreaming of this since I was a child, and now here I am.

The morning passes in a blur, but the game is a fantasy. England bat first, and we get through their top order without much trouble. Adam Gilchrist, who is standing in as captain for Ricky Ponting, gives me the ball and I roll the arm over for seven overs, not giving away too many runs and even getting a wicket, Ronnie Irani caught by Bevo on the boundary trying to hit me into the Torrens.

Chasing 153, we lose Gilly and Jimmy Maher in the first three overs. Damien Martyn and Bevo steady us, but with about 60 runs to get, we collapse. Bevo and pinch-hitter Brett Lee are out within the space of five balls, and I'm out there with Marto. A couple of overs later, he and Andrew Symonds are both out. We still need 49 runs to win in 13 overs when Shane Watson joins me. Suddenly England are favourites.

Stepping up from domestic to international cricket is about so much more than just the standard of play. This is my first time batting in front of more than a few hundred people. I might have dreamed of this occasion, and consciously visualised it a million times – but that gives me no clue as to whether I'm going to enjoy it or not. I think

I will, but I won't know until it's happening. A lot of cricketers, I know, are fundamentally shy and don't relish the attention, but to me it feels normal. With all these people watching, with the gold shirt on, with the blue shirts surrounding me, knowing: *This is the big stage*, it's odd but I don't feel any different. I kind of like it, but am not sure how much yet.

Watto and I bring the game home in ten overs. It's a huge thrill. I know I won't be in the World Cup squad, but I am absolutely stoked with that first game – and I want more.

The Australian one-day team under Gilly are very welcoming in Adelaide. As with my state team, there is a very old-school mentality – if anyone has to carry the stereo from place to place, the youngster carries it and, at the end of a day's play, I have to ask the senior players who wants a beer and go and fetch it for them. I don't mind – that was how it was in Dad's club teams, and at the indoor centre. I loved carrying the stereo in district cricket, because it meant I was getting a game! In the Australian changing room, like any other, the culture of respect for your elders is paramount. I'm used to it, and will do anything I'm asked.

The verbal side of the game also seems, on my first taste, no different. For New South Wales, I have been sledged big-time since my first game, about how young I looked, how small I was. *What are you doing out here? You should be at a blue light disco!* Every team, every game, it was on ... There wasn't anyone who didn't have a go at me, and it's a good preparation for entering the Australian team.

When I was young, I would always say something back, but over time I realised I could never win that battle so I learnt to shut up. And I didn't actually mind being sledged. It was exciting, and it showed these guys cared. In fact, the worst sledging I've seen in my life was in indoor cricket, which I've watched since I was seven years old. After you've seen a few punch-ups in indoor cricket, you'll never be shaken by sledging in an international match.

After the 2003 World Cup, which our boys win in South Africa, I am picked for the next Test and one-day tour to the West Indies, due to Damien Martyn breaking his thumb in the World Cup. I am a reserve for the Test matches, but get a go in the one-dayers. I make 75 and win a man of the match award in our first game, and we have the seven-match series won after the first four.

From there, I keep getting picked for one-day tours to India, Sri Lanka and Zimbabwe, and play in the home one-day tournament and the Champions Trophy in England. From the day I first get picked in the Australian one-day team, I never get dropped, which is a record I am proud of. By late 2004, I've played 34 matches in a world champion one-day team. It's an awesome lifestyle: play the game you love, get paid for it, then go and party with your mates. I revel in every single thing that comes with it.

And I enjoy the fact that my life is organised so that I am free to think about my cricket. Since I was 18 years old and was first picked for New South Wales, I've been looked after by Mum and Dad and managed and mentored by Neil D'Costa. I have people to help me and guide me.

All I have to do is perform and I can keep this dream life going.

Being picked for the Test tour of India in September 2004 keeps the roll going. Due to Punter's injured thumb, I am chosen to bat at number six and make a hundred on debut. Better still, we go ahead and win the match, and then back it up with another in Nagpur, to become the first Australian team to win in India since 1969. It means so much to people like Punter, Gilly, Haydos, Warney, Glenn McGrath, Michael Kasprowicz and others who have been there on so many losing tours, and also to greats like Steve Waugh and Allan Border, who left India empty-handed. I feel privileged just to be in the changing room.

Everything I touch seems to turn to gold. Even with the ball, in the last Test match in Mumbai, a raging turner that is not fit for Test cricket, I can do no wrong. We lose the match, but I walk off in the second innings with six wickets for nine runs. I feel like I'm riding a wave: loving the game, loving being around my heroes, loving the feeling of having 14 big brothers I trust totally. In my first home Test match, I score 141. I have the best seat in the house for Gilly's incredible hitting and positive attitude. I am on top of the world. Little do I know what's around the corner.

I am enjoying myself so much that it takes some time for me to come to grips with how I am perceived from the outside. I'm just a simple Aussie suburban boy living my dream. What's not to like? I read every single word that is written about me, so confident am I that it will be positive. And initially, it is.

There are a few undercurrents that I will see more clearly later – when things have soured – than I do at the time. The Australian cricket team in 2004 looks to me like an all-star line-up. Justin Langer, Matthew Hayden, Ricky Ponting, Damien Martyn, Darren Lehmann, Simon Katich, Adam Gilchrist, Shane Warne, Jason Gillespie, Brett Lee, Glenn McGrath, Michael Kasprowicz. I can't imagine a better team of cricketers has ever been put on the field. It's beyond my comprehension that Australians would not love them, but somehow that's not always the case. There's a lot of public ambivalence towards the team, possibly because they win too regularly – and the ruthless way they do it. On the inside, it's a great environment, but in public we are not universally loved. I would say I find this puzzling, but at the time I'm too happy to care.

The next undercurrent that I don't really get is related to my friendship with Shane Warne. From the first tour we're on together, he takes me under his wing. To my face, all of our teammates go out of their way to make me feel welcome and look after me. I feel like everyone's little brother. All of the boys are unbelievably nice to me. Darren Lehmann even comes out publicly and says that, if it's a line-ball decision between him and me, the selectors ought to look to the future and choose me. It blows me away.

I don't realise, at first, how cliquey the team actually is. I'm too starry-eyed to see it, but there are very clear groups within the team, and everyone knows whose group I am in, because he treats me like gold, he is loyal to me and I am loyal to him. And yes, that might draw some criticism to me. If I were a better politician, I might not let my happiness at being Shane Warne's friend show so much. And as far as I can see, I belong to all the groups. They all invite me out for coffee or drinks. I do have a special relationship with Warney, but I can't see how that could be anything but a benefit.

The first sign of tension is in early 2005, when Warney, on his retirement, hands down his one-day shirt number, 23, to me. I was Australian one-day player number 149, and management made me number 49 when we went to Zimbabwe in early 2004. Warney retires from one-day internationals a year later and says to me, 'I want to hand you my number. I love the way you play the game and think about cricket.'

I say, 'What an honour. Thank you.' I am so in awe of him, it isn't funny. I would wear number 49 to the end of my career with pride, but when Shane Warne hands you number 23, it's the ultimate compliment. I would never consider saying no.

Before long, though, there are mutterings that I'm a bit cocky, a bit presumptuous to wear 23. I never went after it, but that doesn't matter to some people. It dovetails with another coup that I think is a good thing until I realise it might be a bad thing.

Since the beginning of time, old cricketers have been jealous of the financial success of young cricketers. Even Don Bradman was sneered at by senior players because he was suddenly earning a lot more money, through endorsements and newspaper articles, than they had. Since the

1970s, when cricketers' incomes have gone up year after year, new players have come in and earned more than the experienced players. The Chappell generation earned more than the Lawrys and the Simpsons, the Border generation earned more still, and the Taylor–Waugh–Healy–Warne group were lucky enough to get a share of greater and greater income flowing into Australian cricket. And the current era of players will earn more than my generation.

It's just a sign of the times as the sport has expanded globally. The financial transformation of Indian cricket was taking place during my career, and triggered a new inrush of money. After the start of the Indian Premier League in 2008, my generation of players saw their earnings eclipsed by the next wave. It's a fact of life. With professional personal managers and the efforts of the Australian Cricketers' Association, the elite players in Australia saw their incomes rise steeply between 2000 and the end of my career. It's never made senior players particularly happy to see young upstarts come in and earn more, and that wasn't about to change.

Cricketers are often talking about what each other earns. Everyone knows who ranks where, and they are quick to exchange information and find out about each other's contracts. It's a common subject for conversation, and it brings out nearly everyone's natural sense of rivalry and competitiveness.

For me, the moment of realisation comes with a bat contract I get before I'm even a Test player. Due to my one-day exposure in 2003 and 2004, I am identified as a popular cricketer among kids, the demographic the gear manufacturers are most eager to target. Slazenger have just lost Mark Waugh to retirement, and are looking to skip a generation. They offer me $400,000 a year to use their equipment, and almost immediately every player in the Australian team knows that I have a bigger bat contract than all of them other than Punter. I'm getting paid more for my choice of bat than Justin Langer, Matthew Hayden, Adam Gilchrist, Damien Martyn – guys who have played for Australia for over a decade and proved themselves the best in the world. And I haven't even earned my baggy green.

I suspect they might be pissed off, but what can I do about it? I say, good on my manager. I'm not going to go back to Slazenger and say, 'Please, can you cut my contract in half until I've scored 25 Test hundreds and then I can step up to that level.'

When I get my first Cricket Australia contract a year later, I am ranked eighth in Australia, which is higher than I would have thought, given my lack of experience. When I find out that I'm getting $20,000 a year more than Warney, I have a meeting with chief executive James Sutherland and the selectors and ask, 'How am I ranked higher than Shane Warne? I'm embarrassed to be getting more than the guy who brings so much interest and so many people to the game.' They explain that, because Warney has retired from one-day cricket, and I'm playing two formats, the contract money derives from both forms. Warney is ranked near the top in Test cricket, but his lack of a ranking in limited-overs brings him down to ninth overall. I can understand the logic, but am still embarrassed.

Typically, Warney couldn't give a shit about where we are ranked. He doesn't have an envious bone in his body towards me. We never even speak about it. I can tell there is a bit of talking about it behind my back elsewhere in the team.

Through 2005 and early 2006, I sign many sponsorship deals. I do interviews with all media. I lap it up. Because I'm so grateful for the money coming in, I put sponsor commitments first and training second. I even get so busy that I put aside training time in favour of sponsor time. I'm riding for a fall, but I don't see it yet. There are times when my teammates think I am living the high life and am not as dedicated and focused as they are, not as passionate about the baggy green. I don't notice. I'm too busy having a good time.

As the negative innuendo trickles out – *Clarke is earning too much money, Clarke is a cocky upstart, Clarke shouldn't be wearing Warne's number* – I begin to care a little more about what is said about me. When I read stories, my eyes home in on the negatives. Before long, those are the only parts that I remember, and I hang on to them.

For a long time, I am defensive about it. I am my own person. I don't fish or shoot until Symmo gets hold of me, and I don't have a cattle dog. I have tattoos, I buy a Ferrari, and I start going out with a model. When I'm asked what I like doing in my spare time, I say, 'Shopping' . . . and half of Australia groans.

I try to defend myself. *Hang on, I'm a kid from Liverpool. Mum and Dad both worked full-time jobs to put bread and milk on the table, I had to save up two years for $30 for a Mambo T-shirt. I had no silver spoon in my mouth.*

But when I'm seen going out to expensive restaurants with my model girlfriend, with my diamond stud in my ear, some of Australia thinks, *What a dickhead!*

I don't help myself, don't get me wrong. But good-looking women? Show me a 22-year-old cricketer that doesn't like them. Nice food? Show me a guy that doesn't like it. The Ferrari I bought had been in a poster on my wall throughout my childhood. I had a poster of Brian Lara, a poster of Michael Slater, and a poster of that black 355 Ferrari. From six years of age, that's what I always wanted. I didn't buy the car to be a show pony. My parents always said that spending a lot on a car was a waste of money, but I was fixated on ticking off each part of that simple aspiration: meet Brian Lara, bat like Michael Slater, and buy this car. My tattoos may not please everyone, but they're all close to my heart – the first I got was to signify being the 389th Australian Test cricketer – and I'm hardly the first sportsman to get tattoos.

Are my dreams distasteful? To some people, maybe they're western suburbs dreams. But that's who I am. I'm no different from the kid who knew that a big treat from his parents was two dollars to get some hot chips from the takeaway on Elizabeth Drive, and a lunch order for school on Mondays. I set my sights on a reward, and go after it.

I care about my appearance. When I was four years old, I was at a party in new shoes and another kid stepped on them. I ran inside and washed them. When I was a little older, I was too embarrassed to go with Mum into Payless Shoes.

I didn't expect her to take me somewhere else to get nicer shoes. My goal was to save my own money and buy them myself. I didn't ask for anything more, but put the responsibility onto myself.

What does that make me? A kid who was fussy about being clean and dressing nicely, and who knew that his family couldn't afford to get all the things he wanted. It doesn't mean I value playing for Australia any less than the bloke who drinks beer and drives a ute. I'm a product of my times and my environment, and if that makes it hard for people to pigeonhole me or fit me into their definition of the Australian cricketer or cricket captain, I will have to learn to accept that. Times and tastes change.

At some point in that difficult period, when I become captain and there's an innuendo in the general public that I've angled to take the job from Punter, Mark Taylor sums it up. He says I'm the first captain of the generation when there's unprecedented 24-hour scrutiny in social media. It's like the scrutiny of his time multiplied by 50, he says.

Throughout my career, I battle with it. Initially, that spotlight and popularity is so intoxicating, I have no idea there will be a backlash. When it comes, I really care what everyone thinks and don't want anyone to dislike me. When I discover that some of the media dislike me, I get defensive about it.

And to be honest, I still do feel protective of my younger self. Who cares if my tastes did not fit the preconception of the Aussie bloke? Is there really that much wrong with a western suburbs boy with a taste for conspicuous consumption getting the opportunity to live his dream? I can understand that not everyone will like it, but why did they *hate* it so much? Even if I was a smart-arse, which I was, even if I made a whole lot of mistakes, why does that incite so much *anger*? It bothers me for too long.

THE INNINGS

168 versus New Zealand, Wellington, 2010

I was so attached to our family home in Liverpool that I wanted to buy it. It took me several years before I found the same stability in home and family life that I'd had as a boy.

When I first moved out of home, it was into a unit with Leanne at Chipping Norton in the western suburbs of Sydney. We were so close, it seemed the natural thing to do for both of us. I had my first New South Wales contract, worth $25,000 a year, and I helped her begin paying off her mortgage. Like many Australians, we were brought up to place great store in owning our own homes.

After Leanne went travelling to South Africa, I lived with Aytek Genc, also at Chipping Norton. Fifteen years older than me, Aytek had had an impressive career as a professional soccer player, representing the Socceroos three times. He was playing for Sydney United in the National Soccer League at the time, and was making his transition into coaching. I enjoyed spending time with a professional athlete, and he helped me improve my training, diet and discipline.

When I got my first Cricket Australia contract in 2004, I bought my first home, a townhouse at Breakfast Point on the Parramatta River. I was really proud of being able to buy a house at the age of 23. Mum had taught me to be a good saver, and buying a house felt like a special reward. The townhouse was a perfect base for me – not too far from the Sydney Cricket Ground and the airport – and I lived there for several years. Phillip Hughes and other teammates would come and stay, sometimes when I was away, to keep it secure, and we had a little colony of Western Suburbs cricketers and friends living in the Breakfast Point area.

Mum, Dad and Leanne had moved to Cronulla by that stage, and my Nan and Pop lived on the south side of Port Hacking at Bundeena, so with everybody in the south of Sydney it made sense to move closer to them, which I did around 2007. The more time I spent away on tour, the more I missed my family. I also realised more and more how much I owed them for the sacrifices they had made to help my cricket career.

I pined for the days in our swimming pool at the old house, so I wanted to live where I could hear the sound of the water. I was able to buy a multilevel home in Lilli Pilli, on the northern side of Port Hacking. The house was right on the water, and I could dive straight in. I loved nothing better than coming home from tour and looking out of my lounge room, or going to the garage and seeing the car I'd bought. I thought I had everything I wanted.

A number of people had told me the Lilli Pilli house – seven levels, six bedrooms – was a waste for a young single man living on his own. I saw it as a reward, not much different from the $30 Mambo T-shirt I had saved up for as a kid when Mum and Dad couldn't afford it, or the ASICS shoes I would buy, with my own money, rather than go with Mum to Payless Shoes. When I was a boy, my mates all seemed to have money and I didn't. I was strongly motivated to keep chasing success in cricket, and that also meant the material rewards to feed that hunger I seemed to have been born with.

What people meant about the house being a waste might not have been in terms of money so much as in it being too large for one person. The image was: big house, beautiful car, but no one to share it with. The fact was I liked inviting over family and friends for drinks and barbecues all the time. In the back of my mind was a vague idea that I would get married and have kids quite young, and set up a family and be a provider just like Mum and Dad had been for Leanne and me.

I began dating Lara Bingle six months after moving into Lilli Pilli. Before then, I had only had one long-term serious girlfriend, Erina, who I'd met while I was still at school. My dad's cancer diagnosis came the next year, and Lara's dad Graham passed away from liver and pancreatic cancer in 2008. Graham was an absolute gentleman, an easy-going surfer who never seemed stressed out by anything. He and my dad got on very well, as did both of our families, and it was devastating for all of us to see his decline. I missed the beginning of the West Indies tour that year to help her through her grief and also to be with Dad through a tough stage of his cancer treatment. There was never any question for me that family came first, even if it meant risking my place in the Australian team.

Even if I hadn't scored a hundred in Antigua when I returned to the team, I would never have regretted making a priority of the big things in life.

If there was one thing I feel I earned through the years I spent with my ex-fiancée, it's the right to privacy. We were photographed often in what I thought was our private time, we were chased by paparazzi, and then we had to wake up to stories in the newspapers that were total fabrications. Having been naive about how intense the public spotlight would be as an Australian cricketer, I was completely unprepared for the new level it went to when I was seeing her. I was never comfortable with the feeling that people were sitting in cars outside my home with cameras and were watching us, at times, 24/7. I can't remember every episode in the media circus that our life became, but there were a few beauties. There was a photo of us talking once outside the changing rooms at the SCG, with an article saying we were arguing. That was a fabrication. We were only having a conversation. I was so cautious about privacy, if I wanted an argument, I would take it behind closed doors. Another was that we had bought a $10 million property in Coffs Harbour. That would have been clever, as we only went there to visit my grandparents. Maybe the best fabrication of all was the story that her engagement ring went down the toilet. That was another made-up story – the ring was in the safe of my apartment in Bondi. Somebody saw a plumber's truck parked outside the block, and even though it was going to someone else's apartment, it turned into a story that the ring had been flushed away.

Lara and I paid a high price for all of these concoctions, and I think, as a young person, when you pay that price you earn the right to keep sensitive things to yourself. I have been very open about my life in this book, but I feel that I earned the right, through all the violations of privacy that occurred when she and I were together, to draw the curtain. So much stuff was invented about us on a daily basis. I don't know any young couple who could survive when their privacy is under that kind of repeated assault.

In 2010, when we broke up, it made more headlines – in part because I had to again place my private life ahead of cricket. The Australian team was in New Zealand for a three-Test tour, and when it became clear to me that our relationship was falling apart, I had no option. I could have stayed and played, but I know I would have done poorly and let the team down. I had to go home and sort out my life.

I was 28 years old. Anyone who goes through the break-up of a serious relationship at that age, when you are thinking of settling down, knows what a trauma it is. It's devastating for any person, let alone when you are in a fishbowl.

The main reason our relationship didn't work out was that I lost trust in her in a number of different ways. We were going in different directions with our lives. I was constantly committing and re-committing myself to cricket, with my obsessive focus, and she wanted to live a completely different kind of life. I had tried to make it work, but now I knew I had to call off the relationship. I didn't choose cricket over her – I had felt that there was the possibility of working things out and accommodating both of our aspirations – but by the time I was in New Zealand, I was so unhappy it was affecting my life in every way. If it went on much longer like this, I wouldn't have deserved to be with the team. Being as black-and-white as I am, I decided to go home and get my mind where it should be. I couldn't be half-and-half. I had no choice but to do it face to face. I was no good to the team in New Zealand, and I am not the type of person who will break up a serious relationship, in which we had been engaged and were living together, by phone or text.

By then I had moved to Bondi, and when I came home from the tour to break up, the media was camped outside my apartment block. I rang my good friend Anthony Bell, and we cooked up a plan to get me out of there.

Belly and I had become friends around 2003 or 2004 after Neil D'Costa introduced us. He had become my accountant and then my financial adviser, and our friendship grew out of that. He was, outside my family, one of my my closest confidants at that time, the mate I could open up to about my fears and emotions.

Over time, Belly became like a brother to me. He gets on really well with my family, and, like Mum has always done, looks after my money as if it's his own. When we've been out for a drink, he's been another set of eyes helping me out. He grew very close to Phillip Hughes as well, and we would spend some great times out on Belly's 90-foot motor launch, *Ghost*. In fact, he introduces me to the water, through time on *Ghost*, his maxi yacht *Loyal*, and even his rubber ducky. He teaches me how to drive them and encourages me to get my boat licence. My friends become his friends, and his yacht is well named, because he is as loyal a person as I have ever met. In tough times, I am always able to rely on him, and he proved that in spades when he smuggled me away from the media's eyes during my break-up.

He came to Bondi and parked in the garage. I slipped down through an internal lift and climbed into the boot of his car. He exited into the media circus. With all the cameras and microphones on him, he said, 'No, Michael's not in the house.' That's right – I was in the boot.

We went to his house, not too far away, where Mum and Dad came to talk it through with me. I told them how I was feeling, and we came to a resolution there. Belly was an amazing source of advice and friendship in one of the toughest times of my life. Later that year, Phillip Hughes came to my place at Bondi for a weekend and stayed for six weeks; he became the friend I could go and have a beer and talk nonsense with.

I thought I had my freedom when I got on the plane back to New Zealand. But a television journalist, pretending to be a normal passenger, had set up a camera to film me. That's how crazy it was. A Qantas flight attendant said, 'It's illegal, mate, you can't do it,' but the media were out of control. My private heartbreak was public property.

Never has cricket felt like my 'day off' more than in the Test match at Wellington. Once I was in the middle, people couldn't make up stories anymore about what I was doing. They could see me. Cricket was straightforward and out in the open. Funnily enough, that's why it felt like, on the cricket ground, I had some space to myself. My phone wasn't about to ring. If everyone could see what I was doing, they couldn't speculate. My teammates were great, incredibly warm and welcoming, and the coach, Tim Nielsen, was amazing for me. Simon Katich was a great partner for the first couple of hours while I scratched away, and then, through the first afternoon into the second morning, I had Marcus North, a champion bloke, at the other end.

Getting close to my century, my thoughts began to close in about how much this would mean, and I struggled to concentrate. Northy just smiled and said, 'Mate, if you see it, just hit it.' I made 168 and Northy scored 112 not out, which helped set us up for a win, and lifted a mountain off my shoulders. More than anything, that week showed me what incredible family, friends and teammates I had.

After I become Australian captain in 2011, now that I am going out with Kyly, I discover a new equilibrium, if not peace. Maybe it's a maturity that has to come with the captaincy and a serious relationship that will turn into marriage. Maybe it comes from results: in my first two years of captaincy, we win in Sri Lanka, draw in South Africa, beat India 4–0 at home, and win in the West Indies. I put together a run of big scores and have a calendar year, in 2012, that surpasses even Don Bradman. Obviously I find some inner calm and security from these team results, from the praise for my captaincy style, being awarded *Wisden* Cricketer of the Year, and for becoming number one batsman in the world. But more than anything, it's probably just growing up and getting more experience of the world – of which I had precious little when I started out in the spotlight.

By now, Kyly is at the very centre of my life. She loves my family, and the feeling is mutual, with her and Leanne becoming as close as sisters. During the off season, we all box and train together – Kyly and me, Leanne and her partner Craig – and enjoy that healthy lifestyle. I have begun inviting Kyly to come with me on as many tours as she can manage. She is a great balancing influence. She's calm and tolerant, and lenient towards my rigid routines and foibles. If I want to go to bed early and get my required hours of sleep, and get up at a time dictated by my regime, Kyly fits in. She's incredibly kind towards me, even when I'm stressed and anxious and suffering back pain. When I'm out in the middle batting in a Test match, occasionally I'll spot her in the stands and give her a wave. The first Christmas she spends with me on tour, in Melbourne before the 2010 Boxing Day Test match, I give her a present that Phillip Hughes takes note of.

'He must really like you,' Hughesy tells Kyly with his cheeky sparkle.

'Why's that?' she asks.

Hughesy nods at the gift. It's a Louis Vuitton roll-on travel bag. 'He really wants you to be on tour with him. That's how he's telling you.'

And he's right. From then on, Kyly becomes my constant companion not just during the off-season, but on cricket tours.

Neither of us want the pressure of a long engagement, and in the autumn of 2012 we cook up a secret plan. I never had a proper 30th birthday celebration, as I was preparing for my first tour as Australian captain, to Bangladesh. A year later, we organise what Kyly calls 'the 30th birthday you never had', only it's got a twist. We invite a small group of family and friends to come to a resort in the Wolgan Valley, north of Lithgow on the far side of the Blue Mountains, for four days. We invent all sorts of cover stories: Kyly tells her family it's a big event put on by Emirates, a sponsor of mine, and 'we'd love you guys to come'. Her sister is pregnant and needs a lot of persuasion to miss a baby class. It's all very cloak and dagger until, over dinner on the first night, as the entrees are coming out, I stand up in front of everyone and tell them we are engaged. After dessert, a letter is distributed to each of the tables, announcing that we are going to get married tomorrow. Because it's a surprise, and because many of my cricketing friends are away playing in the Indian Premier League, I haven't invited cricket people. It is an intimate occasion. I tell Dad that when he goes to his room, he will find another letter on his bedside. It contains the news that tomorrow, he will be my best man.

I'm told I was booed when I stepped onto the SCG for the first time as Test captain in 2011. I only remember being booed in Brisbane when I walked out to bat against South Africa in 2012. I score 259 not out and get a standing ovation walking off. That's the only time I am aware of being booed by a home crowd. Selective memory! Maybe I am booed more often than that. But by this point, I accept that because of the style of person I am, a lot of people aren't going to like me. I don't care anymore if they don't. I just want to earn their respect. The best way I can do that is perform as a cricketer and help the team to succeed. I believe that if I can steer Australia to winning back the Ashes, getting to number one in the world in all formats, and winning the World Cup at home in 2015, then it will no longer matter what people think of me as a person. They will have to respect me for what I will have done for my country.

By my last tour, in England in 2015, I try a completely novel approach: I decide not to read a single thing about me or the team during the whole Ashes tour. It might be just as well, as I barely score a run and we lose the Ashes with terrible collapses in Birmingham and Nottingham. But I sense, by now, that not reading things doesn't help, because I just imagine the worst.

When I walk down the street, members of the public are always cheerful and supportive. What have I done to turn some of the media against me? I ask myself often, and I approach them for an explanation, but there is no satisfaction, because I'm chasing something that isn't there. I can't make the world see things my way – because it's the world, it's millions of people, and they all have their own minds.

When I retire at the end of the 2015 Ashes tour, the bubble is pricked and I am free. It's incredible, the change in the way I see the world. Now I understand how ephemeral the media is. Things really do disappear from memory after one day. You turn a page of the newspaper, and you've forgotten what you read about who someone is dating and what car they drive. It really wasn't that important. I wish I hadn't dwelt on the negatives for so long or spent so much time puzzling over why I was portrayed a certain way. But I'm glad that clarity has arrived, with fatherhood and life outside the bubble. There was so much to be proud of, and which I am proud of now.

13

THE TWENTY20 REVOLUTION

In some ways, I was in the right place at the right time for the Twenty20 cricket revolution. When the first Indian Premier League (IPL) tournament was contested in 2008, I was 27 years old and doing well with the Australian Test and one-day teams. I had played in a winning World Cup campaign, and we were ranked number one in the world in both formats.

On the other hand, the circumstances never did quite align. I pulled out of the first IPL auction in 2008 to spend time with my father, whose cancer treatment was ongoing. Lara's dad was about to pass away, and I wanted to stay at home for both of those reasons.

As the years went by, this pattern repeated. I put family and cricket for my country first, and later I had to look after my body as my back and hamstring injuries became more chronic. I signed up for the Pune Warriors for part of the 2012 IPL as a replacement for Yuvraj Singh when he was diagnosed with cancer, before coming home early for my wedding to Kyly.

I was busy with Australian international commitments for the first four Big Bash League tournaments, signing marketing contracts in two seasons with the Sydney Thunder with everyone knowing I would not be able to play.

Once I retired from international cricket in 2015, I was keen to play for the Melbourne Stars, but I needed a break from cricket by then and our daughter was about to be born, and the president of their board, Eddie McGuire, agreed that I should spend that time with my family.

Another reason I don't have a front-seat experience of the first years of franchise Twenty20 cricket is that I didn't practise for it. I focused on Test and one-day cricket because I prioritised those formats while playing for Australia, and I could see how I could improve at both without changing the fundamentals of my game. My record in one-day international cricket was good, averaging over 40, playing over 200 games, striking at nearly 80.

Playing Twenty20 until about 2012 was still manageable, from a technique point of view. For Australia, we tended not to train for it because our Twenty20 international games were at the end of seasons. The one tournament where I did have time to train and prepare, we made the final of the 2010 World Twenty20.

But later in my career, my batting would have had to change a lot to adapt to Twenty20's accelerating needs.

You're trying to score boundaries, and hit at 1.5 runs a ball. For practice, guys were doing range-hitting, going to the middle of an oval to hit sixes. I never did that. Those techniques and methods flowed into one-day cricket towards the end of my career, when strike rates greater than 100 became more common, and batsmen were expected to step up to scoring eight to ten runs an over.

Although it didn't play a major part in my career, I like Twenty20 cricket. It has helped the game become more entertaining and widened its appeal. More people come through the gates and watch cricket on TV in all the game's formats due to the Twenty20 revolution, and that has to be a good thing. For people who want a quick fix – three hours of thrills and then go home – it's made cricket accessible.

The IPL has been great for the relationships between countries. The environment around international cricket has become friendlier since the inception of the IPL, because players know each other better. Look at how Australia and India were at loggerheads in early 2008. A few months later, Matthew Hayden and Ricky Ponting were leading the Australian representation in IPL franchises. Andrew Symonds played with Harbhajan Singh. More recently, the Mumbai Indians had Sachin Tendulkar as assistant coach to Ricky Ponting, with Harbhajan in the same team. The after-effects of 'Monkeygate' didn't run very deep, did they? It seemed like the worst conflict in the cricket world at the time, but the effect of the IPL has been to iron out those differences and enhance cultural understanding between players from different nations.

A lot has been said about the threat Twenty20 poses to Test cricket, and that threat is real. This threat comes in two forms. First, the compressed action and big hitting of a Twenty20 match will have an effect on the public's tastes. People who are accustomed to seeing scoring rates of 10 or 15 runs an over and exciting chases might lose – or not develop – the patience for the subtleties of Test cricket. There will always be an audience for the five-day game, but already you can see it narrowing down to the 'cricket tragics', while youngsters and families who want their three hours of night-time fun are committed to Twenty20. If we see audiences in India migrating away from Test cricket in the next five years, then it's time to worry. India's financial strength is currently underwriting cricket around the world, and if people in that country lose interest in Test cricket, then the long game's future is shaky.

The other major challenge to Test cricket that comes from Twenty20 is where players choose the T20 franchise domestic leagues over representing their country.

Playing for your country should be the driving ambition for every cricketer, but sometimes the financial disparity places an undue strain. For Australians, leaving aside the intrinsic benefits of wearing the baggy green or the yellow limited-overs cap, it's easier to prioritise playing for your country, because you are paid well. A top-ten player in Australia will earn fantastic money, and you're representing your country, doing what you dreamed of as a kid. So, for those top Australian players, to turn down an IPL contract is not a big sacrifice.

On the other hand, when Chris Gayle was the highest-paid West Indian player, he was receiving $US100,000 for 12 months. Jamaica, his country, and the other West Indian islands are not necessarily the cheapest places in the world to live. So he certainly wasn't growing rich representing the West Indies. On the other hand, an IPL franchise offers him a $US1.5 million contract to play for six weeks. Adding in his contracts with other T20 leagues, he can make $US2.5 to $US3 million a year – up to 30 times as much as his income with the West Indies. It would be easy for someone like me to say you've got to put your country first, but guys from other countries … well, I can understand why they make these choices. The financial difference between playing Twenty20 and playing for their country is too great.

I know it's scary the way franchise cricket is affecting Tests, but we've got to respect and understand the reasons why. I would like the international cricket community to pool its resources to try and do whatever it can to help players to prioritise playing for their country. I don't believe international T20 cricket has a great future; it seems that the strength of the format is in domestic franchise tournaments. A place in the schedule can be carved out for the main domestic competitions such as the IPL, but otherwise the players should be given no excuse to decide against playing for their countries.

If that means evening payments out across the countries, I say go for it. When Australia played the West Indies in the 2015–16 summer before disappointing crowds, it left an empty feeling to know that there was such a difference between what the two sets of players were earning. When you're playing on the MCG and generating great income, it's both teams who are making the contest and the entertainment, and both teams should get an even distribution of income.

The landscape is changing rapidly, and I can't imagine the new challenges that will arise over the next five to ten years. Is the international game strong enough to sustain all three formats? We'll find that out sooner than we might think.

It was disappointing when, during the 2015 ICC World Cup, it was announced that the number of teams playing in the 2019 version would be reduced. I'm for more, not fewer, countries playing cricket. I want to see Afghanistan, Ireland, the United Arab Emirates, the USA, Hong Kong, China, and every other 'minnow' country given the opportunity to improve their standards by playing against better teams. Why kick them out of the World Cup because their inclusion extends the tournament by two weeks? Those two weeks in 2015 meant that Ireland, the UAE, Afghanistan and Scotland could learn much more about the game and get better.

It's too early to widen the catchment for full Test status, as the five-day game exposes differences in quality too much. Heavy defeats to Test nations could be demoralising.

On the other hand, the shorter formats – 50-over cricket and particularly Twenty20 – have a natural tendency to close the gap and open the possibility for upset results. My view is that children in every country in the world should be able to dream of playing international cricket against the best teams in the world. Let them play! Grow the game. Get more boys and girls playing in any country, any format. Don't press PAUSE on the game of cricket.

A lot of money has been spent marketing the T20 format. Now, I think the emphasis has to go back onto Test cricket. In tennis, Wimbledon is still a very successful tournament despite its 'anachronistic' nature, being played on grass. For most players it's still the pinnacle of a career to win Wimbledon. All the traditions around it are still attached. Test cricket can be our sport's Wimbledon, if it's done the right way.

Where the quality of Test cricket needs to be preserved is in the conditions that are presented for play. Wickets have become flatter. Over the course of my career, the ball has generally moved off the pitch less and less.

One outcome is that cricket is not seeing bowlers of the same standard as when I started. In those years, you had Wasim Akram, Waqar Younis, Curtly Ambrose, Courtney Walsh, Allan Donald, Shaun Pollock, Shane Bond, Shoaib Akhtar, Glenn McGrath, Jason Gillespie and Brett Lee on the international scene. Among spinners, there was Shane Warne, Muttiah Muralitharan, Harbhajan Singh and Anil Kumble leading the way. I don't know why bowling has declined, but pitches and the reduced sizes of grounds, with boundaries roped well in from the fence, have done the bowlers no favours.

Coinciding with this change has been the elevation of batting skills due to Twenty20 and the bats we use now. T20 cricket has helped batting evolve. If the wicket is flat, guys hit it 360 degrees, and the bats are big enough that even if they mistime it, they can get it over the fielders' heads and often over the boundary rope. Bats don't weigh any more than they used to, and I still believe the middle of the bat is exactly as sweet as Mark Taylor's or Allan Border's. But it's the size of the middle of the bat that has grown. Like tennis racquets, shots that used to be mishits are now flying off the bat because the sweet spot is so much bigger. Batters are practising their big-hitting, so bowlers are immediately at a disadvantage, which is aggravated by very flat pitches, white balls that only swing for the first two overs, and roped-in boundaries.

The result is a distortion of averages. As I write, Adam Voges has a higher Test batting average than anyone since Bradman. I fought my arse off to get Adam into the Australian team. But is he a better player than Sachin Tendulkar or Brian Lara? Nobody would say that. Mark Waugh averaged 41 in Test cricket, and he's one of the best players I've seen. He faced tougher bowlers in conditions that allowed a fairer contest between bat and ball. Ian Chappell, David Boon and Mark Taylor averaged in the low 40s. They were, in my opinion, much better players than subsequent batsmen who are averaging higher these days.

In one-day cricket, when I started as a lower-middle-order batsman, the ball was reverse-swinging when I came in. You could easily lose five wickets in the last 20 overs of an innings due to the reverse swing of the ageing ball. That swing disappeared when the authorities changed the rules to allow in two new balls. I felt that some adjustment should have been made to statistics at that point. Dean Jones and Michael Bevan, superstars of one-day cricket, had strike rates of less than 80. They were better players than guys who now have strike rates of more than 120. But the game went through a revolution, and bowlers were the victims.

Sensing they were on top, batsmen improved their mental approach. Huge record-breaking partnerships are regularly seen now, as batsmen keep their feet on bowlers' throats. Batsmen prepare their bodies better, and their mindset has consequently changed. Before I played, certain players would see their role in their team as batting to survive: just hold up an end for the others. During my international career, batting has been about scoring runs. That's the only reason to bat. Your number one concern is scoring runs. Flat pitches have made that easier. If you get in on a flat track, you go as large as you can, because it won't always be this good. There's a real concentration on maximising the potential of opportunities when they do arise. But it hasn't necessarily led to better cricket or even better batting. People might like seeing big scores, but they also like seeing the bowlers have a chance. The balance has to be redressed, or else cricket will become, more than it is already, a batsman's game.

There are many ways of improving cricket as a spectacle, and the first day–night Test match, in Adelaide in 2015 between Australia and New Zealand, offered us a glimpse of the future. I am in favour of anything that increases the appeal of and the audiences for Test cricket. The most important factor that I could see in that match was the evening-out of the contest between bat and ball, because more grass was left on the traditionally batsman-friendly Adelaide Oval pitch. It seems to me that more people were going to watch the day–night Test match because of the timing: they could do it after work or school. Any innovation that brings more people to the game, I'm all in favour of it. If that means playing more day–night Test cricket, that is good.

Another issue that kept bubbling up during my playing career was corruption in international cricket. Gambling in sport is a big problem, and I don't think there is any middle ground. I believe if a player gets caught fixing a result in any way, he should be banned for life. There is no room for it. I was never approached by bookmakers or anyone involved in illegal betting during my career and never knew of any Test match that was being fixed.

There was talk of the 2009 Sydney Test match with Pakistan being the subject of match-fixing, but while I was playing it, I had no idea. Looking back, some of the things that happened there don't look fantastic, but I had no sense of it at the time. In the game before that, at Hobart, Punter was dropped on the boundary by Mohammad Amir before he had scored. To be honest, I have seen much easier catches dropped by much better fieldsmen: take Herschelle Gibbs dropping Steve Waugh in the 1999 World Cup. Cricket is too hard a game for good players to play well for me ever to think about people playing less than their best. Maybe I was naive. Because I know how easy it is to drop a catch, and how hard it is to play cricket, my naivety might have blinded me. But to say I never saw any corruption doesn't change my stance on what should happen if it is uncovered: life bans, no excuses.

It's been widely documented that the 'Big Three' of India, England and Australia have seized control of cricket's revenues and the power over scheduling in recent years. When it comes to knowing whether that's a good thing for cricket or not, it's too soon for me to say. I prefer to judge it by results. Is the cricket world expanding? Is the game attracting larger audiences to all three formats? Are more children taking cricket up? Is corruption being cleaned up?

Is governance improving? Is the standard of pitches and grounds around the world allowing higher quality, more attractive cricket? These are the outcomes I would like to see, so that the game I love is in a better state in the future than when I started.

I am not involved in world cricket politics, so it's hard for me to speak with inside knowledge about the factors determining the game's future at that level. Locally, however, I am doing everything I can. In September 2014, I opened the Michael Clarke Cricket Academy to help youngsters achieve their dreams as I had done. Ever since Mum and Dad had their indoor centre, I wanted to provide a facility to give something back to boys and girls, in return for what I had been given. Initially, Kyly and I bought a property in Berrima, in the Southern Highlands of New South Wales, with a permanent cricket facility in mind. While that project was going through the local government approval processes, the opportunity arose to set the academy up at Scots College in Sydney's eastern suburbs. The school had first-class facilities and classrooms already set up, a modern gym, ice baths, a very sophisticated infrastructure that we decided to lease. In September, October and January we do five-day live-in camps for kids aged 12 to 18, selected on their abilities from all around Australia and the world, including India, China, Singapore, Dubai and Nepal. On Sunday the young cricketers arrive, then from Monday to Thursday they do skills and fitness training, learn about recovery, stretching and mobility, and have night-time educational sessions on nutrition, media training, public speaking, social media, everything that makes up the life of a professional cricketer. We take them on a tour of the Sydney Cricket Ground, which has their eyes boggling. It's certainly not just about batting, bowling and fielding. We do a segment on bullying, for them to realise the importance of the way they act around their peers. Their days run from 6 am to 8.30 pm and then, on the Friday, they have a match. We also do single-day clinics at junior clubs around Australia.

It's something I'm really proud of. Our point of difference is that I am fully involved every day; it's not just something I lend my name to. My goal is to give them the benefit of my experiences. They have my dad and my assistant Sasha Armstrong overseeing it all, with head coach Ben Sawyer leading a group of coaches who have all helped me in some way through my career.

I give away one scholarship to each camp myself, and my watch sponsor Hublot does the same. Spartan, Rebel and ASICS all supply gear. When the kids first arrive, I tell them that my goal isn't for them to be playing for their country but to get the best out of themselves every day. That said, we've had a 16-year-old graduate, Jason Sangha, who got a state contract, and one young woman, Lauren Cheatle, in the Australian team. What I love most, however, is when a parent rings and says their child has come out of the academy a completely changed person, more confident and caring about the people around them.

14

DRIVING THE BUS

It's early 2011, and I am sitting at the Sydney Cricket Ground with a group of men conducting the Australian Team Performance Review, known as the Argus Review after the retired banker Don Argus, who is facing me across the table. He is a straight-talking, trustworthy gentleman with greying hair. More familiar faces are with him: former captains Mark Taylor and Steve Waugh, James Sutherland, and James's predecessor as chief executive of Cricket Australia, Malcolm Speed. They are looking at how to fix our team.

As the review has been brought on by our 3–1 defeat in the Ashes series at home, I could give them an easy answer: I ought to score more runs. I had a terrible summer with the bat, and take full responsibility for that.

But they've moved on. Their questions make my heart thump.

'If you become captain of Australia, would you want Ricky Ponting in the team?'

It almost sounds like a trick question. I don't want to presume anything. Ricky is still our captain.

'I'm very much for that, if it happened,' I say. 'He offers the group so much more than his performance on the field. The bigger picture is the influence he'd have on the players, which we will need.'

I take a deep breath, wondering if I have negotiated the question the right way. Why are they asking me? Has Ricky already stood down? Then they fire in another bumper: 'What do you think about the captain being a selector?'

Whoa, these are big questions for a guy who only wants to score more runs and help his team get back on the winners' list. But I don't see any way out. I can't not answer.

'It's all about accountability. The way I've been brought up to play cricket, the captain has always taken accountability for success and defeat. If I was captain and I had played a big part in picking the players at the selection table, I would be able to stand up when we lost and say, "It's my fault, I stuffed up. We picked the wrong players." I'd be happy to put my hand up and take responsibility for that.'

There is not much response from the other side of the table. I wonder if I've gone too far. Ricky often grumbles about not having enough influence on selections, and I sympathise with him. If you're wearing the results, you should have some say in the make-up of the team. Finally, the only one who expresses a firm opinion is Steve Waugh, who says he's not for it. 'On only one occasion did I not get

Ricky Ponting was the best batsman I played with. I was honoured to share the 2009 Allan Border Medal with him. But we had very different styles of leadership. I wasn't cut out to be deputy and ultimately let him down as vice-captain.

INDRANIL MUKHERJEE/AFP/GETTY IMAGES

LUCAS DAWSON/GETTY IMAGES

HAMISH BLAIR/GETTY IMAGES

TIM CLAYTON/CORBIS VIA GETTY IMAGES

AAP IMAGE/TIM CLAYTON

AAP IMAGE/NZPA, ROSS SETFORD

Above: Andrew Flintoff was the toughest fast bowler I ever faced. His pace and aggression had me ducking for cover at Lord's in the 2009 Ashes series.

Left: I flew home from New Zealand to end my relationship with Lara face to face. When I returned to the side for the Wellington Test, the relief was evident as I hit 168 in a fifth-wicket partnership of 253 with Marcus North.

HAMISH BLAIR/GETTY IMAGES

Left: My friendship with Phillip Hughes really took off in 2009 when he was picked to replace Haydos as opening batsman in South Africa. They were big shoes to fill, but Hughesy slipped into life as a Test cricketer like he was born for it and scored twin centuries in his second Test.

Right: I never dreamed of being captain. But when I was thrust into the role of vice-captain in 2008, chairman of selectors Andrew Hilditch backed my attacking style of leadership.

KRYSTLE WRIGHT/AFP/GETTY IMAGES

Australian captain. My first game as Test skipper was as stand-in for the 2011 SCG match against England after Ricky fractured his finger. I was proud but didn't want to do anything to make it look like I was angling for Punter's job. We lost the Test, and the Ashes.

PHIL HILLYARD/NEWSPIX

KYLY CLARKE

Left: Date night. Kyly Boldy and I were in the same year at Westfield Sports High. We reconnected over a drink in 2007, and romance blossomed in 2010. I was going through a rough patch, and Kyly's warmth and compassion touched me deeply.

LAKRUWAN WANNIARACHCHI/AFP/GETTY IMAGES

Above: A sharp catch in Galle against Sri Lanka in 2011 gave Nathan Lyon his first Test wicket. These reflex movements became excruciating as my back deteriorated.

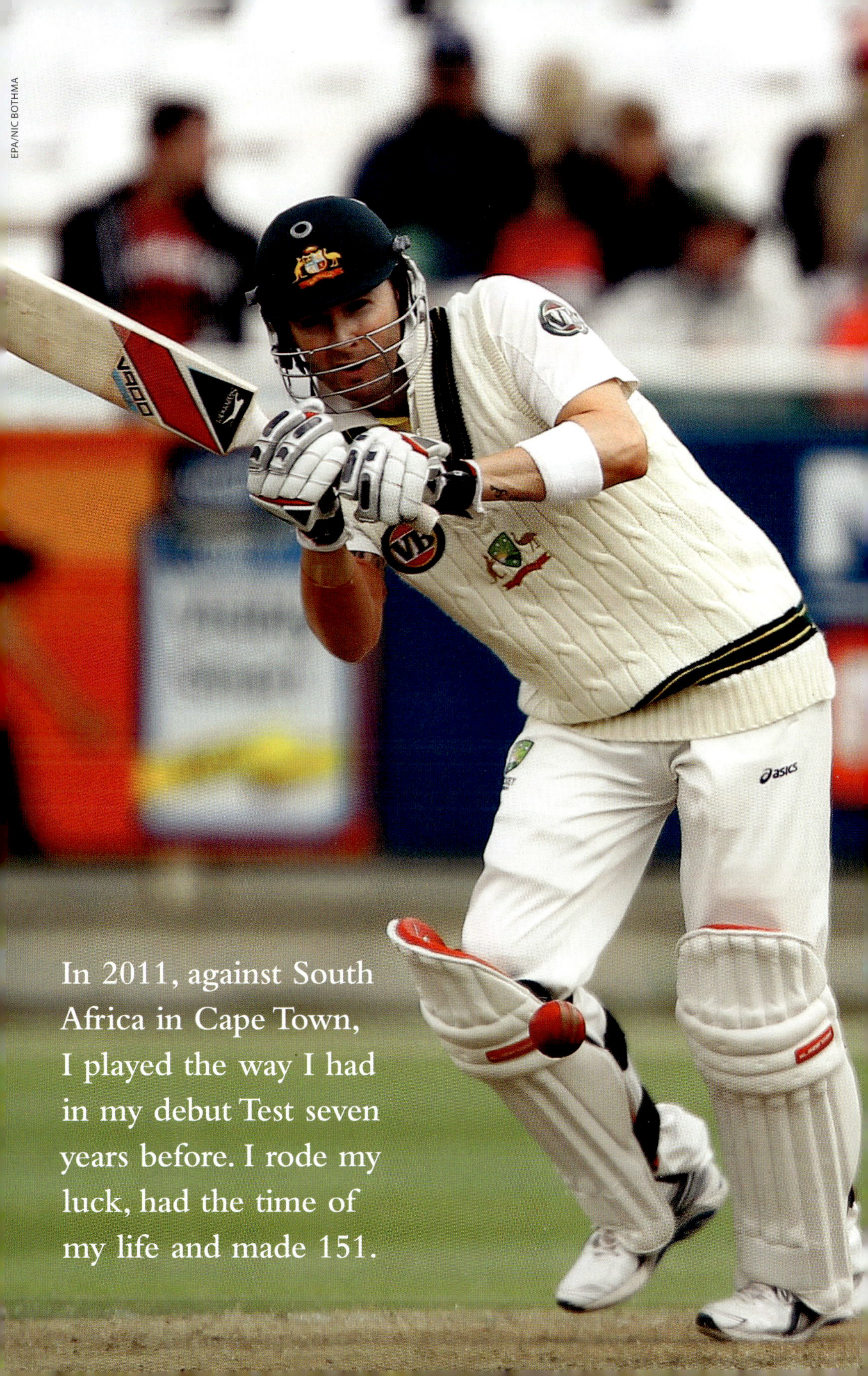

EPA/NIC BOTHMA

In 2011, against South Africa in Cape Town, I played the way I had in my debut Test seven years before. I rode my luck, had the time of my life and made 151.

GRAHAM CROUCH/GETTY IMAGES

Our dismal early exit from the 2011 World Cup derailed Punter's reign as captain. We won this match against Kenya, but our loss to India in the quarter-final left us hungry for redemption in the 2015 tournament at home.

GRAHAM CROUCH/GETTY IMAGES

AP PHOTO/AIJAZ RAHI

RYAN PIERSE/GETTY IMAGES

Above: Captaincy is a 24/7 job. After 'Homeworkgate' I had to rebuild the team's morale. The Mitchell Johnson who came back post-suspension was a different bowler. His hostile spells sent a warning shot to the world that Australia was coming back.

Below: Ricky Ponting was my captain for eight years. When he resigned as captain in 2011 and endorsed me as his successor, I was glad he stayed on as batsman.

LAKRUWAN WANNIARACHCHI/AFP/GETTY IMAGES

CHRISTOPHER LEE/GETTY IMAGES

I got on with Mickey Arthur as coach. In the end, he took the rap for the team's failings.

329
NOT OUT

The Sydney Test against India in 2012 was magic. I watched the ball closely and let it come. Everything I'd learned and worked on came together – as 329 not out. It's the highest Test score at the SCG, my home ground – a record I cherish.

HAMISH BLAIR/GETTY IMAGES

Cement
Zuari

329 NOT OUT

AAP IMAGE/PAUL MILLER

AP PHOTO/ROB GRIFFITH

AP PHOTO/ROB GRIFFITH

AP PHOTO/ROB GRIFFITH

AP PHOTO/RICK RYCROFT

230 v SOUTH AFRICA, ADELAIDE

CAMERON SPENCER/GETTY IMAGES

106 v SRI LANKA, MELBOURNE

RYAN PIERSE/GETTY IMAGES

HAMISH BLAIR/GETTY IMAGES

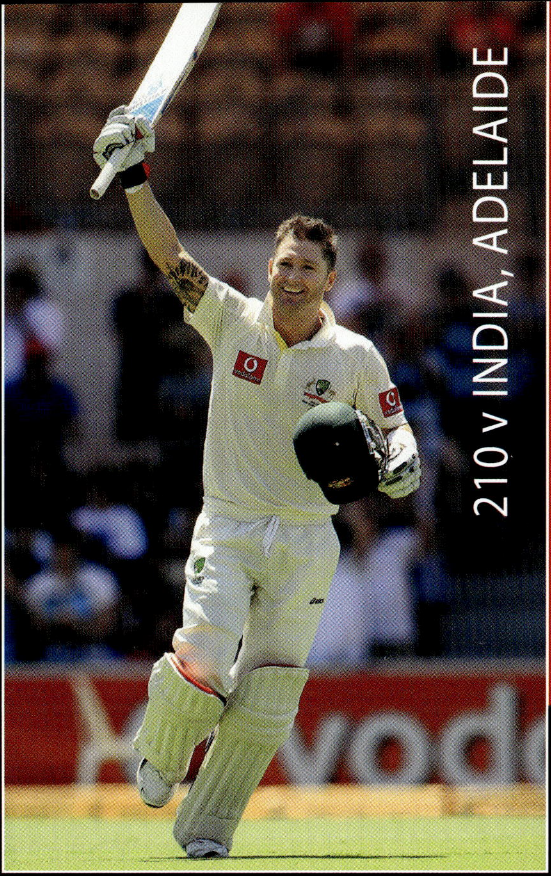

210 v INDIA, ADELAIDE

After the 329* I went on a run of big scores in 2012 that the media labelled 'Bradmanesque'. After 1595 runs in the season I was named *Wisden* Cricketer of the Year. Best of all, the team was winning. I was leading from the front and loving it.

259 NOT OUT v SOUTH AFRICA, BRISBANE

AP PHOTO/TERTIUS PICKARD

I married Kyly, my best friend, on 15 May 2012.

ALL PHOTOS COURTESY KYLY CLARKE

PUNIT PARANJPE/AFP/GETTY IMAGES

Above: The year I couldn't get enough cricket. I played my only season of the Indian Premier League with the Pune Warriors in 2012, four days after my wedding!

ROBERT CIANFLONE/GETTY IMAGES

Above: Some welcome advice from Test legend and national selector David Boon at a nets session in 2012.

SCOTT BARBOUR/GETTY IMAGES

Left: I've never seen a selector as a boss. John Inverarity had the air of the school headmaster he used to be. I never handled his assertions of authority well.

SCOTT BARBOUR/GETTY IMAGES

Above: My fourth Allan Border Medal came after the epic 2012–13 season. My cricket had come a long way since my first AB Medal in 2005 – so had my haircut!

Below: Chatting with Steve Waugh on the eve of the Third Test against Sri Lanka, January 2013. Steve's ability to fight hardest when the Australian team needed him most was a hallmark of his leadership that I always tried to emulate.

CAMERON SPENCER/GETTY IMAGES

Above: With former Test captains Steve Waugh and Mark Taylor for the 2013 Australian Ashes squad announcement. I was leading an inexperienced line-up, a team in upheaval, through the most challenging period of my career.

the eleven players I wanted,' he says, 'even though I wasn't a selector.' I can see how that happened – he is Steve Waugh. I am not sure if I, as captain, would have the same kind of personal authority from outside the selection room.

It's been an interesting interview. I don't quite know what to make of the captaincy questions. In my three years as vice-captain, I have led Australia in a caretaker capacity when Ricky was injured in one-day series against Bangladesh and the West Indies, in occasional one-day internationals elsewhere, in the ICC World T20 event in the West Indies in 2010, and in one Test match, the last we played, against England here at the SCG. But on every occasion, I felt like a stand-in and didn't want to do anything that made it look like I was angling for the job. I hope my answers to the Argus Review haven't created the wrong impression.

A couple of months later, after we come home from a disappointing early exit in the 2011 World Cup, Cricket Australia's operations manager Michael Brown and public affairs manager Peter Young drop in to my unit at Bondi. They tell me that Ricky stood down earlier today, and that Cricket Australia is inviting me to be captain of Australia in all three formats, starting with a coming one-day tour to Bangladesh. I'm gobsmacked. My first thoughts are about letting my parents and grandfather know, and my next thoughts are for Punter. I still don't want to step on his toes. Michael and Peter say that he is available for selection for Bangladesh as a batsman, and that he has endorsed me as his successor. That means everything to me.

If I'm to be captain, I will use what I have learnt from Ricky and others. I know that if I impose myself too strongly from the start, people will say I've been too eager to get the job . . . but, stuff it. If I hesitate, we might lose games, sink even lower than our current ranking of number five in the world, and I'll be on the scrapheap. I have to be decisive straight-up.

For all my thoughts about how to lead, my first serious challenge is a rolled ankle the day before we're due to leave for Bangladesh. The morning of the flight out of Sydney, I can't even put on my shoe. In normal circumstances, I shouldn't be going. When I get to the Qantas Club I am sitting with one foot in a black shoe and the other in a black sock.

I get Alex Kountouris's attention.

A couple of days before, I rang our team physio to tell him I'd hurt my ankle but it would be all right. Since then, it's only got worse. Now, in the Qantas Club, I whisper, 'Lexy, I've f—ed my ankle, it's really bad now.'

'What do you mean?'

I lift up my trouser cuff and show him. My ankle looks like it's swallowed a volleyball.

He's got a look of total horror. 'What the f— happened?'

'I was running round my house trying to get to my fridge,' I say. 'I was barefoot, and I rolled my ankle.'

'You can barely even stand,' he says.

'I'll be fine, mate. I'm going.' I am full-time captain of Australia for the first time. No way am I not going.

In Bangladesh, I tape my ankle for the four games in Fatullah and Mirpur, and we win them all. I manage a hundred in my first game as full-time captain, Watto follows up with a record 185 not out off 96 balls in the second match, and Huss makes a century in the third. In our clean sweep, we play some fantastic cricket.

I feel like the players back me. I say to Tim Nielsen, 'If we keep doing the same things, we'll keep getting the same results. Let's change a few things up. For starters, I'd like to be involved in all the decisions that affect the team.' To the players, I make it clear what our goals are, and that we're going to chase them hard, starting in this series.

I don't feel any different as a player, except I am free to do tactically on the field what I couldn't do before. I hope that I can get more out of these players on the field, including Ricky. I never feel any problem with our former captain being in the room, and don't buy into the criticism that his very presence can undermine me. True to his character, Ricky is a brilliant teammate in Bangladesh and contributes some handy runs.

Through the winter, there is more time to think. We're starting off a low base. There is a lot of talk about getting more young players in and around the squad, which I don't necessarily think is the best thing for our team. We've had enough turnover for the moment. Our captain for my whole career has just stood down. The transition since the 2006–07 Ashes, when we lost so many senior players, has given us a hit. The public, the media and possibly the players all thought we would roll on, and in their last years took guys like Damien Martyn, Justin Langer and Jason Gillespie, the support cast around the superstars, for granted. We had bad luck with the next generation. Guys we thought would be there for years, such as Simon Katich, Phil Jaques, Andrew Symonds, Stuey MacGill and Brett Lee, aren't there anymore. None has been easy to replace.

Off the field, the structures around the team are about to go through a revamp: Tim's job is going to be readvertised, and the selection panel headed by Andrew Hilditch is going to be dumped. The Argus Review will restructure our team along the lines of the England team that has just beaten us, creating a position of performance manager which will be held by former Wallaby Pat Howard, who comes across from rugby, where he was general manager of the Australian Rugby Union's high performance unit. There's a lot ahead of us. But I stress to the players that it will be up to *us*, and we have to clear all that other noise from our heads.

The other thing I will not shirk is the tough and direct conversations, which are going to be all the more important now I am a selector. I am black or white, never grey. I won't sugar-coat things. This is partly my personality and partly a result of experience. I hate when people say nice things to my face but I later find out they have been dogging me behind my back. One of the reasons I trust cricketers like Warney and Hughesy and my closest friends is that they will tell me things straight. Some others ... I thought they were my mates, but they weren't.

That said, your greatest strength is always the source of your greatest weakness. My direct way of speaking has got me into trouble ever since I was a chirpy kid in the classroom, and it continues to do so while I'm captain. Regularly I walk away from conversations thinking, 'Okay, that went well', when the other person is still reeling because I've been too direct with them. Dad has always said to me, 'It's not what you're saying to your mother, it's *how* you're saying it, it's your *tone*.' I've found it a hard thing to manage – being straight without hurting people's feelings. But I feel, from the start, that I have the CA board's full support and knowledge of the way I am. Chairman Jack Clarke and his successor Wally Edwards know what I'm like, they know it isn't going to be a walk in the park. I'll voice my feelings and drive the team hard.

So that's the initial landscape. My first major assignments come later in 2011, when we tour Sri Lanka and South Africa for combined Test and one-day series. We go without a coach, as Tim Nielsen has not reapplied for his position. The tours are a microcosm of my whole four years in the job: a roller coaster. We mix some fantastic cricket with some of the worst days in Australian Test history.

In Sri Lanka, Huss has the series of his life and some of the less experienced guys really make waves – Shaun Marsh and Phillip Hughes with hundreds, Nathan Lyon with five wickets in his first innings as a Test bowler, Trent Copeland hitting paydirt with a wicket in his first over, and Ryan Harris leading the overall wicket-taking. One of the first major decisions I make is having Shaun bat at number three with Ricky at number four, for the Third Test match in Colombo. It's in the best interests of the team, with Shaun having made a century at number three as Ricky's replacement in the Second Test at Kandy. In my opinion, he is a specialist top-order batsman and a future long-term number three for Australia, with Ricky playing more of a senior mentoring role below him. In a couple of conversations, I talk to Ricky about it, and he is very supportive and more than happy to do what is best for the team. We win the Test series and also the one-dayers, where I'm the leading run-scorer and Punter isn't far behind.

In South Africa, we come into the Tests on a roll after winning the one-day series there, and Graeme Smith asks me to have a bat on a wicket that will suit fast bowling.

THE INNINGS

151 versus South Africa, Cape Town, 2011

By the time I am Australian captain, I am more or less self-coaching with my batting. In 2008, Neil D'Costa moved to India to take up a position with the Vidarbha Cricket Association, so our meetings aren't so frequent. He and I still have occasional chats about batting, and Dad is still around once he's recovered from his cancer treatment, always making himself available to feed the bowling machine. In some ways he is still my main coach, reminding me of things I used to do. 'You're jumping back instead of cruising back.' 'You're not getting close enough to the ball.' Just little things.

Within the Australian team set-up, Justin Langer has been batting coach since 2009. Justin speaks to Neil about what to look for in my batting, and that is helpful. Justin is an outstanding batting coach, very dedicated to helping all the players in the team, and his attitude and commitment are the same as a coach as when he played. His efforts go a long way to taking us back to number one in the world. I use Justin and Vinnie Nielsen a lot, and will later use Michael Di Venuto when he replaces Justin in 2012. But I don't have a coach in the way I had Neil when I was growing up.

When you encounter conditions such as we get on the first morning of the Cape Town Test match of November 2011, you need to know your own game. You can have the best coaching in the world, but when the pitch has been sweating for two hours under the covers and then, when it is uncovered, it is hit by a rain shower, and you're facing an attack of Dale Steyn, Morne Morkel and Vernon Philander – then you have nothing but your own resources to rely on.

I come onto Newlands at three for 40. Little do we know what mayhem waits for both teams on this pitch, but we know it's favouring the bowlers. Shane Watson, Phillip Hughes and Ricky Ponting have got out early, and I have trouble laying bat on ball with Steyn swinging it late and fast.

As soon as I get out there, Graeme Smith brings on Morkel to replace Philander. Like Andrew Flintoff and Steve Harmison, Morkel's height makes him particularly awkward to face. Steyn is the best exponent of swing in the world – both conventional and reverse – but Morkel gets such bounce, every ball feels like it's hitting the splice of the bat and I can't get forward. The sky is overcast, the ball is keeping its shine, and batting is a nightmare.

Shaun Marsh is battling away and doing well at the other end. Warney's words come back to my mind: the better the bowling, the more positive you have to be.

After half an hour, I get in behind one from Steyn and drive it back past the stumps for four. That's a Ponting-like shot. As captain, I have seen Punter lead from the front so often, I'm craving my chance to play an innings that salutes him. This has got to be it, today.

Jacques Kallis comes on to bowl before lunch. Grateful to have survived Steyn, I go on the attack. This looks like one of those days when you have to get them before they get you, and, if Kallis overpitches, I'm hopping into it. Then I go after Morkel as well. As an innings, this is much more like the way I played in my Test debut seven years ago. See the ball, hit the ball. Poke around and you're just waiting for the good one to get you out.

I have a lot of luck, too. Edges fly past fielders and when I miss, I miss by a fair way. It's a cavalier kind of innings, but it has to be, as the wickets are falling fast at the other end. At one point, I have hit 20 runs off 20 balls from Steyn; his figures to the other batsmen are 58 balls, four wickets for nine runs. A cover-driven four off Kallis brings up my hundred, and after play reporters are asking if it's the best I've played. I'm not in a position to judge, but it's probably the best Test hundred I've made on the worst pitch.

On the second day, I start at 107 not out, and end up with 151 in our first innings, almost at a run a ball, before I get out slogging at Morkel.

How much the captaincy has changed me is clear in how little joy I get out of this innings. I appreciate that for others it ranks highly. But today, not for me.

What happens next defies belief. It still feels like a dream – a nightmare. I start the day batting in my first innings, and by stumps I've batted in my second, we're all out, and the South Africans are in . . . again! Twenty-three wickets in one day. Nobody has seen anything like it.

The highest highs and the lowest lows. I know, from batting on that strip, how tough it is. South Africa have no answer for Ryan Harris and Shane Watson, and we take fewer than 25 overs to bowl them out for 96. We're jubilant when we come off before tea, nearly 200 runs ahead. It's just a matter of keeping our foot on their throat.

Watto is lbw to Steyn on the third ball of our innings, and then the horror begins. Punter and Hughesy follow, and I'm only in for a quarter of an hour before Philander traps me. Huss goes next. While I'm still taking my gear off, Hadds follows his plan to whack the first ball out of the ground, but it doesn't come off.

I feel like I want to press PAUSE, but there is no button. An unstoppable momentum is dragging us along, like we're pinned down under a runaway truck. The changing room is stunned. Dead silent. Devastated. People are coming and going like the walking dead, padding up and unpadding. We are all out for 47, Australia's lowest score in more than 100 years. Our first innings is overshadowed by the humiliation of our second, and our loss of the match from what seemed an unbeatable position.

By the time we go back into the field, we're still unable to accept what's happening. We go through the motions, but the stuffing has been knocked out of us. The next day, it doesn't take Hashim Amla and Graeme Smith long to knock up the 236 runs South Africa need to win. We look like a cricket team, but we are eleven ghosts, unable to believe this reality.

Life smacks us between the eyes between the Test matches, when cricket writer Peter Roebuck dies. I knew him personally, but Ricky and Huss had a lot more to do with him and express their sorrows to the travelling press. We are all in a state of shock over what happened on the field at Newlands, and Roebuck's death adds to the sense that we are in some kind of alternative universe.

But what I love about our team is their ability to recover when they have been counted out. In the Second Test, at Johannesburg, we limit South Africa to 266 in their first innings before Watto and Hughesy put on a brilliant counter-attacking opening partnership. Pat Cummins, a teenager playing his first Test match, rattled through the South African second innings with six wickets just when they looked like they were getting away from us, and we are left with a target of 310. Punter, Usman Khawaja, Mike Hussey and Brad Haddin lay the foundation, and then Mitch Johnson, who is playing with a broken toe, and Pat Cummins bring it home. I have contributed a grand total of 13 runs, but I'm stoked. Talk about a roller coaster: all out 47 one week, winning with a record run-chase the next. I don't know if my nerves will stand it.

To see Pat Cummins hit the winning runs and so many excellent efforts from the boys to square the series shows me that something has changed in my mentality. When I was young, I certainly loved winning, but it was always mixed with how I felt about my own performance. Now, as captain, I feel that I am happier when we win and I don't care if I fail. If I succeed personally but the team loses, I have a hollow feeling. That Cape Town hundred might have been one of my finest days as a batsman, but ultimately it means nothing to me. The Johannesburg match is one of my favourite memories.

Through those two tours, I gain more confidence in my role as the team leader. Maybe it helps that we don't have a permanent coach, only our bowling coach Troy Cooley in an acting capacity. I am very clear about where I want to take this team. I think we are a lot better than fifth in the world. The senior players, rather than the staff, take much more ownership of the team, as I work to get their ideas flowing, and I try to make the leadership work more like it did when I made my debut. Ricky has noticed a change in me, with my greater involvement in team discussions and all the 'little things' around media and administration that a captain has to do. He is surprised, as I did not show much interest in those matters as vice-captain. But it wasn't because I was not wanting to help. It was because I didn't want to be seen as interfering.

Now, with the fetters off, I encourage the players to go about their cricket freely and positively. I try to innovate in my bowling choices and field positions, and tell the players that they are all there to participate – it's not required that the bowlers bowl and the batsmen bat; I am just as happy for Pat Cummins to hit the winning runs and Shane Watson to take the crucial bag of wickets, if it gets the job done.

In my man-management style, I want to be different from Punter. When we were on tours under his captaincy, he was unbelievably committed: his door was always open to every member of the team. We could always go to see him whenever we wanted, and he would be receptive. But when he went home, he would turn his phone off or not answer your call. I had thought, *If I'm captain, I'm not going to do that. Friendship is 24/7 and I'll always answer my phone when a friend calls. You don't pick and choose, and when you're at home you make time to talk or catch up.*

Little did I know how busy you are as captain of Australia – when you get home, you want to maximise your time with your family. But I don't know that yet and, when we are at home in 2011, between tours, I am constantly on the phone to teammates, checking how they are travelling, seeing if they want to catch up. As much as I admire Ricky, I make it clear that my style will be different. Not better, just my own. There's no right or wrong, but this will be my way.

Off the field, I want to work on team culture. I'm already nostalgic about my early days in the team, how much we used to do as a group. When I arrived in the West Indies to join the Australian team in 2003, the first person I ran into was Stuart MacGill. 'How are you?' he said.

'I'm all right.'

'The jet lag's a killer.'

'I think I'm all right.'

'You won't be. Come with me.'

He took me to the swimming pool area, where the boys were jumping in, swimming, having a great time together, and fixed me up with a rum and coke. From feeling nervous about being there, within minutes I didn't want to leave. And it cured my jet lag.

Team culture is hard to define. Touring overseas is difficult. You have to learn to live out of a suitcase, eat hotel food, go in and out of airports every few days. You miss your basic comforts of home – just going to the fridge and knowing what's in there seems like a luxury – and you spend a lot of time on your own. Touring the world with teammates brings you out of yourself, but those challenges are even more daunting when you're a junior member of the squad. As a youngster, I knew I had to be last on the bus, last to take a seat in the changing room, and if I was upgraded to business class on a flight, I had to surrender that upgrade to a senior player. It sounds harsh, but I loved it: it gave me a part to play.

When it came to information from the team manager, in those days Steve Bernard wrote it on a piece of paper and slipped it under your door. The team looked after the team, and the manager organised the logistics.

What I loved most about the Australian team then was that the players were their own coaches. When you walked to the middle, you had spent so much time with your batting partner learning the game, you knew him better as a result. If Darren Lehmann gave me a kick up the arse, or

Punter helped with my batting, or Symmo wanted a night out, those were better solutions than any coach could provide for you.

After play, you weren't on your mobile phone, you were getting ready to meet all the team in the hotel bar for one drink at 7 pm before organising where to go for dinner. If it was the end of a Test match, you would be talking cricket all night with your opponents. You used to get as excited about the prospect of an all-night victory celebration as you were about the game itself. On days off, some of the boys would go fishing, or play golf, or go out for lunch.

Now that I'm captain, I can see in painful, sharp relief how much that world has changed. Those card games on the bus have gone quiet, as a lot of players are now on their PlayStations or Nintendos. Others are busy tapping on their phones, which they've been on since the end of play.

Now there is a staff member for everything, and the manager doesn't need to slip some paper under your door because you have the team app, with alerts, to structure every moment of the upcoming week down to the last detail. What you eat for breakfast, who your batting partner and bowling partners are in the nets, exactly what time you'll be doing what. Bowlers know in advance what net they will bowl in, with what ball, for how long and to whom. There will often be a sponsor event, a gym session or a team function. If you're not training on your skills, you're doing fitness work. Every moment is accounted for.

If you're going for dinner, there will be a WhatsApp alert. If you're out at a function, you all leave together, there's no hanging around to socialise. A tour is not a working holiday; it's work.

And young players are made to feel as comfortable as anyone. You can sit anywhere, on a plane or in the changing room. You don't need to defer to the senior men, and if you get an airline upgrade, that's yours to keep. And the stereo? The physiotherapist carries the stereo.

If I sound like I'm wishing to live in the past, that's not what I mean. Cricket has always been an individual game in a team context, and if it's more individualistic now than ever, that is the type of structure that appeals to my personal strengths. I like structure. I like planning. I like committing myself to preparation. My personality likes the rigorous and methodical approach to touring now. But . . . but . . . in my heart of hearts, I *loved* touring more in my early days.

Maybe the pendulum has swung too far towards professionalism, or maybe I'm just wishing I was young again. Either way, as a captain, I would like to do more to rekindle the old-fashioned notion of a team.

As a captain, however, I will soon find that my power to change the system is more and more limited.

I enjoy being on the selection panel at first. Late in the year, the Hilditch-led panel is replaced by a new panel with

John Inverarity as chairman. John is the centre of gravity in the panel after Greg Chappell is made National Talent Manager, and soon Rod Marsh joins the group.

I've known John and Rod since they were coaches when I was at the academy, and have always got on well with them both, though our new relationship as selectors and captain places a new perspective on things. In one of our first chats, John and I are in a hotel, and he's sitting in the restaurant when I come in.

'Michael,' he says, and indicates for me to sit in front of him.

'Hi John,' I reply, but I remain standing. I think, *It's not going to work this way*. I feel like the principal is telling me to sit in his office. John has that way, developed from being a school headmaster for many years. I don't handle those outward signs of authority well. Whenever John tries to speak down to me, my fur stands up. But aside from those surface tensions, I feel really comfortable talking to him and think we get on well, as long as we're talking as two men rather than a schoolboy and the headmaster.

I've never seen any selector as my boss. I always believe my career is in my own hands and if I score enough runs, I think the selectors will have to pick me. My belief is you shouldn't have to suck up to anyone to move forward in the world.

I was a great admirer of the way Andrew 'Digger' Hilditch handled his role as chairman of selectors, which only briefly overlapped with my captaincy. The first time

I was given the role, for a Twenty20 international against India at the MCG in 2008, Merv Hughes, who I like and respect enormously, was the selector on duty. He walked into the changing room before the match with a piece of paper showing me the batting order and who was opening the bowling.

'What's this?' I said.

'This is the batting order and what the selectors want to see happen today.'

'Merv,' I said, 'ring Digger and tell him he's got to find someone else to captain Australia.'

I tore Merv's piece of paper up. This wasn't the under-10s. I wasn't walking out onto the MCG with a piece of paper telling me what to do. (If you ask my dad, he'll say that I was not accepting instructions when I had a chance to captain the under-10s at Woodlands Park, either!)

Sure enough, Merv phoned Digger, who called me. 'Sorry about that, Michael,' he said. 'You're the captain, you make the calls, that sheet's what we're thinking, but it's only a guide.'

Never a great one with authority, I got on very well with Digger, who supported my style of captaincy. With John, I enjoy having a voice inside the selection room, and he always listens to me, though I can tell he is not a huge fan of the captain being a selector.

It is tough to have your loyalties tested and divided, and this is the conventional argument against a captain being a selector. For example, I am very close friends with both

Brad Haddin and Matthew Wade, who will contest the wicketkeeping position over my first two years as captain. The selectors might worry that I would endorse a decision as it was made, but then run off to my mate and say, 'I didn't really back it.'

I am not like that. When a decision is made, I am quite comfortable with telling the player. Even if he is my mate, and even if I didn't agree, I deliver the decision as if it is my own. But I don't know if Inver has complete confidence that I can separate the captaincy from the friendships and, if I can, whether it will cost me the trust of my teammates. Clearly it cost me Symmo's.

The post-Argus change does not only involve the captain being a selector. The head coach is on the panel, too, and by the time we come back from South Africa at the end of 2011, we have a new coach.

15

CAPTAINS AND COACHES

In 2011, Australian cricket was trying to climb out from the wreckage of the Ashes defeat at home and an unacceptably early exit from the World Cup. The Argus Review came and went and I was appointed captain. James Sutherland and Pat Howard asked me, 'How do you see the captain–coach relationship?'

To me, it depends on the individuals. I've been told that Allan Border preferred to share responsibility with team coach Bob Simpson, who 'drove the bus'. When Mark Taylor became captain in 1994, he was a forceful figure who enjoyed running the team. Simmo was moved on, replaced by Geoff Marsh, who was a faithful ally for the skipper, a 'practice captain' who was a caring father-figure for the younger guys in the team.

When I started playing for Australia, I had one tour under Steve Waugh's captaincy, but my captain for eight years was Ricky Ponting. For half of that time, the coach was John Buchanan, a different kind of guy, not a former Test cricketer, who brought a left-field approach to the job. Then Ricky wanted to put his stamp on the team, and Vinnie Nielson took over the hands-on side: fielding drills, throwdowns and wicketkeeping skills. But by 2007, when Vinnie came in, the support staff had grown much larger and the demands on both captain and coach were more complex.

The Argus Review vacates the job, and Vinnie goes back to Cricket South Australia. So in 2011 we will be having both a new captain and a new coach. I want to make things straightforward and simple again. I say to James and Pat, 'If I'm captain, the wins and losses go against my name. I will be accountable for them.'

Cricket Australia appoints Mickey Arthur, a South African former first-class cricketer who played that supportive, pastoral role alongside Graeme Smith's captaincy. They were a successful partnership, steering the Proteas to a win over us in Australia in 2008–09 and taking their country to number one in the world.

I didn't know Mickey well when he was coaching South Africa, but when he joins our team at the beginning of the 2011–12 summer, we immediately click. He is a kind, gentle soul, softly-spoken and highly intelligent. He is quite a big man and has the appearance of a smiling, welcoming, bald teddy bear. The chemistry between us is comfortable, and the support staff try to blend different characters in so that we have the right combinations.

Alongside Mickey is Steve 'Stumper' Rixon. Stumper is a fantastic bloke, an ex-Australian Test wicketkeeper and successful coach of New South Wales, where I got to know him as a youngster, and New Zealand. Where Mickey has the easy-going man management skills, Stumper is old-school, rough around the edges but as honest and straight as anyone I've met. I believe Stumper would be the ideal coach for the team on purely cricketing matters, whereas Mickey's strengths are in taking care of a lot of other issues involving media and off-field management. They should be a perfect combination, but instead CA gives Stumper the more token title of fielding coach. I'm happy that he's involved, but would prefer, for the sake of support staff dynamics, to see him in a more senior role as Mickey's assistant coach.

On the range of soft-to-tough, I probably stand in between Mickey and Stumper, which, in my view, makes us a good team. When a player needs a particular kind of conversation with one of the leadership, he should be able to find one of us on his wavelength. It's true that I'm not the type who will take a troubled player out for a one-on-one dinner for a heart-to-heart and give him big hugs, but nor was Punter, and nor, I suspect, were our predecessors. On tour, I have plenty of time to talk with any player about anything that is on his mind. My door is always open. I do make a priority of my preparation during Test matches and I'm not often seen out and about during the course of a big match, but I'm a strong believer in each person having responsibility to lead his life as he wishes. I oppose 'booze bans' and curfews, that treat adult cricketers as if they are children needing constant supervision. So I bring to the role a mixture of emphases: I'm very intense about our preparation and our cricket time, but I'm also relatively relaxed about giving players freedom in their downtime.

For a year, the new set-up produces brilliant results. The team is going through a phase of renewal, with David Warner, Nathan Lyon, James Pattinson and Mitchell Starc making their Test debuts in my first home series as captain, against New Zealand. The Black Caps hold us to a drawn series, but then, against expectations, we smash India 4–0. I find the best streak of form in my life, scoring a triple-century in Sydney and a double-century in Adelaide. Punter and Huss, who have been under some pressure for runs, surge back to form with huge scores in Sydney and Adelaide. Warner and Ed Cowan get off to a flying start as the opening pair, and it's a great summer for the new regime.

THE INNINGS

329 not out versus India, Sydney, 2012

I am always nervous before I bat, but this time I'm even more jittery than usual. We have had a so-so start to the season, squaring a series with New Zealand before getting away with a win in the First Test against India in Melbourne. In my first home summer as Australian captain, I want to make a statement. The New Zealand result wasn't good enough. We have to beat India. But I have made very little contribution with the bat so far.

On match morning, I have an important conversation with Kyly. With my nerves building up, I am very short with her, as I have been all week. I don't know what's wrong with my batting. It feels like I've lost my mojo.

'Listen,' she says. 'If you do the same things, you will get the same result. If you know your winning formula, concentrate on that and what you have to do to achieve that. You know your routines, who you talk to before you go out, what song you sing in your head when you're happy batting. Why don't you just stick to that formula?'

I don't say a lot, but it gets me thinking. Captaincy has been such a huge job, it's distracted me from that formula and those routines that work for me personally.

I drive to the SCG with Mickey Arthur. He's in tears as he reads an email he's received from John Inverarity two days earlier. Mickey hasn't wanted to show it to me, but we are so close, he can't hold it back any more. John has made it clear that he's worried about my batting: that I have technical deficiencies and am not the player I used to be. I say very little. I'm very thankful to Mickey for having the courage to tell me. He wouldn't want to hurt me at any stage, let alone on the morning of a Test match. I give Mickey my word that I won't tell Inver I've seen the email. I take the information inside myself. Earlier in my career, I might have exploded. But after everything that has happened, I take the criticism quietly and let it fuel my fire.

The first-day SCG pitch is helpful to the bowlers, and 13 wickets fall: ten Indian, three Australian. It seems like it's going to be a fast-developing Test match when I join Punter in the ninth over of our innings about an hour before stumps. India have been dismissed for 191, and we are already three for 37, with Zaheer Khan bending the ball about.

At first, I'm in trouble. Ishant Sharma bowls a very fast bouncer, and I misread it, going forward to block it. It flies over my head. My eyes are shut as it goes past. I'm frozen. If it had been on line, my helmet would have been sitting in the grandstand.

Punter comes up and says, 'Are you all right?'

'I didn't see it,' I say.

'No shit! You went forward to a ball you should have been ducking!'

I tell myself to just see the ball and hit the ball, be positive, no matter what the situation.

Throughout my career I've been criticised for losing my wicket too easily, for being over-aggressive, but when I look back at my best innings they have all been examples of positive intent. You might occasionally die by the sword, but you live by it too. Pulling myself together, I hit two boundaries from the next four balls; when the speedy Umesh Yadav comes on, I hit him for three in a row. I guess you can get out when you're playing your shots, but the game is about scoring runs, and I feel that if I go into my shell I'm offering myself up to the next good ball.

After play, Kyly and I go to a friend's place for a delicious lamb dinner. It helps to further lower my anxiety levels. Ricky and I are both not out in the forties when we recommence on the second morning. As I've said, I love starting a new day with some runs in the bank. Immediately, I feel better than last night. The pitch has settled. My stance, my balance, my lack of head movement – everything feels like it's in alignment. I'm standing still and not trying to overhit balls. Everything's going along the ground. I'm feeling my confidence and courage flow back.

And then, at some point of the second day, it turns to magic. I'm watching the ball closely, letting the ball come to me – everything I've worked at over the years is coming together. I also get a mysterious feeling of a returning past inside me: it's like the 23-year-old who batted at Bangalore in 2004 has come to life again, seven years later. But it's even better than that. Whenever the Indian bowlers drift onto my pads, I don't miss a ball. I honestly think that I score runs off every single ball on middle and leg stumps. That's a direct result of all the work I put into straightening my game up after I was dropped.

I get to my hundred just before lunch. Ricky is 99 not out at the break, and when we resume I find it hard to get off strike for a few overs. I nearly run myself out trying to get him his hundredth and, when he eventually plays one down the ground and takes off, he has to dive to avoid being run out himself. But he gets there, and it's a special moment. I'm actually feeling that I want him to make runs even more than I want to myself. His position is being widely discussed, and my biggest wish is for him to put the critics back in their box. He's done that now.

To bat with, Ricky is always very calm. If I miss balls or hit them to the fielders early in the innings, I get frustrated easily. Ricky will come up between overs and say, 'Just keep hitting the middle of the bat, don't worry where the ball goes. If you keep hitting the middle, it will find the gaps.' Throughout my career, he is always in before me and I gain confidence simply from walking out to join him. In our conversations, he keeps it to cricket. He talks about the bowler, the wicket, what's next. He counsels patience and structuring your innings. That time in the middle has, from the start, been the best coaching I could get as a batsman, and now, at the SCG, we're reaching a kind of fruition of those eight or nine years we have spent together in the game.

We have put on 288 by the time Punter slices a catch to Sachin Tendulkar at backward point, but the afternoon keeps getting better and better. Mike Hussey cover-drives his first ball to the boundary and our momentum doesn't miss a beat. As I go on, I can hear the words Brian Lara spoke to me after I got dropped from the Australian team. 'When you get back in,' he said, 'make big hundreds. That's what will stand you in good stead when you have tough times again.' Today, I think that this is my chance. Everything feels so good, and I'm not feeling any fatigue, not even when I go past 200. Thanks to all of the extra physical conditioning I've done with my personal trainer Duncan Kerr, I am not going to fall victim to what, in these conditions, is the major obstacle to posting a big score: your own mental and physical weariness pushing you into poor decisions.

By the end of the day, I'm 251 and we have pushed out to a lead of nearly 300. The third day is Jane

McGrath Day, and the fact that I have a cleanskin bat – I'm in between sponsorships with Slazenger and Spartan – gives me the opportunity to put McGrath Foundation stickers on a high-visibility piece of real estate. The whole of the SCG is decked out in pink, and it's a great sight from the middle.

Batting with Huss is always enjoyable. He is very intense, always worried about the next bowling change, and this gives me a chance to calm him down. One of the best things about our partnerships is that we like to rotate the strike. When either of us is in trouble, the other comes down the pitch and says, 'Get a single, I'll face him.' And in this partnership, that's how it works. Our running is fast, we turn twos into threes, and our communication is strong. Not once do I fear that we will run each other out.

I am not motivated by a sense of history, by which I mean I don't bat for records. I'm not aware that when I pass 287, I've made the highest Test score on the SCG, but that's a lovely thing to be able to say in my home town. I do know that Brian Lara's world record Test score is 400, but that's the furthest thing from my mind by the middle of the day. I'm thinking that, with Virender Sehwag, Rahul Dravid, Sachin Tendulkar and V.V.S. Laxman, India have incredible batting firepower, and the way this pitch has settled, they could do anything. We need to leave ourselves enough time to win the match even if India make a massive second-innings score. When Huss reaches his 150, that's enough. Our lead is 468 and we have two and a half days remaining in the match.

It turns out that we don't need that many runs or that much time: Ben Hilfenhaus leads a hard-working bowling unit, grinding the Indians down, and we keep their second innings to 400, to close out an innings win. I get a little icing on the cake by dismissing Tendulkar myself. It's a great week. To look up in the stands and see Kyly and my family and friends clapping and cheering makes it even more special.

We follow up with a tour of the West Indies, where we retain the Frank Worrell Trophy. There's a glitch in our plans when Brad Haddin has to leave the tour because of the illness of his young daughter Mia, who has been diagnosed with neuroblastoma, a cancer-like condition. Matthew Wade slips into his place straight away, though, and scores our only Test hundred in the Caribbean.

Everything seems to be sailing smoothly from my point of view. Being a selector is not something I enjoy all the time, because I feel that I'm doing the work full-time and yet only getting one vote out of five. The accountability I sought is not there.

I'm especially pleased with the way Mickey Arthur sees his role in selection meetings. He backs my preferences, even if they're not his first choice. He sees his role as to provide a strong and stable voice but ultimately fall in alongside the captain. I feel that he reinforces me. Mickey's great strength is his caring nature. He doesn't want to hurt anyone's feelings. But as we head into the next home season, 2012–13, I glean that when Mickey has to make the inevitable tough decisions, some of the players who find themselves on the wrong side of them begin to talk about him behind his back, and this steadily boils up. There is also a growing sense in the team that Mickey has his favourites, who manipulate him, and those outside this perceived circle fume along in the background. Something is building, but, because I am so fond of Mickey, I am slow to see it.

THE INNINGS

259 not out versus South Africa, Brisbane, 2012

Through the year of 2012, when I make 329 against India in Sydney and 210 against them in Adelaide, 259 not out against South Africa in Brisbane and 230 against them in Adelaide, I only use two bats in Test cricket. I'm a big fan of sticking by my favourite bat when it's going well. I break a bat early in my triple-century in Sydney, but from then on I use the same bat for all of the remaining Test matches this year.

I use it in the Brisbane innings against South Africa, who I rate highly because they are the best pace attack in the world, bowling at us on a fast, bouncy pitch at a time when we are well behind in the match. The zone I'm in that year is hard to comprehend and impossible to reproduce. Facing Dale Steyn and blocking a ball that races past him for four – that's when you know you're batting at your peak.

None of these innings is without luck, but I am always trying to score runs, even when, in Brisbane, I come to the wicket with our team at three for 40 in reply to South Africa's 450. The game has been slowed down due to the loss of the second day's play to rain, but there's no question that we are in a mini-crisis when I go out and join Ed Cowan.

The South Africans give us a torrid time with short balls and a bit of chat, but once we survive that tricky twilight session, Ed and I feel increasingly comfortable. I sense some psychological dominance – or, if not dominance, the clear message has gone out to the South African bowlers that if they bowl a bad ball, we will try to score off it. That puts the pressure back onto them.

The Gabba is such a beautiful place to bat: fast outfield, true pitch. The quicks feel quick, and the spinners get bounce. Adelaide, where I make the other two double-centuries that year, is my most productive ground in Test cricket, but the pitch there is a lot flatter than this. In Brisbane you have to bat really well to make runs, but it will reward you with full value for your shots.

This innings is the best example in my whole career of becoming aggressive to get myself into the game. I think, *If I block, I'm a wicket waiting to happen. I have to change something. Put them under pressure.* I'm not going to look at the scoreboard. Any bad ball, I have to make sure it goes for four. I hear that good-omen song in my head, 'When the Saints Go Marching In'. People say when you're at your best, you think nothing. I try to think something. If I leave it to nothing, a negative thought might creep in.

So between balls, I'm talking to Eddie, on point, trying to anticipate what the South Africans will do next. Or I look around the ground and point out a lengthening beer snake, a beach ball getting caught by security, a fight between fans. I keep that mental traffic going.

I'm delighted to be at the other end when Eddie makes his maiden Test hundred. Ed and I have played a lot of cricket together, ever since we were juniors, and he has worked as hard as anyone to get to this level. He's thrilled as well, and our 259-run partnership (followed by one of 228 with Mike Hussey, who makes another hundred) steers us safely past the South African total. It doesn't result in a win, as that lost day cuts the match too short for us to force the issue, but I'm pleased that against the best fast bowling attack in the world, I've produced my best. It's what I saw Punter do so often, and what I would like to make a hallmark of my captaincy.

16

THE SCAPEGOAT

For Mickey Arthur, the crunch comes during the 2012–13 home summer. A chain reaction of events, and alterations in the management structure of the Australian team, end up on Mickey's doorstep.

In November 2012, after his two big innings against India kept the wolf from the door, Punter is struggling for runs. At 37 years of age, he becomes a target for relentless media pressure. After we draw our first two Test matches against South Africa at home, I get wind that John Inverarity wants to talk to Ricky in Perth, where we will be playing the series decider. John confides that the other selectors have made their minds up that Perth will be Ricky's last Test match, whether he scores nought or a hundred.

I am shattered. Ricky has been in almost every Test and one-day international I have played in. I idolise him:

how successful he has been, how competitive, how hard-working. In the two seasons since I've been captain, he has made it comfortable for me to have my predecessor around. Some people warned that it would be a tricky situation, but Punter has made it easy all the way. I still have a bad conscience about what a poor vice-captain I was to him, so I want to make up for that by being a good captain and looking after him.

It's less than 12 months ago that he made those brilliant Test hundreds in Sydney and Adelaide. In my view, he is the second-best batsman, after Don Bradman, that our country has ever produced. I don't believe in fairytales for myself, but I do for Ricky. I want him to play the summer, win in India and in England, and do his lap of honour at the SCG next year after we win the Ashes again. And I think Punter is still good enough to help us achieve all those things.

I put this to John. In our selection meeting, the senior figures are adamant that Punter has to go. I am so emotionally attached to Punter, I cannot be part of any decision to drop him. It wouldn't matter anyway, as I am obviously going to be outvoted, and, as it happens, Punter independently comes to the realisation in Adelaide that he's had enough.

Even then, I don't give up. When we land in Perth, I try to talk him out of retiring. Next year, in India and England, we're going to need his experience. But it's to no avail. I can see in Ricky's eyes that he has passed through to the other side. In his mind, he has made the decision and is coming to terms with life after cricket.

I am in tears during the press conference in Perth where Ricky makes his decision public. I describe the upcoming Test with South Africa as our 'grand final', as we haven't beaten them in a series in Australia since 2006. But that all pales into insignificance behind the retirement of Ricky Ponting. I can't believe it. He has been the soul of the Australian cricket team for 17 years. How will we go on without him?

We play the Test match in Perth as if we've already had a limb amputated. In two sessions on the second day, Dale Steyn hammers us with the ball and Graeme Smith and Hashim Amla bury us with their bats. We surrender meekly, considering the stakes of this Test match, but the focus is less on our performance than on the nation's farewell to Punter. It's a terrible on-field performance, one that I have almost wiped from my memory.

Punter's retirement is like the first tiny crack in an ice sheet. It looks fine on the surface for so long, and then suddenly it's in pieces. As a captain, I'm like anyone else: my strength is that I'm always looking forward and outward, thinking about match tactics, wanting to drive on to the next practice session, the next match, waking up every day looking for ways for myself and my team-mates to become better cricketers.

Because I'm not introspective, this can mean I skate over potential negatives. When someone is feeling down, I sometimes lack the patience or sensitivity for a session of soul-searching. I'm more likely to say, 'Come on, let's go out for a drink', or 'Let's go and hit some balls.'

The end effect of this is that I'm unaware of how some players are growing unhappy during this summer.

We defeat Sri Lanka in Hobart, but then Watto and I both have fitness problems before the Melbourne Test match. He has a calf issue and I have a strained left hamstring. Before the game, there's an agreement that he can bowl if used sparingly, and I give him the ball on Boxing Day. Three overs later, he's broken down. It doesn't affect the team's performance – Watto and I, running like a pair of wounded soldiers, put on 194 on the second day – but there's a mood of unease in the changing room that is at odds with a Test series victory.

The next shock comes from Mike Hussey. At the MCG, after the Test is finished, Huss tells Mickey and me that he's had enough. The New Year's Test in Sydney next week is going to be his swan song.

Unlike Punter, Huss is under no immediate pressure to score runs. He's had another solid summer. But he is 37, six months younger than Punter, and dreads the pressure that bubbles up every time a player of his age has a couple of failures. He's sick of that feeling: *Are they going to drop me? Why is the press talking about my position again?* We all know what that feels like. It's a nasty, nasty feeling. He and his wife Amy also have four young children, and understandably he doesn't want to leave his family for six months next year. I appreciate that he is going out on his own terms, and can see that he's not asking for Mickey's or my opinion. He has made his mind up.

It's a massive loss. I look Huss in the eye and say, 'Mate, if that's what you want to do, you've been a great bloke to play with and you've had a great career. Thanks for everything you've done.' But in my mind, I'm thinking, 'This is a blow for India and the Ashes. How the hell are we going to replace Huss?'

In Sydney, things are further complicated. Huss is only retiring from Test cricket at this stage, while making himself available for the home one-day international series coming up against Sri Lanka and the West Indies. But John Inverarity says, 'We're not going to pick you for the one-day series, we have to look to the future, but we will give you a farewell game in Perth if you want it.' I am not part of that decision at all, and am with Huss when John tells him during the Sydney Test match. I'm stunned into silence, and so is Huss. Neither of us can say anything. Finally, Huss decides that he doesn't want to be a charity case, and retires from ODIs as well.

And then, to ice the cake, during the first innings of Huss's farewell Test match, I run him out. It's totally my fault, and when the decision comes down I'm on my haunches saying, 'What have I done? What have I done?' Huss is very good about it, laughing it off as he leaves the wicket, but I am so dirty at myself I can barely hear him.

As all of this is bubbling along during the SCG Test match, I don't even spare a thought for the consequences of another decision I've made: another of my ill-fated Sydney parties.

Before the Melbourne Test match, before Huss's announcement, I approached James Packer and asked him if the team could go out on Sydney Harbour on his boat, *Seahorse*, to celebrate the end of the Test summer. We have done this before, and it's been an amazing night. He graciously consented, and said the boys' partners were also welcome. Due to safety concerns and the number of very young children several of the players have, it's agreed by management that it will be a no-children night. I have told the team, and those with children have gone about organising babysitters.

Our team manager, Gavin Dovey, who took over the role in 2011 from the long-serving Steve Bernard, sees the storm approaching before I'm aware of it. 'I'm a bit worried about the night on the boat being the night of Huss's last Test match,' Gavin says to me. It doesn't cross my mind that there is any problem. I have never been one for compulsory celebrations. The party on the boat will go ahead, but if anyone wants to opt out, they are entirely free to do so.

During the Sydney Test match, Huss invites friends and extended family members to Sydney, and Amy comes with their four kids. Gavin's worries are borne out when Amy is adamant that if it's a no-kids night on the boat, she will not come. Gavin and Huss's manager, Neil Maxwell, try to talk Amy around, but to no avail. Meanwhile, Huss decides that he will stay with Amy, the kids and their family and friends. But he doesn't want to cause a division in the team or any undue fuss, so he doesn't let anybody know before the end of the game that he won't be coming on the boat. I am unaware of the details of all these conversations, but Gavin updates me at the end of the game.

It's all really nice in the dressing rooms: we win the match early on the fourth afternoon and have hours to have a drink together and sing the team song with Huss for the last time. Gavin Dovey and I organise for John Williamson to come in and sing 'True Blue' live. This is the signal for coming together to sing the team song. Huss says a few words, receives some gifts from the team, and hands over the songmaster's job to Nathan Lyon.

Early in the evening, Gavin announces the plan that we will go back to the Quay West apartments and get changed, then walk down to the wharf at Circular Quay to meet the boat. Kyly and I go home to get ready, and travel from there to the wharf. It's all good until we realise that, at the hotel, Huss has told some of the boys he won't be coming on the boat. He's happy to celebrate with his family at the hotel, and doesn't want to interfere with the boys having a separate end-of-season party. He has told them that he would just like to retire with a minimum of fanfare, and a focus on his family.

The complications arise when the team gathers in the hotel lobby to leave for the cruise. When they hear that Huss is staying behind, Shane Watson and Peter Siddle say they want to stay with him. When I hear about this, I have no problem with that either. Watto is carrying an injury he picked up in Melbourne, has missed the Sydney Test, and probably wants to look after his body. Sidds is by this time a non-drinker, and would prefer a quieter night.

That's all okay by me. I've always been the one to send out a text saying, *Boys, we're going out, if you want to come, meet downstairs at 6.30, if you don't want to come, that's fine.* I have never believed in manufacturing team harmony through compulsory events. If you didn't want to come, you would have a shit night anyway. If you wanted to come, you'd have a good night. It wasn't complicated. Or it shouldn't be.

So we go out on the boat, minus the Husseys, Watto and Sidds. We make a last-ditch effort to get them all to come, putting in some phone calls. But Huss repeats, on phone, that he wants to be with Amy and the kids, and he has nothing but good wishes for our party. We have a good night, and the next morning Huss meets with Gavin Dovey and makes sure he will get the message out that he never intended to go on the boat and was happy with the way the night turned out. It's really a small thing, a minor miscommunication.

How did it then blow up? Again?

A few days later, some outsider circulates an email telling a story about a team bust-up over the boat trip. This person seems to have an axe to grind with me, because the gist of the email is 'Michael Clarke split the team by making them go on James Packer's boat instead of celebrating Mike Hussey's last Test match'. As with the Kato thing three years before, this story is built on pre-existing opinions about me. I am the eastern suburbs wanker with the high-rolling friends, while Huss is the salt-of-the-earth family man.

I'm not too bothered about that, because I know there was no conflict between Huss and me over the boat party. What does annoy me is that somebody outside the team knows details about our arrangements that can only have come *from inside*. The dots have been joined to create a completely false story – that I tried to use Cricket Australia powers to enforce mandatory attendance on the boat – but what concerns me more, at the time, is how any of it got into the hands of some malicious anonymous individual who obviously dislikes me. (Further investigations suggest that this person is an outsider to the team who barely even knows me.)

Again, I make what is, in retrospect, the error of not coming out in public and making a strong statement about what really happened. I am so mad about how things got twisted, I don't trust myself to stick to the script. What I should do is cool down, explain exactly how things happened, preferably side by side with Huss, and throw a bucket of cold water on the malicious email. Instead, I angrily brush it off and tell myself that if I say nothing, it will go away. As with the Kato episode, it doesn't.

The innuendo leaves a sour taste to what was, at the time, a fantastic night. When we were at the SCG, it was all about Huss, and when we were on the boat, it was all about the team. But once the ugly and false email gets out into the press, it becomes all about how I have divided the players into factions. Because of the myths that have been built up around my falling-out with Andrew Symonds and what happened to Simon Katich, it's added to the Michael Clarke rap sheet.

Of the relationships that had deteriorated since I had been captain, I did everything in my power to rebuild my friendship with Symmo, but he didn't want it. I never had any bad blood with Kato, but, as I have explained, the public image around our relationship proved too big a barrier when his contract wasn't renewed. The main relationship within the team that I did know I had to address was with Shane Watson. I heard that Watto did feel that we had somehow let Huss down by going on the boat without him, and this was one of the issues that would be mentioned two months later when things came to a head in India.

Watto and I had played together since we were both in under-19s representative teams. We went to the Australian Cricket Academy in the same intake, and were close mates there. I got on really well with him, and the way we related to each other never changed throughout our careers. I never disliked Watto as a person. He was such a nice guy, it was impossible to not like him. Whether we played with or against each other, we were always friendly. You can see pictures of us right through our careers, celebrating winning back the Ashes in 2013–14, winning the World Cup in 2015, and many other great victories, and none of that is faked. Person to person, we never had a bad moment.

Because we were the same age, the media built us up as competitors from early in our careers. There was never anything in that. I was a specialist batsman who bowled a little, whereas Watto was a genuine all-rounder, who bowled at up to 145 km/h early in his career, and was among the most destructive limited-overs batsmen Australia has ever produced. We were quite different kinds of players, with different roles in our teams, but I guess you can't evade those comparisons and contrasts when you come up through the system together. It never produced any antagonism between us.

We broke into the Australian one-day international team around the same time, in 2002–03. I made my Test debut in 2004, Watto in 2005. The team we entered was quite factionalised, but as youngsters neither of us belonged to any senior-player group. We were both just happy to be there.

I spent a lot of time with Andrew Symonds and Shane Warne, and Watto was very close to Brett Lee. But I also hung out with the rest of the guys – anyone who would put up with me!

My closest friend turned out to be Shane Warne, and he was also tight with Watto, bringing him into his Rajasthan Royals IPL team for their successful first few years. Nothing that came between Watto and me had anything to do with team factions in those years.

Little misunderstandings can grow over time. I can only speak for myself, and I'm sure I had a lot of habits and ideas that would have irked Watto. Like nearly every Australian cricket follower, I desperately wanted him to fulfil his obvious potential. No batsman could dominate attacks like he could, and no bowler was as dangerous in conditions that suited him or as economical in tough times. He had the potential to be as phenomenal an all-rounder as Jacques Kallis.

Injuries interrupted his early career, and changed the way he had to prepare for cricket. When I became a senior player and then captain, I got an insight into how those injuries had affected Watto's preparation. I thought that if we had a running session, we should all run together. But Watto, due to his history with injuries, would go off and do his own thing, often with his personal physio, Victor Popov. We would do a running session and he would do a bike session, which annoyed the support staff, who were trying to bring us all together. Maybe we should have had broad enough minds to accept that one size did not fit all players. But due to my own beliefs, I was hell-bent on the team sticking together and preparing as a unit, and the way Cricket Australia had structured the support staff was reinforcing this view. I wasn't criticising him or whingeing about him. Other players would say, 'Why isn't Watto with us?' I would defend him, but I assume it was one of those things in the atmosphere of the group, over the years, that wedged itself between Watto and the group.

We all thought he was a better player than his stats ultimately showed. I don't place much store in statistics. Watto averaged 35.20 with the bat in his 59 Test matches, and 33.68 with the ball. Those are figures that compare pretty well with the likes of Andrew Flintoff and Ian Botham, two great all-rounders, but Watto would no doubt feel that he could have averaged higher with the bat, and influenced more matches and series the way those great all-rounders did. As a selector for two years and as captain for four years,

I was always in favour of picking him when he was fit to play as an all-rounder.

I happily own those decisions, and feel that he contributed enough to our team to warrant those selections. Nonetheless, I was regularly having to defend his selection to other players. He was invariably given a chance, whereas batsmen like Phil Hughes and Shaun Marsh were the first to be axed, and there were plenty of others who didn't get a go at all. Selections, by their nature, cause resentment, because someone has to miss out. Watto, due to his class as a player, never seemed to be the one to miss out. And yet the way people interpreted his body language, he didn't exude the joy you would expect from someone given so many chances.

I repeat that none of this was Watto's fault. He was trying his best, and we are the way we are. He had a way of trudging around that was purely a result of his build and his appearance. The body language was a superficial thing that he didn't intend at all, but others would get frustrated and interpret it as a sign that he didn't care. This wasn't true. He cared as much as anybody. You would have to care immensely, to go through the amount of rehab he endured to get on the park. But when someone would say, 'Get him off the field if he doesn't care,' I would have to defend him again, and the rumblings among the team added to the atmosphere.

There's no hiding from the fact that I wanted to be a strong captain and could rub people up the wrong way. I said straight up to the team, 'If you're not going to get on this train, get off.' It was all about getting the team back to number one. If you weren't on board, get out of the way. I was very driven by that. My greatest achievement was getting the team back to number one in South Africa, but I sacrificed relationships for it.

Is this what happened between me and Watto? I'm not sure. We didn't have arguments and we didn't thrash it out. But something would leak to the media, like the boat story, and it was turned into how I was not getting on with some teammates, and I was having a war with Watto.

A few weeks after the Melbourne Test match and the boat episode, we go to India for a four-Test series. Watto is my vice-captain. Our relationship is the same as it's always been, which is to say, on the same footing as my relationship with 90 per cent of the players I've played with. We sit in the changing room and chat, we chat on the field, we practise and play together, we go out for team dinners and functions. On this tour, Phillip Hughes, Matthew Wade and Brad Haddin are the players who are also my close friends outside cricket, but that happens in any team, and I don't think we are factionalised on the tour.

Although I'm aware of his feelings over the boat and Huss's retirement, I don't go into this tour thinking there is any bridge to build with Watto. The boat party just didn't seem like a big issue. My focus is on getting him on the field as an all-rounder, so that his talent can help us win games. I get worried before some matches that he's going to break down – and then very frustrated if he does. That drives me nuts. But it would be the same with any player. You just want them to be at their best.

While we were winning matches during the 2012–13 Australian summer, these and other issues were swept under the carpet. That's the nature of sport. When you start losing, however, it's a different matter.

India pump us in the first two Test matches, in Chennai and Hyderabad. Watto doesn't bowl, which increases the strain on our bowling unit, who are struggling against some determined Indian batting on unhelpful wickets. I want him to bowl, but he says he can't risk injuring his calf again, and the selectors continue picking him as a specialist batsman. If he's being picked as a specialist batsman, then that takes the bowling side out of the equation. He isn't scoring as many runs as he would like – though he is not alone in that.

We are a dispirited and disappointed team after the Second Test, which we lose by an innings. I make a hundred in Chennai and 91 in Hyderabad, but my back is starting to play up, which I have to fight against if I want to keep up a happy and resolute face for our inexperienced team.

And we are outrageously inexperienced: Ed Cowan, Phil Hughes, Glenn Maxwell, James Pattinson, Matthew Wade, Moises Henriques, Nathan Lyon, Usman Khawaja, Steve Smith, Mitchell Starc, Xavier Doherty and David Warner – 12 out of a squad of 15 – are on their first tours of India as Test cricketers. A huge load rests on myself and Watto, as the captain and vice-captain of course, but also as the only regular members of the team with Test experience in India.

On the day the Hyderabad Test match finishes, I have lunch in the team hotel with Mickey Arthur, Gavin Dovey and John Inverarity. A number of issues come up: players wearing non-regulation uniforms, being late to meetings, leaving change rooms in an unacceptable state, and showing disrespect to people who are helping us. We are exasperated with the slipping standards, and believe there is a direct correlation between that and what is happening on the field.

As chairman of selectors, John raises some queries we will have to face for the Third Test in Mohali, among them Watto's lack of runs. John has always been adamant about having Watto in every single team, yet I'm getting frustrated with him breaking down when bowling, or, as on this tour, refusing to be considered as a bowler. I'm not saying not to pick him. I am saying, 'Pick him when he's fit.' The medical staff, who I am seeing every day, are asking, 'Why do we make this mistake over and over again?'

Other players are also frustrated with him having run his own show fitness-wise. He has his reasons for this. When he feels that he isn't getting what he needs from the team staff, he pays for his own separate treatment. But whatever the reasons, it creates a division within the team.

I organise a centre-wicket practice at Hyderabad on the notional fifth day of the match, and again it's clear that some players are giving everything to the session while others are going through the motions.

Mickey, meanwhile, is trying his best to rally us. When the team arrives in Mohali for the Third Test, which we need to win to keep alive our hopes of retaining the Border–Gavaskar Trophy, Mickey tells everyone that he wants them to contribute ideas. We are being outplayed. He says, 'I want to hear two positive things and two negative things about how we're going from all of the team.' It doesn't matter if they tell him in person, by email, on a piece of paper, whatever. But over the next few days before the Test match, Mickey wants feedback, a request that would be common in any professional sporting team.

On the eve of the Mohali Test match, Mickey calls a meeting of the support staff, plus me, at the Marriott Hotel in Chandigarh where we are staying. He announces, 'Four players still haven't got back to me by the deadline. What are we going to do?'

I don't know who the four players are, and I don't know if anyone else in the room apart from Mickey does before the meeting. There is a lengthy discussion among the staff about general standards slipping. They say that there is no unity in the way the team is preparing for matches, and that guys are getting away with disciplinary infractions that should not be occurring at the highest level of sport. I don't know if it is Mickey's soft, relaxed approach, or my fanatical style of preparation, but whatever the cause, we are not getting the message through. Until now, I haven't realised how frustrated the support staff have been. Meanwhile, we are getting flogged on the field and everyone is looking for answers. The meeting is the explosion of a volcano that has been bubbling for some time.

Finally, the team doctor Peter Brukner, who has worked with ultra-professional Australian Football League and English Premier League teams, says to Mickey, 'You've got to take a stand. This rubbish has been going on long enough. They think you're not tough enough, Mickey.'

It is open for everyone to share their opinion on a sanction. The most popular option is to rule those four players ineligible for selection in the Third Test. Mickey reveals who they are: Shane Watson, James Pattinson, Usman Khawaja and Mitch Johnson. Usman and Mitch have not played in the first two Test matches, but due to our performances they are in the reckoning for the third.

There is almost unanimous support, from the staff, for a one-match ban. I am pissed off in general about losing, and the staff have convinced me that too many blokes in this team are acting like they couldn't care less. The argument is not just to punish the four players, either. It's to say to the other squad members, *Good on you for making an effort*. I say to Mickey, 'Whatever you decide, I'll support.'

The only one in the room against taking a firm stand against a one-match ban is Alex Kountouris, who thinks it's too harsh a punishment and will have negative ramifications in the group. He thinks a ban is going to be hard to communicate to the public. As usual, Alex will prove to be right on the mark.

In his heart, I don't believe Mickey wants to ban the four players. The vice-captain being one of them makes it particularly sensitive. But there is such a strong feeling among the staff that Mickey has to act, or he will lose all respect. He has been told that Watto has been criticising him behind his back, and he knows that having gone this far, he has to follow through or else he will look weak and the disciplinary problems in the team will only get worse.

So Mickey, Gavin Dovey and I set ourselves up in a hotel room and hold individual meetings with each of the four players. Mickey is the one to break the news. He hates doing this, it's so far out of his comfort zone as a person and would cost him a lot emotionally. In a few weeks, it's going to cost him his job.

The four players are shocked, disappointed and angry, all in their own ways. Patto is shattered at missing a game for Australia. He and Usman are pissed off, but it seems that they are most angry at themselves for forgetting to get back to Mickey. I try to help and support them as much as I can, telling them that it's only one match and they will bounce back.

Mitch's and Watto's responses are directed more at the three of us on our side of the table. Mitch is extremely angry. 'I f—ing forgot! What do you want me to do?'

Watto goes off his brain. He's furious at Mickey and me. His line is, 'We're being dropped for something as small as this, while there are other blokes in this group who have done much worse and it's been let go.' From a justice point of view, he isn't wrong. This is not a hanging offence. But this is where Mickey has decided to draw the line in the sand. The punishments are a signal to everyone in the team, including people who, as Watto says, have done worse things than him.

I knock on his door later, to placate him. I go into his room and assure him how important he is to the team and how much we need his leadership. It doesn't do much good. Watto's wife, Lee, is expecting their first child, so he has that on his mind. He will fly back to Australia for the birth, for which he has been given permission. So it turns out that he has been banned for a match that he would have missed anyway.

I support Mickey in taking a stand. If I hadn't supported him, there was a chance for me to back Alex's line in the staff discussion. Swayed by the strength of feeling among the support staff, I'm fully behind Mickey. But then, as has been happening so often, communicating the decision to the world turns into a shambles. Mickey makes the announcement that the four players are not going to be considered for the next Test, and focuses only on the 'homework' assignment instead of explaining that this is the culmination of a lot of disciplinary looseness over time. Soon after, James Sutherland rings me from Melbourne.

'You have to do the media, Michael.'

'What do you mean? I didn't make the decision. It's Mickey's job. He does media all the time.'

'You have to tell the world,' James insists. 'It hasn't been communicated the right way.'

He's right – we have let ourselves down with the way we have communicated this – but I hate having to step in now, and feel caught between a rock and a hard place. To explain it to the players has been unpleasant enough. I'm sure, given my determination to drive the bus, some of the players think that I have been behind the whole thing and have pushed Mickey into it. That's not true. But if any players believe that already, they're going to be convinced when they see me taking accountability for it in public. I tell the media that it's not just the assignment but 'stuff off the field that's unacceptable for the standards an Australian cricket team ... We can't accept mediocrity here. Maybe I am biased, but there is a big difference between this team and other cricket teams. If you play for Australia, there is a lot that comes with that, and standards, discipline, culture are all a big part of what we're talking about.'

When the Test match gets started, I win the toss and four of our guys – Ed Cowan, David Warner, Steve Smith and Mitchell Starc – dig in and produce some outstanding batting in the first innings. But ultimately, it's not enough. I promote myself to number three in the first innings and make a first-ball duck. Down the order in the second, I'm little better as we collapse. Only Hughesy, with his best innings in India, gives our innings respectability. It's another horrible loss, made even worse by knowing that the outside world is taking the piss out of us for what they're calling 'Homeworkgate'. The idea that four Test cricketers have been sacked for not doing their 'homework' makes us a laughing stock.

As if this isn't disastrous enough, my back is thoroughly gone by now. It's been deteriorating for weeks, and the stress of the past week has finished the job. The medical staff say, 'Get home for some tests and treatment. You need to get it right for the Ashes.' I fly home as the Fourth Test in Delhi gets started, and am criticised for 'abandoning' the team. Watto flies back into India, back into the team, and is named captain. I'm feeling at my lowest since I was dropped by Australia seven years ago. The thing I am proudest of in my Test career is that I have not missed one match through injury. Given the underlying state of my back, it's a real achievement. Not many people know about it, but I regard that ability to present myself as fit to play for Australia as a greater personal feat than any of the wins I've contributed to, or scores I've made.

And now that's gone.

We lose in Delhi too, and Mickey is about to become the scapegoat for our failures. As I watch the Fourth Test on television from Sydney, I am in no doubt that the 4–0 series loss is the responsibility of us players, not Mickey. Some of the batsmen, like Ed Cowan and Phillip Hughes, have worked and worked and worked until they found a way to make runs by the end of the series. For the team, it's unacceptable to bat first in all four matches, getting the best of the conditions, and not once make 500. We had to lift, collectively, to fill the experience gap left by Punter's and Huss's retirements, and instead we drifted in the opposite direction, letting the 'one-percenters' become 'ten-percenters' and costing us Test matches. Results-wise, it is the worst tour by an Australian team since 1970.

At the end of the tour, Watto stands down from the vice-captaincy after discussions with Pat Howard. Brad Haddin is selected for the 2013 Ashes tour, and he will be my deputy. Watto and I have had a number of chats where we've talked about where he wants to go with his cricket and how to make amends for an unproductive Indian tour.

For myself, the break between India and the Ashes is filled with rehab and training. I drive from home in Cronulla to my physio Steve Giulieri's practice in Beecroft twice a day to work on the MedX machine, a contraption that has become as familiar to me in the past few years as my own bed. I sit in the MedX for short bursts while it bends me backward and forward, and then I do more treatment before another turn on the MedX. Steve is a saint, working out of his normal hours. His outlook is always positive, and I couldn't get through this without him – in fact, I doubt I would have played for the past three years without him. Once I'm stronger, I have an intensive 'boot camp' with my personal trainer Duncan Kerr, who has known me since I was 17, in the Southern Highlands, something we do for two weeks a year in various locations. It's always a great way for me to focus 24/7 on my physical and mental preparation. Duncan is a solid and loyal friend who always finds a way to get the most out of me. Then I head up to Brisbane for a couple of weeks at the Centre of Excellence, practising with the Ashes squad members who are still in Australia, rather than playing in the IPL or in county cricket.

I also offer to stand down as a selector, something that was raised in a conversation I had with Rod Marsh and

Allan Border during the Indian tour, but James Sutherland refuses. It was a big reform of the Argus Review to make the captain a selector, and James wants to stick with it, despite my misgivings and those of several former Australian captains.

Over time, I've grown dissatisfied with the captain–selector role. I have been doing the full-time job of being a selector, and am seen by the players as determining their futures, with all the negative feelings that brings, and yet I am only having one vote out of five and don't believe I exert much influence, even with Mickey supporting me. I only ever get what I want if I have the chairman onside.

By 2013, it has turned into the worst of both worlds. I am distrusted by some players because I am on the panel, I'm fully accountable for our wins and losses, and yet I am not actually very influential. It's got to the point where, in selection meetings for the 2013 Ashes tour, I walk in with three players in my head who I want to be on that tour, and I get none of the three.

If I don't have the support of the chairman and the senior selectors, what's the point in taking the heat for their decisions? As I said to James Sutherland when I offered to resign, 'You can't expect me to be accountable for results if I have no say in the team selection.' We are living in a different world from when I became captain in 2011.

Physically, I am on the mend until four days after our arrival in England. I spend two days resting after the long flight, and then we have two practice games for the Champions Trophy, the one-day series known as the 'mini-World

Cup'. We haven't been treating it as such: 90 per cent of our training in Brisbane was with red Dukes balls, and all the media questions I've been asked since my arrival in England have been about the Ashes. The Champions Trophy is being seen as something to get out of the way before the real tour begins.

Before the second practice match in Cardiff, I go to the nets early. While facing some throwdowns I jump to avoid a short ball, and feel the nasty old grab in the right-hand side of my lower back. It knocks the breath out of me. The pain is bad, but nowhere near as sharp as the mental realisation of what this means. I'm going to miss the Champions Trophy, and will be wrestling with this for the whole tour. I go to hospital and receive four cortisone injections. The injections, as always, relieve the pain. Alex locates a MedX machine in London, and I'm driven back there for as many days of treatment as I can fit in.

I'm in London while the boys go down in their first Champions Trophy group game, against England at Edgbaston, on Saturday 8 June. A bunch of them go out to a bar that night. I am unaware of anything untoward having gone on when, the next morning, I'm joined by Phillip Hughes, Matthew Wade and David Warner at a charity event put on by Shane Warne in London. Nobody mentions anything to me about their night out.

Those three players return to Birmingham for the next game. At a fines meeting – a light-hearted tradition of touring teams that we've reinstated for this England tour – Matty Wade, as head of the committee, sanctions Watto for wearing a sweater rather than a training top at practice. It's meant in jest, but Watto blows up and refuses to pay the fine.

Meanwhile, players have spoken to Gavin Dovey and said, 'Mickey Arthur should ask David Warner what happened on Saturday night.' Mickey confronts David, who admits that some English players were at the bar, and a party wig was being passed around. England's Joe Root put the wig on upside down and David, apparently taking offence at what he saw as an anti-Muslim slur, took a swing at him. David says he texted Root the next morning to apologise, and also spoke by phone to Root's teammate Steve Finn. They concluded that everything was sweet and it wouldn't go any further.

It's Monday night by the time Mickey finds out, and he's not happy. As the one who laid down the new standard of behaviour in India, Mickey feels personally let down by Davey, who he has a lot of time for. Mickey calls me on the Tuesday morning in London. I'm absolutely ropeable. It's not just what happened, but the fact that now I feel like I am the last person in the entire squad to know about it. I'm furious with Davey for not telling me on Sunday.

When I chat with a number of the boys on the phone, I'm also angry at what they're telling me about disharmony in the squad. Blokes are muttering about each other and about Mickey. Watto is still seething at what happened in India and what he perceives as inconsistencies in punishment: that he copped a major sanction for what he believed was a minor offence in India, and now feels picked on by the fines committee. The most troubling thing for me, being a few hours away from the team, is that Mickey's bold action in Mohali clearly hasn't brought about team unity and discipline. It has only set off a new chain of unwanted consequences.

Mickey and I agree, in that phone call, that we should try to work out an appropriate disciplinary action within the team. But immediately, Cricket Australia come over the top of us and take it out of our hands. They will take any further step, which ends up as a ban for Davey lasting until the First Test at Trent Bridge. As this match will run back-to-back with the Lord's Test match, it effectively means he will miss the first half of the Ashes series. Once his ban ends, he will join an Australia A team touring southern Africa while we play England in Nottingham and Lord's. It's a harsh but fair punishment. His actions in the bar were unacceptable for an Australian cricketer and a further indication of slack standards in the group.

I step up my training and medical treatment, desperate to play in our first Ashes tour game against Somerset in Taunton next week. At the Royal Garden Hotel in Kensington, where we're staying, I join the boys in the bar, to watch a rugby game on the other side of the world between Australia and the British Lions, and then go out for an early dinner with Kyly.

As we're walking out, I see James Sutherland and Pat Howard are in the reception area looking tense. They beckon me over and say we need to talk. We make a time for me to come back to the bar after dinner. I'm not surprised to see them, as they came to England to see how the Australia A team under Darren Lehmann are going. Their faces are tight as they invite me to sit on a stool in a quiet corner. Immediately I suspect something is up. They begin with some small talk before getting to the point.

'Tomorrow we're going to Bristol,' James says, 'to let Mickey know that he's no longer required as our head coach, and we're going to offer Darren Lehmann the job.'

I am too dizzy to speak. I literally have to stop myself falling off my stool.

'I don't know what to say.'

Sacking Mickey? That was the last thing I thought James and Pat would want to talk about.

'We wanted you to be the first to know,' James says. 'How do you feel about it? How will the team handle it?'

I can't even hear him above the noisy thoughts rushing in my head.

'Mickey's going to be shattered,' I say. My first thoughts are for him, how he will feel. My second thoughts are about how much planning we have done together. Mickey and I have grown very, very close. The first Test match is 18 days away.

'Are you sure it's the right time?' I say. 'We've done so much planning together for this series.'

There's no point me pleading for Mickey to be retained. James and Pat have already decided. They begin speaking positively about what Boof can bring to the job. Both on and off the field, the team's performances have been heading south. I see this as entirely the responsibility of the players, and me as the captain, and I don't believe Mickey should take the rap for that. But James and Pat can't sack the entire team at this point. Their action is to move on Mickey.

'Also,' James says, 'we're happy to accept your resignation as a selector now.'

In the circumstances, that brings relief more than anything. Whether I remain a selector or not seems irrelevant at this moment. I have to take stock. Eighteen days to get myself fit and rebuild our approach to the Ashes without Mickey. I am stricken for him, knowing that his mother is very sick in South Africa.

That night, when I get back to the room and sit there unable to sleep, my phone lights up. Mickey is calling from Bristol. Normally, we chat several times a day. But Pat has told me to say nothing to Mickey, as he is going to give him the bad news in Bristol tomorrow morning. I look at the phone, wondering whether I can lie to Mickey and have a normal conversation.

I can't. I let it ring out.

As soon as Mickey has spoken to Pat the next day, he texts me. We speak soon after. I tell him how terrible we, the players, feel for him, and confess to a sense of guilt. Our performances are our fault, but he has paid the price.

There's worse news to come. I am devastated for Mickey when I hear that as he is flying home to Perth, his mother has passed away. Immediately, Mickey and his family rush to South Africa.

I feel unmoored without him. We have had a great relationship for two years. I trust him, he trusts me, and we complement each other well. He has been the warm father figure for the team, and I've been the gadfly driving them to work harder and get intense about preparation and tactics. Until the Indian tour, with me leading and Mickey supporting, that was going well. Or at least I thought it was. On that tour, when he decided he had to show strength, it began to unravel for him.

I thought Mickey was unfairly scapegoated. When we look back, Mohali will be seen as a turning point in team behaviour. Mitch Johnson, who had been lacking hunger and was troubled by injury for two years leading up to it, will be transformed. The Mitch who comes back in late 2013, having been banned for a match in India and then left out of the Ashes tour, is a different person. The amazing player and athlete inside him, the real Mitch, will come out. Everyone in the team will see it, and his transformation will inspire us all. Not that Mickey will ever get any credit for it, but Mitch's renewal, and with it the team's, started when we hit rock bottom in Mohali.

After Mickey's sacking, he and I continue texting and speaking for the next three weeks. The team plays quite well against some ordinary opposition in our two warm-up matches, and then we fall agonisingly close to pulling off a miraculous win in the First Test at Trent Bridge. It's one of those sliding-doors moments: if we are able to get those last 15 runs and win the match, I believe we go on to win the Ashes comfortably. But when we fall short, it steadies England's self-belief and shakes ours, and we melt away badly in the Second Test at Lord's.

On the eve of that match, I'm rocked again. Mickey has lodged a legal claim against Cricket Australia. They only offered him three months' severance pay when he had another two years of his contract to run. Somehow, his statement of claim has leaked into the media and the most explosive part, which is all over the papers, is that Mickey says he had to be the 'meat in the sandwich' in the 'feud' between me and Watto. He says I called Watto a 'cancer' on the team.

I am so angry I can't speak. It's the morning before the Second Test. I send Mickey a text telling him that it's bullshit. I try to call him, and we play phone tag for a few hours but don't talk. Publicly and privately, Mickey will deny leaking the statement, but that's hardly the point.

For me, the main thing is that I did not say that. What I did say, two years earlier – before the 'Homeworkgate' saga – was that I felt there were a number of players in our group whose behaviour was like 'a tumour, and if we don't cut it out, they'll become a cancer'. I was referring to several players who were letting standards drop and weren't behaving like Australian cricketers, who were whingeing behind the coach's back about his decisions. It had been dealt with, and was not directed personally at Shane Watson.

Now it is being re-cast as something new and fresh and personal between me and Watto. It was a private conversation between me and Mickey, and I had trusted him to keep it that way. I have never leaked anything he has said to me, not to a soul, let alone to the public, and I feel betrayed.

The next thing I do is go to find Watto himself. He and I have covered some distance in improving our communications since India, and now this stuff from Mickey could wreck it. I find Watto in the restaurant having breakfast, surrounded by his wife Lee and other family members. I walk straight up, stand in front of them and say, 'I'm really, really sorry that this shit has happened and it's in the media.' I am nearly in tears. I don't try to justify it or explain what I said two years ago. I just have to apologise.

When I'm finished, Lee thanks me for coming up and speaking to them. I don't know if they accept my apology or hate me. We then go to Lord's to practise, and get smashed in the Test match.

There will be no difference afterwards, either for better or worse, in my relationship with Watto. Face to face, we will always be civil, and we will tour and play together for another two years. No change. We just get on and deal with it and try to win matches for Australia.

Mickey, on the other hand, I wouldn't speak to for the next three years. He lost my trust, and trust was the foundation of our relationship. It would take me a long time to forgive him.

He said later, about his time as Australian coach, that he had not been able to run things his own way. He blamed the constant involvement of Pat Howard, but the truth was that the system of leadership was changing around us. When I became Australian Test captain, I envisaged being a leader in the Mark Taylor–Ian Chappell mould. Mickey was helpful in supporting me, but Cricket Australia saw things moving in a different direction, where the powers of the Test captain were to be steadily narrowed down. Mickey's removal clarified that. The capacity of James Sutherland and Pat Howard to come in and decide on the coach without asking the captain beforehand was a big neon-lit message to me. Removing me as a selector was another. Restoring the authority of the captaincy, as I had envisaged it in 2011, was not what Cricket Australia had in mind.

As the system changes in 2013, I feel left behind. Ian Chappell is saying to me, more and more, 'The Win–Loss record goes against your name. So why aren't you taking the boys for a beer? Why aren't you choosing the bowling coach? Why aren't you choosing this player?'

All I can say is, 'Mate, it doesn't work like that anymore. I'm not in charge of any of that. I'm in charge of tossing the coin and whatever happens on the field. The rest is up to others.'

Chappelli can't work that out. When he was captain, the captain was boss. And I have trouble adapting to it as well. In my first two years, I brought back the idea of past players joining the team camp in the lead-up to a Test match and presenting debutants with their baggy green. In Melbourne, I asked Dean Jones and Bill Lawry to be around the boys. In Adelaide, I invited Greg Blewett and Jamie Siddons. I love reintroducing that tradition. That is my personality, how I am helping us get to number one in the world, how I was brought up, how I saw my grade captains and my dad lead their teams, how I saw Warney at Hampshire. Nothing would happen in the team without the captain having the final call.

Now it is different. Darren Lehmann is coming from a system in Queensland where the coach runs the show. And that is what he demands when he takes the Australian job. Boof, who had no enmity with Mickey and feels bad to be taking the job in those circumstances, has stipulated that if he is to become head coach, he wants the power to shake things up and run the team his way.

This means a further scaling down of the captain's role. From here on, the coach is going to run team meetings. The coach will decide who presents a cap to a debut player. The coach will make key staff appointments. The coach will remain a selector. There are a million and one things they have taken away from the captain so that I can focus on what happens on the field, but I want those things! I was not expecting to be moved down the food chain, halfway through my captaincy. I feel that the captain's role is not something that stops at the boundary line, as the things you do off the field flow directly into the things you do on it.

None of my grievance is personal. I always liked Boof. When I started in the Australian team, he was a senior player I looked up to, and I was always grateful for his positive comments about me as a batsman in my first year.

As shattered as I am for Mickey, I look forward to working with Boof. We have a good honest relationship with each other, and even though we will have some tough conversations in late 2014, I have unwavering respect for him as a person and a cricketer.

But in 2013, it is late in my life to accept such a sweeping change to the system. The hierarchy now has a pyramid of James Sutherland, Pat Howard, John Inverarity and Boof all above me, telling me to get the best out of my players. Pat Howard comes from rugby, where the coach runs everything, so he doesn't see a problem. In rugby, the captain is the boss on the field, and the coach is the boss off the field. Simple.

But that's not the way I see the game. Cricket is different from other sports. You spend five days on the field with your teammates – it's not a 90-minute game with the coach controlling the moves. In football, the coach has a bird's eye view of the whole game and can see it from a commander's perspective. In cricket, the captain is on the field and has the advantage of a close-up perspective and better feel for the game. There are little moments and changes in the dynamics of the game that you can only perceive if you're out there. You can see things developing before they happen. In cricket, you can sense momentum shifts and changes in behaviour, from bowlers and batsmen, that can't be sensed from afar. For example, on the last afternoon of the decisive Test match in Cape Town in 2014, the game that could take us to world number one if we win, I choose to go to Ryan Harris for the final overs. From afar, the coaching staff in an air-conditioned box might have been looking at Rhino and thinking he was busted, his knee was gone, he couldn't bowl another over. I go up to Rhino and say, 'How are you going?'

'How do you reckon?' he says.

'I know you're rooted, like everyone on the field,' I say, 'but we've got two choices here. Either you bowl now, or I do.'

He grabs the ball out of my hand and bowls the decisive over, dismissing Dale Steyn and Morne Morkel to take us to number one.

It confirms my certainty that there are things on the field that only a captain can know. Cricket is not football, and a coach can't pull the strings in our game.

On the 2013 England tour, Boof and Gavin Dovey try really hard to inform me what is going on, and include me in the loop, but I want to be accountable and so I want input. Mickey didn't make a decision without asking me. That is what I am used to. But it's different now. I still struggle to accept it. How can you employ your support staff without the captain's input?

How can you not select Steve Smith – as happens in Zimbabwe in 2014 – when he is one of the first players the captain would choose? The non-selection of Smithy is the only time my public mask really slips, and I give the selectors a serve. It wins me no friends at Cricket Australia, and that friction is about to get a lot worse with my physical problems in late 2014.

It isn't about personalities. Halfway through my captaincy, the system around me changes. One thing is for sure: I am no longer driving the bus.

17

THE ARTS AND CRAFTS OF CAPTAINCY

One of the most important things Neil D'Costa told me about cricket was, 'Don't just watch the batter bat and the bowler bowl. Watch the whole game of cricket. Why is the game drifting? What could you do?' As a kid, I learnt to watch the whole canvas. There's so much more to the game than the batsman and the bowler, and when I became Australian captain I got the chance to develop and express my ideas about how to influence matches.

Winning was always my prime concern. As I grew up watching sport, I liked how there had to be a winner and a loser, and I was not afraid to risk losing if it increased our chances of winning. If that meant a surprise declaration or some ultra-aggressive batting in a second innings to set up a run chase, I was happy to take the gamble.

One example is the first match of a three-Test series against the West Indies in Barbados in 2012, where bad weather affects the first and third days of play. The West Indies take two days to score 449 in their first innings and we are five wickets down and 200 runs behind at the end of the third day. With so much at stake, the safe option would be to shut things down and let the game peter out over the final two days. Our tail does better than expected, with Ryan Harris and Nathan Lyon adding 77 runs for the last wicket. But it is a slow grind, and just before tea on the fourth afternoon, we are still 43 runs from overhauling the West Indies' total.

I see an opportunity. With large, slow-moving first innings taking up the first four days, I think it's worth the risk to declare while behind. I call in Ryan and Nathan just before tea. Nobody expects it. In 14 balls before the break, Ben Hilfenhaus dismisses the West Indian top three, and the match is suddenly alive. We get them out for 148 by lunch on the fifth day, and then Mike Hussey and Shane Watson bat very positively – yes, risking a loss in order to win – and we reach the target of 192 with three wickets to spare. It's a memorable win, and sets the tone for a series victory. More conventional decision-making, accepting an apparently inevitable draw, would have left us at risk of losing the series, but instead, we end up walking out of Barbados with a lead.

If you're going to play to win, you need to take your players with you. A captain who takes risks without the backing of his teammates is headed for disaster. I am fortunate to lead a team in which every player is ready to put his personal success on the line if it is going to help us win.

In the Ashes Test match in Adelaide in 2013–14, we are in a commanding position at stumps on the third day. We lead by a massive 530 runs. David Warner is 83 not out and charging towards his second hundred of the series. But I'm worried about the weather forecast. As we leave that afternoon, the groundsman says to me, 'There's some rain around.'

'How bad – next two days?'

He says yes, and the next morning the clouds are closing in. He tells me there is plenty of rain on its way.

The circumstances press on me. Three months ago, we lost our third straight Ashes series, and are absolutely sick of it. We've just won the first Test match in Brisbane, and a devastating Mitchell Johnson spell has put us well on top here. When you are as hungry to win matches as we are, it tears your guts out to let one slip by. From the position we're in, to *not* win this game would be as morale- and momentum-destroying as a loss.

But there's the matter of taking a personal achievement away from David Warner. Since his arrival in the team, he has brought just the kind of positive intent I want to see at the top of the order. From the first ball of the day, he and Chris Rogers have formed a partnership where they are constantly looking to score runs. There is no target run rate we have in mind, no set job to 'see off the new ball', just an overriding understanding that the batsmen's aim is to score, not just survive. David has been right on board with that, and so has Chris who, coming into the team at the age of 37, has shown incredible courage to adapt his game to be a more fluent scorer when we need it. His strike rate has been higher in his return to Test cricket than it was in first-class cricket. There have been several examples of him going out of his comfort zone in second innings when we've needed to accelerate. It's not his natural instinct, but he'll do it for the team. My task is getting him to share in my belief that he can do it. I say, 'If I didn't think you could do it, I'd bat you at number seven. But you're good enough to play for Australia, and that means you're good enough to do more than just take the shine off the ball.' Helping to bring out this new capability in a senior batsman is one of my greatest satisfactions as a captain.

Davey, on the other hand, needs no encouragement to score runs, but I've had lots of chats with him where the public facade of his immense self-belief has cracked. It happens to all of us. The outside world thinks you're a Test cricketer and you're always super-confident, but it's not so. I've had many a night when I've lost my self-belief, and a pep talk from Shane Warne – 'What are you talking about, you're playing brilliantly, you're one of the best batsmen in the world!' – brings it all back.

There's a time with David Warner when we're practising to play South Africa in Australia in 2012–13. In the nets, he's wearing a chest guard and an elbow guard in preparation to face Dale Steyn and Morne Morkel. I go up to him and say, 'What are you wearing those for? You never miss a ball! Get them off!' He does, and the removal of the protection seems to remind him that he is good enough to not need it.

I try to play the confidence-building role that Shane Warne has played for me for that whole generation of younger players coming through, the guys that haven't played as much international cricket, because I know what it's like to feel shaky inside and be less than willing to let it show.

On this morning in Adelaide, it's not a matter of pumping up Davey's confidence, but of getting him to buy in to the team objective even if it means sacrificing what should be the straightforward completion of a Test century.

'If we don't declare,' I say to him, 'you get another hundred, and that's great, you deserve that. But the weather forecast is really bad and we need all the time we can get to bowl England out.'

It doesn't surprise me when his response is immediate. 'If you think that's what's best for the team, then declare. I'm all for it.' I appreciate the trust he has in me to make the right decision, and I also have enhanced trust in him. As it turns out, we win the match with two sessions to spare. But it does rain through those sessions, and if we'd kept batting for Davey's personal milestone, events might have unfolded quite differently.

Trust between players and captain is essential, especially if the captain is to make decisions in a spirit of adventure. Steve Smith is a cricketer who is in and out of the Australian team for three years from 2010 to 2013, and many outsiders say disparaging things about his potential as a Test cricketer. For the group of young players that I see as the long-term future of Australian batting, my job as captain is to transmit my belief in them, so that they believe in themselves. That kind of mentoring was the greatest gift I received from the Australian team I entered in 2003 and 2004, and one of my key aims as I become a senior player is to pass that on. I can see something unique in Smithy. He is as good a player of spin as anybody we have, he's a brilliant fielder, and he bowls more than handy leg-spin. We have to keep faith in players who are so talented in all three facets of the game. That's why I get so angry when Smithy is not picked in the one-day team in Zimbabwe in late 2014, and unleash publicly on the selectors for the only time. If you stuff young guys around, you can set them back years. Fortunately, the selectors' commitment to Smithy in the Test team remains firm in those years, and he turns into one of the best batsmen in the world by 2015. And when he goes out at Lord's in the second Test of the 2015 Ashes series to belt a quick fifty to set up a declaration, I'm proud to see another batsman in our team willing to risk personal failure if it's going to help the team win.

As a leg-spinner, Smithy lacks no self-belief. In fact, he often makes the team laugh with his claims that he has dismissed such-and-such an opposing batsman so often, he *must* bowl to him. During the Ashes in 2013, when Ian Bell is scoring three hundreds against us, Smithy is in my ear. 'I've got Bell out nine times before, he's my bunny!' Someone has looked up the stats: Smithy has got Bell out twice before, and once was in a limited-overs slog. But I give him the ball, and he gets Bell out in a critical situation in Adelaide.

Winning Test matches is about taking 20 wickets, and I don't care who takes them. If it's Smithy, Mike Hussey or

David Warner bowling, a wicket is a wicket and there are any number of ways to skin a cat. I'm different from Punter in this way. He thought, *Batters are paid to bat and bowlers are paid to bowl*, but I don't care if it's the tail-enders who score our runs and the batters take the wickets bowling half-track leg-spinners. The end – winning a Test match – justifies any unorthodox means.

Take us to Hobart, December 2012. Fifth day of a grinding Test match against Sri Lanka, made a battle of attrition by a lifeless wicket. We have left ourselves a day and a bit to bowl them out and take a 1–0 lead in the series, but I let us down late yesterday by dropping Kumar Sangakkara at slip off Nathan Lyon.

All through the morning and afternoon sessions of the fifth day, we have to work our butts off to get even the sniff of a breakthrough. The Sri Lankans know what they have to do, and are taking no risks. Thilan Samaraweera, a tall and solidly-built right-hander with a Test average of 50, starts as a stumbling block but soon begins to look like a huge brick wall.

I remember 2008, when I was bugging Punter to give me a bowl on the last day of that Test match against India at the SCG. He waited until the very end to put me on, and I snared the last three wickets to close out that Test match. I'm unable to do that now due to my back, but I sense that the Sri Lankans are feeling too comfortable. The crowd at Bellerive is small, but can get very vocal when given a little encouragement. Just before tea, I decide to change things up. I turn to our wicketkeeper.

'Wadey? Next over.'

'You're joking?'

'I'm serious. I've faced you in the nets. You'll get a wicket for sure.'

And I can see Matthew Wade's face change from surprise to certainty, *Yeah, I'll get a wicket!*

Instantly, I have become Santa Claus and given two young men the happiest day in their lives. Wadey has been bowling every day at training, and he fancies himself in the nets with his medium-pacers. There's a lot of laughter on and off the field. Everyone's laughing because the keeper is bowling, and the crowd's loving it because Wadey is a Tassie boy. It changes the pace of the game, which has to stop while Wadey takes the pads off and Phillip Hughes puts them on. Hughesy, who has kept wicket throughout his junior and club career, definitely fancies himself with the pads and gloves.

I'm thinking, *If Wadey goes for 20 off this over, we lose nothing. But you never know your luck. It's worth a try.* And, *If I was the batsman, just trying to get through one more over to tea, I'd be hating this.*

It doesn't work immediately – Wadey bowls a tidy maiden, Samaraweera blocks every delivery, and Hughesy leaps about but doesn't get to actually glove one ball – but my aim is just to change the atmospherics in the ground and jolt the batsmen out of their comfort zones. After tea, the wickets begin to fall and we claim the match.

On the field, I captain like a batsman. That is, I'm trying to see the world through the batsman's eyes and anticipate what is going to disturb his concentration. *What does he not want now? What's his weakness?*

Because every batsman is different, and because I study them all, this makes my tactics unorthodox and sometimes eccentric.

Crowd atmospherics and scoreboard pressure are just as important. A team might be two for 250 but if they're chasing 500, they're not cruising, they're still 250 behind. If they're playing away from home in front of a hostile crowd, there are times when you want to mobilise the pressure that the batsmen will already be feeling.

I love to get the crowd involved. Sometimes, like in that match in Hobart, I'll turn around and start a conversation with them from the slips cordon. A year later, in Perth, when everything is turning sleepy in the intense heat and Kevin Pietersen has set himself for a big score to save the 2013–14 Ashes for England, I put Mitchell Johnson on and rev up the crowd by motioning for them to start up a slow hand-clap.

To know the opposition, as a captain, is essential. The more information you have about an individual batsman, the better. During the 2013–14 Ashes series, even if a bowler is bowling well, I often give him a rest if I don't think he is about to take a wicket. My number one goal is getting batsmen out. 'I want to try someone else for a couple of overs,' I say, and am blessed as a captain in that the bowlers respect my instincts. If the batsman is terrified of Mitchell Johnson and unable to score runs, he might be more likely to take risks against the bowler at the other end.

This is why bowlers working in partnerships is so important: they can create opportunities for the guy bowling at the other end.

As with batting, your captaincy ideas are worth nothing if your players aren't buying in. The best bowling attack I played with as a young man was Glenn McGrath, Jason Gillespie, Brett Lee and Shane Warne in 2004 to 2006. As a captain, the best bowling attack I had was Mitchell Johnson, Ryan Harris, Peter Siddle, Nathan Lyon and Shane Watson in 2013–14.

One thing those two attacks share is variety. As a captain, I love having options at my disposal. Mitch Johnson is the greatest X-factor you could have. Not only is he super-quick and unpredictable with the ball, he can also take the freakish one-handed catch, pull off a direct-hit run-out from nowhere, or score a quick half-century or century. The challenge has been getting him to believe in himself as much as I believe in him. When he comes into the team in 2013 after a lay-off from cricket, he's bursting with new self-belief, and with it comes the extra 10 km/h in pace that terrifies the English batsmen, as well as the all-round confidence to match his supreme athleticism.

During the 2013–14 Ashes series, I only bowl him in short spells of one to four overs. Our plan is to attack batsmen early in their innings and I don't necessarily care about his control. I just want him to bowl as fast as he can at them, and then take him off. I don't care if I bowl him in ten spells a day, this is the way I think I can get the most impact out of him. To his credit, he accepts it, even when he's taken two wickets in a spell and clearly doesn't want to be taken off. He backs my judgement.

What this means is that we need his bowling partners to play their roles. Ryan Harris I also want to be aggressive, but his greatest strength is his accuracy and his ability to bowl long spells. Peter Siddle, who is the workhorse, builds pressure from his end so the batsmen have to try and score their runs off the other bowlers. Shane Watson complements the three fast bowlers by being so hard to score off. In Adelaide, he bowls maidens for almost an hour, a spell which precipitates the collapse of wickets when Mitch comes back on.

As full-time fast bowlers, Rhino, Mitch and Sidds will run through a brick wall for Australia, even when their bodies are spent. People don't realise how hard it is to be a fast bowler. Look in the dressing room and see the blisters, the bleeding ingrown toenails, the bruised heels, not to mention the underlying strains to knees, ankles, hips, shoulders, backs and necks, and you see how fast bowlers are definitely underpaid and overworked.

Rhino is an out-and-out champion with the figures to prove it. It's a great shame that injuries stopped him from reaching his peak until his thirties. I loved seeing him in my team. And Sidds was the icing on the cake for that attack. He could bowl long spells, keeping his line and length consistent, uphill or downhill, with or against the breeze.

You can be the cleverest captain in the world, but of course it will mean nothing if you don't have bowlers who can execute the plans. Sometimes I had to adapt our bowling plans to the attack that the selectors have given me, but I am more than happy with the combination of Johnson–Harris–Siddle–Lyon–Watson, which doesn't change for the entire five-match 2013–14 series. They know the English batsmen, they know our plan, and each bowler knows his job and his zones. Once we have had our discussions, I don't have to tell them anything. The only specific order I give the fast bowlers is, 'When the tail-enders come in, you do not hit those stumps. You bowl short.' They love it. Mitch Johnson absolutely laps it up.

The reward for them – aside from the results – is that they have my total trust. Whenever one of them says, 'Skip, can I have another slip?', or 'Can I have deep square leg back?', I agree to everything. 'Tell me what you want and you'll get it,' I say. The sweetest words a bowler can ever hear from his captain.

Plans have to be malleable. We have one plan against a batsman at the start of his innings, another plan if he makes it to 30, another if he makes it to 80, and so on. These plans in turn will vary depending on conditions: the pace of the pitch, the outfield, the weather, the state of the game.

Fielding positions play a big role in executing these plans, and also as a tool to get in the batsman's mind. If the bowler is aiming at the stumps and trying to get the batsman out lbw, there's no point in having seven men on the off side. So I'll think about using a catcher anywhere the batsman might hit the ball. But when the set plan doesn't work, I might try to make something happen. There's a cricket textbook for where fielders go but for me, the key is to put them where you think they can get a catch. So I will put a fielder in an unusual position where he has planted a question in the mind of the batsman, who can now see him out of the corner of his eye every ball. *Why has Clarke placed a fielder there? I've never seen anyone there, and now he's all I can see! What's he up to?* It also helps the bowler to know that I'm adjusting the field to suit his plan of attack and give him another avenue to take a wicket.

As a bowler, I've always seen myself as the type to bowl only when conditions are conducive, when the pitch is very slow or deteriorating. It's not complicated: I just put it in the area and let natural variation play its part. Some will spin, some will go straight on. Sometimes, as in Dominica on my last tour of the West Indies, I'll indulge myself and go on a bit longer if conditions suit and the batsmen will give away their wickets. In one-day cricket, I like to use part-time bowlers like myself to sneak a short spell and get off before the batsmen get used to us.

But I am not good enough to be a frontline left-arm spinner dictating terms to batsmen. What I am is a batsman-watcher, placing myself in his head. *He wants to hit over mid-wicket, against the spin. That's risky for him. Okay, I'll bring mid-wicket in and tempt him to play that shot.* Next thing, he goes for it, and there's a chance he can top-edge a catch. I want to tempt him to play a shot he is not comfortable with; I want to do something that will force him to change his plan.

At Test level, many batsmen's greatest strength is their concentration. At their best, good batsmen are not thinking about anything. So I will try things to get the batsman's brain moving, cause surprise, and shake him out of that cruisy thought-free zone. The variety offered by a good spin bowler is crucial to winning this battle. For example, in the 2013 and 2013–14 Ashes series, we more or less nullify Alastair Cook as a scorer of big hundreds (during those series, he doesn't make any centuries and averages in the low 30s). We've done it by challenging him to score runs in his least-preferred zone, by tempting him to drive between point and mid-off, and I also became aware that he prefers pace to spin early in his innings. So, at the MCG in 2013, I bring on Nathan Lyon in the third over from the southern end. Everyone's thinking, *What the hell is Clarke doing? He's put England in to bat, and he's bowling his off-spinner in the third over?* But I know that Cook's preference, like most batsmen's, is not to be playing spin with the ball turning away from him at any time, let alone when the ball is new. He wants to be facing pace. I am not scared of doing the unorthodox. Spinners can change the tempo of the game and the tactics, even if the wicket isn't turning. You can use spinners and part-time bowlers in lots of different ways, not just to come on and trundle in for a token over.

In the field, my captaincy is largely based on my knowing, as a batsman, how difficult it is to play 360 degrees around the wicket and be equally good at every shot. For instance, I love to cover-drive and score a huge proportion of my runs there. But I also get out a lot playing that shot and nicking. So, if I was captaining against me, I would feed that shot, content to give up runs early in my innings but confident of taking a wicket. Not many teams do. They see me hitting fours through cover, and redirect their attack to my body, where I might not look as comfortable but I am less likely to get out.

I can only think of one opposition captain who worked out what makes me really uncomfortable. Early in my career, Stuart Law, as captain of Queensland, puts in a very short, unorthodox cover-point when I'm batting. Michael Kasprowicz comes in and bowls back of a length outside off stump. They know I can't resist hitting it, and if one ball bounces a bit more, I'll hit it in the air. I make a few runs through that area, but a couple of times Queensland get me out caught by that fielder. I hate having him there. If I was captaining against me, I would have a fielder there all the time.

My own preferences guide my field placings. I always have some sort of method to my madness. Conventional wisdom says that an 'attacking field' means a bunch of slips fieldsmen. That may be so in Brisbane or Perth, but in different conditions, such as on slow wickets in India or the West Indies, that's not the case. As a batsman, if I have a slips cordon and the pitch is slow, all I'm seeing are the gaps to hit through in front of the wicket. But if I have fielders in front of my eyes, at silly mid-on or in a cordon of close mid-wickets, I'm wary of them.

But it's not about me. I think like a batsman, but I must think like *this* batsman. I play spin bowling well, for instance, but it would be a great weakness to think other batsmen are the same. My liking for spin is irrelevant. Does the present opposition batsman like it? You have to read the game that's in front of you, not just imagine what you would do. You're using your knowledge of how you feel pressure when you're batting, how it builds to where something has to give, and you translate that to the batsman at the crease. In my case, it might be having a series of balls I'm leaving outside off stump. I begin to fall across. Then they duck one in, and I'm out lbw. I have to use that knowledge to our advantage, but there's going to be a different breaking point for every batsman.

One of my favourite dismissals is Mitchell Starc bowling Brendon McCullum in the first over of the 2015 World Cup final. As a group, we don't actually talk a great deal about the opposition before this match. We are more focused on the certainty that if we play our best – batting, bowling, fielding, attitude – we will beat any team. We know the conditions, we have the best team, we only need to control our side of the game and we will win.

But as captain, I still study the opposition. Away from the group, I spend an hour and a half watching footage of the New Zealand captain and opener before the final. He belted 50 off us in our preliminary match in Auckland, and I watch that video closely. Two days before the final, I say to the bowlers in the team meeting, 'Guys, very simple. All we are doing to McCullum is bowling yorkers.'

They're surprised. 'What? From ball one?'

From examining the footage, I've seen that new-ball attacks have gone at McCullum as they would at any other batsman, whereas he's treating the scenario as if it's the last five overs of the innings. Maybe we should bowl as we would at a guy in that situation.

I say, 'If he's trying to smack us out of the park at the death, we try to bowl yorkers. But he plays like that from the beginning of the innings. So let's bowl at him from the beginning as if we're bowling at the death. The difference is, Starcy is bowling 150 km/h, swinging the ball, bowling yorkers. Imagine facing that when you're starting! We should bowl full, and straight at the stumps. If he misses, we hit.'

The challenge for McCullum is to counter this kind of attack. Okay, he can get down on one knee and ramp it over the wicketkeeper's head in the first over. If he has the courage and skill to do that to Mitchell Starc, I will stand and applaud him. One of the best innings I have ever seen was back in 2004, when Sachin Tendulkar put away his cover drive and scored 241 in Sydney. No way would I have had the discipline to do that. That's why he was a step above everyone else – the discipline to say, *I've got out to that shot three times in the series, I'm not going to play it again.* I could only have held off on my cover drive for my first 20 or 30 runs, and then would have felt confident enough to get back into it. Sachin did it for the whole innings, over two days. *What a freak,* I thought. *That is a batsman right there.*

So if Brendon McCullum can adapt to 150 km/h straight yorkers and smash us around the park at the start of a World Cup final, I will be the first to congratulate him. Instead, Starcy is good enough to execute the plan, and his dismissal of McCullum in the first over really does set the tone for the match.

Instilling confidence in young bowlers is different from working with more seasoned players, as the younger ones usually take a few seasons to establish themselves in the team, so they are battling for a sense of belonging as much as executing their on-field plans. Mitchell Starc comes into the Australian team in my first year as captain in 2011, as do James Pattinson, Pat Cummins and Nathan Lyon. Together with Josh Hazlewood and Mitchell Marsh, who will make their debuts a couple of years later, they comprise the nucleus of as good a bowling attack as Australia has ever had. Pattinson and Hazlewood are both skilful, tough and talented, and get better every time they play. Cummins never plays another Test with me after his man-of-the-match debut in Johannesburg in 2011, but I am sure he will be there for a long time. Starc was always identified as a very special bowler but, like anyone, he probably didn't realise how good he was at first. In 2012–13, he gets very frustrated by the selectors' policy of managing bowlers' workloads, leaving them out of Test matches even when they are fit and in form. After winning us the match against Sri Lanka in Hobart in December 2012, Starcy is unhappy at being rested from the Boxing Day Test. I say to him, 'Don't set your sights on getting into the Australian team for this particular match. You should be aiming to be the best bowler in the world for the next ten years.' I think he is that good, and within four years, after Mitch Johnson and Ryan Harris retire, Starcy is probably the first bowler picked in all three formats for Australia and, I believe, on the verge of being the best in the world for a long time.

I am also extremely proud of the progress Nathan Lyon made between 2011 and 2015, because when he came into the Australian team he was not a naturally confident person, and he knew he was about number 11 on the list of spin bowlers our selectors had tried since the retirement of Shane Warne. Being the Australian Test spinner was turning into a poisoned chalice.

Lyono came into the Test team at the same time I became captain. Whether he was better than the other available spin bowlers was not the most important thing to me. There had been five years of trial and error, and we'd all had enough of it. I was sick of the revolving door, and I was sick of a bowler like Nathan coming in with that revolving door in the back of his mind. For his first 20 to 25 Test matches, I just wanted the selectors to keep picking the same spinner so I could build a relationship with him. My way of ensuring this was bringing him on to take tail-end wickets if he didn't have any dismissals already. I wanted him to read in the paper the next day, *Lyon two-for* or *Lyon three-for*. I wanted him to look up at the scoreboard and see 2 or 3 next to his name instead of 0. I wanted him to be taking enough wickets that the selectors would keep picking him.

So when the tail-enders came in, I would say, 'Lyono, you're on.' Someone else would go, 'No, bowl the quicks both ends.' I would reply, 'I want Lyono full of confidence, because on another day I am going to need him.'

Self-confidence was his biggest stumbling block. We brought in Shane Warne, Stuart MacGill, Greg Matthews and other former Test spinners to tutor him in practice sessions, and he had a terrific mentor in John Davison, a former Sheffield Shield spin bowler on our coaching staff.

I pushed Lyono in Shane Warne's direction in England in 2013, not for his technique so much as to give him confidence. Warney was an absolute freak with the bluff and the mind games. 'Tell the press you've got six different varieties of balls,' Warney said. 'You've only got one? Doesn't matter. Say it anyway. Be prepared to change. Change the field, change your angle, slow the game up. There doesn't need to be a reason for it. You're trying to play with the batsman's mind, get him asking questions.'

Part of his shyness was expressed in a reluctance to bowl over the wicket. Even though he had all these advisers telling him he should do it, Nathan was the one who had to perform when his team needed to win and 40,000 people were watching. That day-five situation used to petrify him, because of the expectations. He was better on day one than day five. But that changed by 2014, when he took seven wickets in the last innings to bowl India out in Adelaide on a dead-set batting track.

He still resisted bowling over the wicket from the beginning of his spells, but I nagged away. For the first couple of years, Lyono would say, 'Set the field, and I'll bowl in those areas for you.' I didn't want that. I wanted *him* to be asking *me* if he could bowl over the wicket, and I wanted him to be *telling* me he wanted a certain field. Eventually, he got to that stage and I couldn't have been prouder.

By the end of my career, I could open the bowling with Lyono – bowling over or around the wicket, down breeze, into the breeze, it didn't matter. He had always been a good enough bowler, but now he knew it. When I see Lyono bowling over the wicket to begin his spell these days, I think, *How far you've come.*

To instil confidence in a player, to free him up to walk out and play his way, gave me the greatest satisfaction of my years as a captain. Confidence really is everything. When we went to Bangladesh in 2006, on the back of hard home and away series with South Africa, many of the boys were cooked. Warney? They'd have been better off not taking him on the tour, and it showed with his bowling on the first day of the series. He wasn't happy, and his confidence evaporated. But then, when we looked like losing and really needed him, he roared back.

Similar with Punter. He got out so often to New Zealand's part-time medium-pacer Scott Styris, we used to laugh about it. But put Punter up against Wasim Akram, Shoaib Akhtar or Curtly Ambrose, and he was so confident he would smack them around, it was self-fulfilling.

When it came to the 2015 World Cup, confidence was precisely the challenge. I know that if Glenn Maxwell goes out and bats as if he's having fun in the local park, he will score 100 off 80 balls and win us the game. Guys like David Warner and James Faulkner are similar. Their natural state is to believe they are invincible. The trick is to give them that freedom, to build them so high that self-doubt can't reach them.

Throughout the 2015 World Cup, we break the rule against not thinking too far ahead. Instead, I want those young guys to think that there's a big concert coming up at the MCG, the whole world will be watching, and they are the stars of this show. They aren't scared of it – they *want* that front page. Five games out from the final, they can see themselves there. They have so much self-belief, the results in all the lead-up games take care of themselves.

That's when I love the captaincy and wouldn't swap it for any job in the world.

THE INNINGS

161 not out versus South Africa, Cape Town, 2014

During my Test debut, I took my helmet off at 98, even though the Indian fast bowlers were on, because I'd promised Dad I was going to be wearing my baggy green if I ever made my first hundred for Australia. Did I care about being hit on the head? Not a chance. Twelve years later, I had become worried about helmets. After Phillip Hughes died, the thought was unavoidable: *You can die playing this sport*. Before then, I did not fear short-pitched bowling one bit. I may have looked uncomfortable at times, but I was not scared.

When Morne Morkel launches a four-over spell of constant short-pitched bowling at me in Cape Town in 2014, I have no fear. I am more concerned that I haven't scored many runs in a series that means everything to me.

The ICC world Test rankings have their critics, but when I accepted the job of Australian captain, those rankings were our benchmark. We were ranked fifth, and I vowed to take us back to number one.

Through all the ups and downs and criticism, I told everyone in the group that if we kept the faith and made good plans and stuck to them, we would get back to the top. It was an obsession. And now, in this series against South Africa in South Africa, after we've beaten England 5–0 at home, we have the chance to go number one. But only if we win in Cape Town.

In Centurion and Port Elizabeth, the results have split both ways. Mitch Johnson and Davey Warner have been stars for us, with Ryan Harris, Nathan Lyon, Chris Rogers, Shaun Marsh, Steve Smith and Alex Doolan all pitching in at times. Conspicuously absent has been myself: I've barely been able to make a run, whether on the bouncy pitch at Centurion or the wearing, reverse-swinging deck at Port Elizabeth.

On a sunny first morning at Newlands, the top order gets us off to a flyer: we are two for 138 when I go out in the 32nd over. Davey is in the form of his life, and while it would be nice to strap in and enjoy the ride, I'm not batting well at the beginning. I am so desperate to help us win, I'm tight and nothing is coming easily. For the first half hour, the attack of Steyn and Kyle Abbott is pinning me down, while Davey flows along to another hundred.

Graeme Smith, who has a lot of emotional support behind him, having announced that he will be retiring after this Test match, brings on Morkel. In his first over back, he bowls me four short balls in a row; the fourth hits me in the ribs.

RYAN PIERSE/GETTY IMAGES

Leading the boys out for the First Test at Trent Bridge in the 2013 Ashes. We lost by 14 runs, but the amazing tenth-wicket world record partnership between Ashton Agar and Phillip Hughes lifted our spirits and inspired us to dig deep. I was desperate to reclaim the urn on English soil.

MICHAEL CLARKE

Left: I never took my form for granted. I'd do a two-week 'boot camp' with personal trainer Duncan Kerr every year. It was a great way to focus on my physical and mental preparation, particularly for the 2013 Ashes tour.

THE DAILY GRIND. TEAM PHYSIO ALEX KOUNTOURIS WENT ABOVE AND BEYOND TO KEEP ME FIT TO PLAY OVER THE YEARS, SPENDING COUNTLESS HOURS MASSAGING, STRETCHING AND DOING STRENGTH WORK ON MY DETERIORATING BACK.

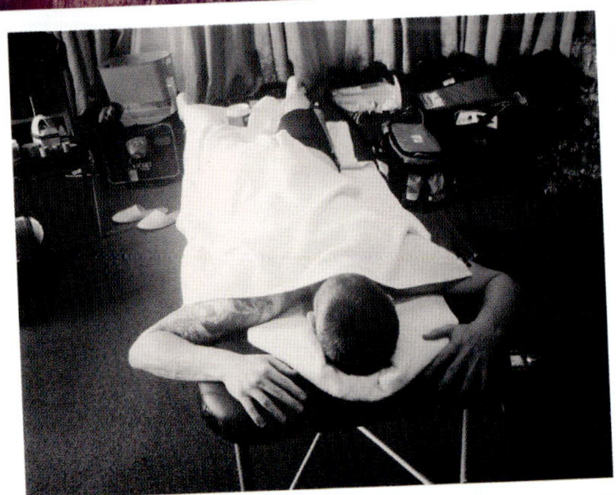

MICHAEL CLARKE

BETHANY CLARKE/GETTY IMAGES

Above: David Warner should have been swinging his bat in the first two Tests, but when he let his fists swing at Joe Root in a bar on Ashes eve he was suspended. It was a disappointing opening note but I stood by him, knowing he'd come back stronger.

RYAN PIERSE/GETTY IMAGES

Left: Watto caught Ian Bell on the first day at Trent Bridge. Things were looking up.

Below: Her Majesty Queen Elizabeth II began proceedings for the Second Test at Lord's. Understandably, she took a shine to our lion-hearted fast bowler Ryan Harris!

ANTHONY DEVLIN – WPA POOL/GETTY IMAGES

Below: Darren Lehmann's 11th-hour appointment came with the power to shake things up. Under Boof, the chain of command started with the coach.

RYAN PIERSE/GETTY IMAGES

Right: Ryan Harris (left) was a matchwinner and could've been up there with Lillee and McGrath but for injury woes.

Below: I'm very proud of the progress Nathan Lyon made under my captaincy. He was far from confident when he joined the Test XI but he's come a long way.

MIKE HEWITT/GETTY IMAGES

RYAN PIERSE/GETTY IMAGES

Results weren't going how we wanted but team unity was strong. We never stopped trying to win, fighting hard all the way but often falling just short.

RYAN PIERSE/GETTY IMAGES

The 2013 Ashes was far closer than the 3–0 result. Our rebuild was working.

MARTIN RICKETT/PA WIRE

MICHAEL STEELE/GETTY IMAGES

STU FORSTER/GETTY IMAGES

I made 187 in the Third Test at Old Trafford, the first time in the series we were able to establish a stronghold. I'm confident we would have finished England off, but steady rain put an end to our dream of retaining the Ashes.

RYAN PIERSE/GETTY IMAGES

Above: Selection dilemmas. Rod Marsh had been a mentor since my academy days but, as selector and captain, we didn't always see eye to eye.

GARETH COPLEY/GETTY IMAGES

Above: I was never one for milestones, but my 100th Test was very special. After we won the WACA Test, the boys presented me with this photo, framed. It's one of my treasured possessions.

RYAN PIERSE/GETTY IMAGES

Above: Even when chaos reigned, I always had the neatest corner of the locker room.

AFTER DAD'S CANCER BATTLES, I VALUED EVERY SECOND OF HIS COMPANY. WE WENT FROM FATHER AND SON TO THE GREATEST OF FRIENDS. HE WAS BEST MAN AT MY WEDDING.

MICHAEL CLARKE

GARETH COPLEY/GETTY IMAGES

My 100th Test in Perth was also England captain Alastair Cook's 100th. But the honours would be mine as Australia went 3–0 up to reclaim the Ashes.

RYAN PIERSE/GETTY IMAGES

RYAN PIERSE/GETTY IMAGES

Left: The 2013–14 series got off to a rocky start when I told Jimmy Anderson to get ready for a 'broken f—ing arm' after he sledged debutant George Bailey.

Right: The Ashes were won, but it wasn't over. On Jane McGrath Day, during the Fifth Test in Sydney, I revved the boys up for what was to be the final day of play.

RYAN PIERSE/GETTY IMAGES

STEVE CHRISTO/CORBIS VIA GETTY IMAGES

MARK KOLBE/GETTY IMAGES

My catch of Boyd Rankin off Ryan Harris ended the Sydney Test and sealed my second 5–0 whitewash as a player. It was a landmark Ashes series win for the team.

RYAN PIERSE/GETTY IMAGES

Above: Beating England 5–0 at home was one of the proudest moments of my time as captain.

MATT KING/GETTY IMAGES

Above: Rejoicing in our whitewash of England with fans at the Sydney Opera House. It was a welcome reprieve from the many off-field issues weighing me down.

CARL FOURIE/GALLO IMAGES/GETTY IMAGES

MORNE DE KLERK/GETTY IMAGES

Making Australia the number one Test nation was my obsession. At Newlands, I was hit in the ribs, elbow and jaw. My thumbnail was shattered and my shoulder was broken. But I hung on.

MORNE DE KLERK/GETTY IMAGES

Below: I was 92 not out at stumps and slept on the physio table that night. The next day, I fought on to 161 not out.

CARL FOURIE/GALLO IMAGES/GETTY IMAGES

MICHAEL CLARKE

HUGHESY, WARNEY, PATTO AND ME ON A HIGH IN THE CHANGE ROOMS AFTER THE WIN IN SOUTH AFRICA.

Below: In the final hour I threw the ball to Ryan Harris and asked for one last effort. He delivered, and we were the number one Test nation. It was the crowning moment in the team's rebirth.

©RYAN WILKISKY/BACKPAGEPIX VIA AAP

PHILLIP HUGHES DIED PLAYING THE GAME WE LOVED ON 27 NOVEMBER 2014. I LOVED HUGHESY AND STRUGGLED TO DELIVER THE TERRIBLE NEWS AT A PRESS CONFERENCE.

MARK KOLBE/GETTY IMAGES

SAEED KHAN/AFP/GETTY IMAGES

Below: I wanted my eulogy to Phillip to be something Greg, Virginia, Jason and Megan Hughes could hold onto – that day, and into the future.

CAMERON SPENCER – POOL/GETTY IMAGES

I was injured, grieving and at war with selectors when we took to the field in Adelaide. But I had Phillip's spirit with me as I fought to 128.

AAP IMAGE/DAVE HUNT

RYAN PIERSE/GETTY IMAGES

Left: After selectors publicly questioned my mental and physical fitness, I doubled my efforts to return. But my frustration with Cricket Australia continued to eat away at me.

RYAN PIERSE/GETTY IMAGES

MICHAEL DODGE-IDI/IDI VIA GETTY IMAGES

The 2015 World Cup was a fairytale finish to my 245-game ODI career. In front of 93,000 MCG fans, I scored 74 from 72 balls to steer us past New Zealand in the final and win Australia its fifth World Cup.

RYAN PIERSE/GETTY IMAGES

Left: We won the series 2–0 but the Tests in the West Indies left me empty before the 2015 Ashes. Sad, lonely and angry, I sealed myself from the team.

WE SQUARED THE SERIES WITH A 405-RUN WIN AT LORD'S AND CELEBRATED IN CLASSIC AUSTRALIAN FASHION. BUT THE HIGH WAS SHORT-LIVED.

MICHAEL CLARKE

RYAN PIERSE/GETTY IMAGES

Left: My fourth series in England got off to a shaky start when we lost Ryan Harris to injury before the First Test. New vice-captain Steve Smith and I had plenty to think about as the Ashes got off to a fiery start in Cardiff.

Trent Bridge was the worst wicket I saw in 12 years as an international cricketer. But I couldn't imagine the capitulation that unfolded: Australia all out for 60.

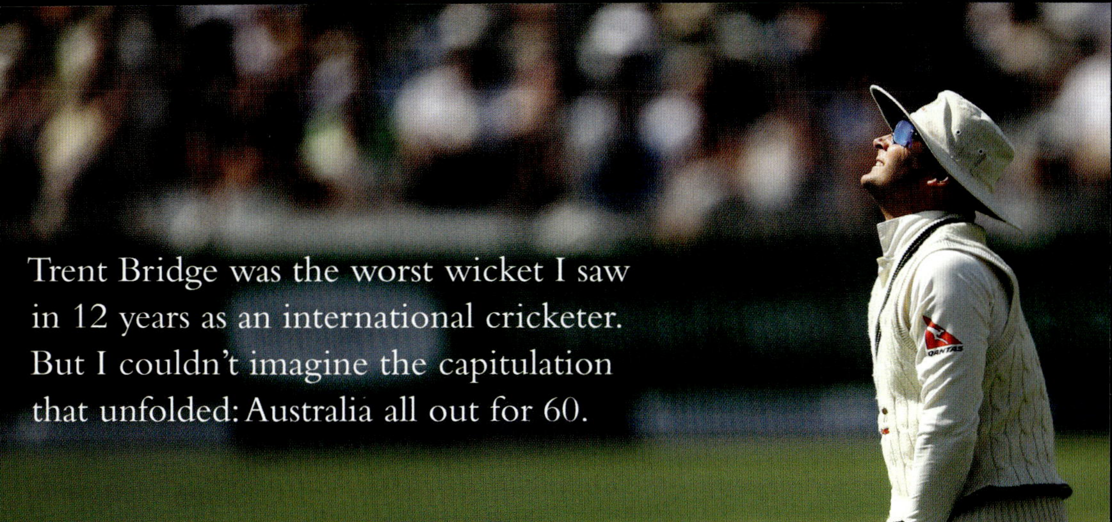

RYAN PIERSE/GETTY IMAGES

RYAN PIERSE/GETTY IMAGES

Left: My head was not in the game. I couldn't shake the fear of getting hit and killed. My batting helmet had become a prison. I announced my retirement from cricket after losing the Fourth Test – and with it, the Ashes.

Below: My 115th Test and final innings for Australia. I was grateful to Alastair Cook and the England team for the guard of honour they formed to farewell me from the game.

GARETH COPLEY/GETTY IMAGES

Right and below: My angel was born on 16 November 2015, five weeks premature. Kelsey Lee came into our lives at the perfect time. She melts my heart. It was a special moment, having my daughter with me for a last lap of the SCG in January. She slept the whole way.

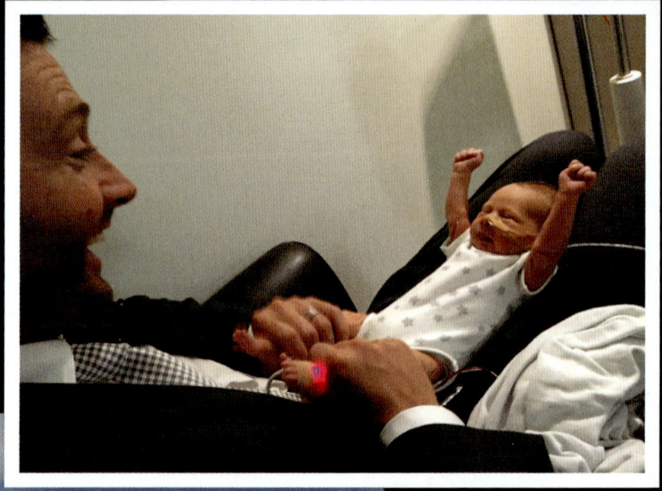

KYLY CLARKE

MATT KING/GETTY IMAGES

Below: Deep down I'm still the little boy who slept with his bat. So when my old club team Wests invited me back to Pratten Park in February 2016, I couldn't resist.

JASON MCCAWLEY/GETTY IMAGES

JONATHAN NG/NEWSPIX

Left: After retiring in 2015, I took stock of what was important to me. When Kyly and I revisited our school in May 2016, I realised how far I'd come, and how free I felt.

KYLY CLARKE

Smith has a fine leg and deep square leg out waiting for the hook. In close, he has a short leg and a leg gully. On the off side is a third man and a deep point. Smith has arranged the field so I can't play the hook, pull or cut without taking maximum risk.

Morkel's next over is all short balls. I weave inside the first, duck the second, get hit on the forearm by the third, dodge the fourth, and fend the fifth away for a single. The South Africans have sensed and homed in on my uncertainty. I'm not going to play the pull or hook shots, so they feel they can attack me with impunity.

In Morkel's next over, I stand up and block the first two balls, but the third rears up and I can't get out of the way. It cannons off my shoulder into the side of my head. I throw my bat down and check that I'm all right. When I face up again, I glove a ball in the air, but it falls safely. He can't keep going for long at this pace and intensity. I'm just trying to outlast him. I need to get off strike, but can't. Luckily, balls are missing my gloves or my edge or popping past short leg.

During Morkel's next two overs, Davey manages to get most of the strike, and then Smith takes him off, leaving me to assess the damage. Straight away, I know that my shoulder is seriously hurt. Alex Kountouris has already come on more than once, worried about my forearm, which he thinks could be broken. I see my right thumb is bleeding when I take my glove off.

Seeing the damage to my forearm and thumb, Alex says, 'Can you even hold the bat?'

'It's my shoulder that's hurting most.'

'Your shoulder's fine!'

'No, my shoulder's the problem.'

More than anything, he's worried about a concussion from when I was hit on the jaw, or even a broken bone. He's asking me if I know the score and so on, to see if I'm thinking straight, and I keep talking about my shoulder. It doesn't reassure him, and he's considering whether I ought to come off.

But I am never going to come off the field. I *have* to score runs. My mind is strong because I have something very clear in front of me that I want to achieve.

I play through the pain and, in the parts of my body where there is no pain, the lack of feeling and power. By the end of the day, I've made it to 92 and we are three for 331, a satisfying position. But there won't be any rest for me. Until after midnight, I am with Alex in the team room at the hotel, being iced and treated. The shoulder is broken, I'm sure, and the forearm and thumb could be as well. I go to bed at about one o'clock, but three hours later I'm back in the team room and relying on more of Alex's treatment and medication, which includes a local anaesthetic injected into my thumb so I can hold on to my bat. I doze for a little, then wake again, then doze off, able to grab only occasional moments of sleep before the team bus is ready and waiting to go back to Newlands. By then, I'm also suffering from extreme nausea due to a reaction I've had to some painkillers Peter Brukner has given me, and feel like throwing up constantly.

There is commentary on the toughness of this innings, because people saw me get hurt. It's all out there in the open. But I go through pain and need treatment every single day by this stage of my career. With what I've been through with my back and hamstrings, getting hit by short-pitched bowling is not the worst. The pain is ever-present now; what makes this innings different is that the causes of the pain are visible to people watching.

Walking back onto Newlands the next morning, adrenalin, excitement and love of the contest do more for me than all the medication I'm taking. Needing to clear my mind for the task ahead, to do a job for the team and myself, has the effect of numbing me. I spend 25 balls on 99 before making that hundred. I get exactly what I want: a decent personal contribution to a team score that sets up the match for us. Davey backs up with a second-innings hundred, and the combined bowling effort of Mitch Johnson, Ryan Harris, James Pattinson, Shane Watson and Nathan Lyon gets us that all-important victory, and the number one ICC ranking, in the shadows of stumps on the fifth day. I can't express how much that means to me. It's a crowning moment, for sure.

But also, in retrospect, it's bittersweet, because this was one of the last Test matches I played when I was still innocent, when I had no fear of dying while playing the game I love.

18

HUGHESY

It's a Tuesday morning in November, the first day of an important Sheffield Shield round leading up to the first Test match of the summer. But instead of playing, I'm at home and my head is buzzing with irritation. All the little annoyances that have been simmering away over the past couple of years feel like they're coming to the boil this week. Ian Chappell, when asked why he quit the Australian cricket captaincy, said he'd got fed up with all the people he wanted to tell to f— off. He had been in the job for four years. There is a long line of post-war Australian captains – Hassett, Benaud, Simpson, Lawry, the Chappells, Taylor, Waugh – who have reached their limit in this job after about four years.

I have now held the captaincy for almost four years.

I've come home for a shower after a rehab session at the Sydney Cricket Ground. Over the past few days I have been battling with so many people, it feels like life is one long argument. With the Cricket Australia hierarchy, I've been having some very tough conversations, often not fighting them so much as feeling puzzled and a bit let down by the line they've taken, considering how well they know me.

At issue is my fitness for the First Test in Brisbane against India, which is less than two weeks away. It goes without saying that for such a big series, the first spark in a summer that builds all the way up to the World Cup in five months, I am going to do everything in my power to get on the field.

The problem seems to be that CA have decided, after ten years, that they're going to stop trusting me to know my own body. In ten years in the Australian team, with a degenerative back complaint that I've had since I was a teenager, I have only missed one Test match through injury. I've put myself through torture to fix my back and my hamstrings, and I have always come right when I've declared myself fit to play.

This morning, it's all come to a head. A month ago, during Australia's one-day tour of Zimbabwe, I aggravated a left hamstring strain which I initially incurred in a one-day match against South Africa in Perth. Rod Marsh, as chairman of selectors, wants me to prove my fitness by playing in the Sheffield Shield round starting today, for New South Wales against South Australia at the SCG. The Cricket Australia medical staff have told Rod that there is no way I can get through a four-day game without risking re-injury. They've ruled me out of the Shield game.

I can totally understand that view. The risk is too great. But at the same time, I want to find a way of playing a game somewhere so that I can prove to myself that I will be fit for the Test match.

Pat Howard told the selectors a compromise could be reached. He suggested I play in a two-day match between India and an Australian XI in Adelaide, also starting this week. If I get through that, Pat told Rod, I should be considered available.

I hadn't been consulted, and neither had the CA medical staff, when this deal was discussed. I was too busy working on my recovery. Every day, I have to travel to my physio Steve's practice in Beecroft, in the northern suburbs of Sydney, to get onto the MedX machine. It's horrible for Kyly. She'll say, 'What are we doing today?' And I'll reply, 'Driving to Beecroft and back.' I'm irritable and angry, and not fun to live with, but Kyly has the ability to stay tranquil. Eventually I calm down and say, 'I'm sorry, I'm not having a good day with my back.' As inconvenient as it is, we both know that for the past ten years, the MedX has been the silver bullet for my back, the only regular treatment that I can rely on to get me right. There isn't one in Adelaide.

Flying to Adelaide would not be great for my injury, but it's the time away from the MedX machine to treat and strengthen me that could set me back.

On top of that, in Adelaide I would be facing an international attack highly motivated to take me down. One twist to avoid an Ishant Sharma bouncer, and my back could be gone – not only for the First Test, but potentially for the whole summer, which means a World Cup on home soil.

Once again, the Cricket Australia medical staff step in, saying that I'm not ready to play in Adelaide and face an international attack. What next? Alex and I come up with an alternative plan: that I stay in Sydney, get treatment on my back every day, and play in a club match for Western Suburbs this Saturday. Alex knows, and I know, that this would be a perfect testing ground for my back: facing first-grade bowlers and being close to treatment, including the MedX. If I can't get through a club match, I can accept that I will definitely not be fit for the Test match.

Pat Howard gives me a flat no. 'If you don't play this game in Adelaide,' he says, 'you're unavailable for the Test match.' He's fed up himself, having had to persuade the selectors to agree to my missing the Shield match.

'Pat, your own medical staff have said they don't think I'm ready to play India in Adelaide.'

'All right then, you won't be considered for the Test match.'

'Won't that look silly,' I say, 'because I'll be playing in this club game on Saturday, and I might make some runs, and yet you'll be telling the Australian public I am not available for the Test match.'

'That's right.'

'Okay, let me understand,' I say, containing my anger. 'If I go to Adelaide, field in slips all day without touching a ball, then get out for a golden duck, you're going to pick me for the Test match?'

'Yes,' Pat says.

'But if I go out and make 100 for Western Suburbs and run around in the field all day, doing everything, even if I bowl, you will consider me unfit?'

'Correct.'

At 33, I know my body better than anyone, except perhaps Alex. I just need Cricket Australia to follow the same procedures they have followed for the past decade, to trust that I know my body, that I'm honest with Alex, and that together we will know whether I am ready to play. They have placed that trust in me throughout my career and I have never let them down. But the people and policies are different now. They are not taking my word for it, nor Alex's.

I make one final plea. 'Pat,' I say, 'that's not fair. I have never let my teammates down by playing in a Test match when I'm not fit. Ever since I've played for Australia, I have been trusted on this. I know I can play in this club match and satisfy myself whether I'm fit or not. I've done it for 100 Test matches. I know I can't make it to Adelaide. But if I can stay in Sydney, I believe I can get myself right for Brisbane.'

It falls on deaf ears. The upshot? Cricket Australia ban me from playing club cricket even though their own physio has told them I was 100 per cent fit to play for Wests. So I will not be considered for the Test match.

None of it has been making sense, and I'm fuming. Word has leaked out to the press, and some of the cricket journalists are writing that James Sutherland, the chief executive of Cricket Australia, and other powerbrokers are running out of patience with me. The feeling is mutual.

I've been down to Moore Park this morning to do running drills with Duncan Kerr, my personal trainer. While I was there, one bright spot gave me a momentary lift. As we crossed the road and walked past the SCG, we peeked through to the Sheffield Shield game, which had started. South Australia were batting, and Hughesy was opening. If there's going to be one silver lining to all of this, it might be that Hughesy gets my Test place.

As we look through the gate, I see that he is into the twenties. Perfect! I'll go home for a shower and change, then come back to watch him bat. I know he's in for a big one. He loves punishing his old Blues teammates. He'll make a hundred and the selectors will have to pick him.

I finish off with Duncan, and it's only a ten-minute drive home. I have a shower and plan to go back to the SCG for the after-lunch session.

When I get out of the shower, there are five missed calls on my phone. Strange. A couple of them are from Malcolm Conn, at Cricket NSW. Malcolm and I go a long way back. When he was chief cricket writer for *The Australian* and then *The Daily Telegraph*, we would be blueing one minute about something he'd written, and the next minute we would be collaborating, with him ghost-writing my columns for the paper. It typifies the up-and-down relationship I've had with the media through my entire career. Malcolm is a very straight-shooting type, however, and we were always able to bounce back from our disagreements quickly. He has now moved from journalism to our side of the fence, as a communications officer for Cricket NSW and Cricket Australia.

I'm moving around my bedroom getting my things ready to go. 'What's going on?' I ask Mal.

His voice is flat. 'Have you heard about Hughesy?'

'What?' I laugh. 'Has he got a hundred already?'

'He's been hit on the head and a helicopter's about to land on the SCG.'

I stop moving. I'm almost too shocked to speak. 'Is he all right?'

'We don't know.'

Everything else empties out of me. All the arguments that have been spinning around my head for days and weeks, everything that has been driving me crazy and putting the cricket world into a lather – it's all gone. There's nothing in me except one thought: *Hughesy*.

I must run every red light between home and the inner city. I'm going like a race car driver. My heart is in the pit of my stomach, set off by the word *Helicopter*. What did Mal say? *A helicopter's about to land on the SCG?* It sounds bad. I don't let my thoughts go any further than that. *Hughesy*.

In the car, I speak to Dave Thompson, the Cricket NSW operations manager.

'He's not at the SCG,' he says.

'Where's he been taken?'

'He's been put in an ambulance and is going to St Vincent's Hospital.'

I change direction and whiz to St Vincent's, which is only a few minutes from the SCG. Out of my mind, I park in the ambulance area and run into emergency. Tim Nielsen, my old Cricket Australia coach who's now South Australia's head of high performance, and some other SA Cricket people are there.

'Where is he?' I say to Tim.

Before he can reply, a member of the hospital staff grabs me. 'He's been taken for a CT scan. Come through, his family's in here.'

As I'm being taken to the room where they are waiting, Hughesy is being wheeled past on a trolley. He looks normal. There's still a sheen of sweat on his face, and his hand, when I hold it, is hot. He has a scratch on his face from where he fell forward onto the pitch. I notice a little bit of facial swelling, but not much. My first thought is, *He'll be right.*

Hughesy's mum Virginia, his brother Jason and his sister Megan are all in tears. When I come into the room, they get up and we're just hugging and crying for a long time. Virginia's asking me a lot of questions about what happens next. I don't have a clue. All I can say is, 'He's in the best hands.' They begin explaining the shot Hughesy was playing when he was hit. New South Wales were bowling short to stop Hughesy scoring. He went to hook a bouncer but got through his shot too early. The ball hit him in the back of his head or the top of his neck, just beneath the rim of his helmet. He was 63 not out.

At this stage, we're unaware of what is going on in the outside world. Everything has shrunk down to this hospital ward. We don't know that they have called off the game entirely, as none of the players could bring themselves to go back on the field. Nor do we know that the full round of Sheffield Shield matches around the country, and the Indians' game in Adelaide, will be abandoned. It's not the time for cricket. Nor will it be for a long while.

When Hughesy is taken up to the next floor for more scans, we follow and are put in another waiting room. It's all a blur. Virginia's barely able to speak, she's crying so much. Greg, Hughesy's dad, is up at his farm near Macksville on the North Coast. Someone has rung to organise him a flight down, but there are no seats out of Coffs Harbour, so the plans have been changed and he's driving to Port Macquarie to fly from there. The family are worried about him getting misleading news over the car radio or a television in an airport terminal. They just want him here.

A surgeon comes to us, sits us down, and says, 'We've had the scan results. There's been a bleed and we've got to release the swelling as quickly as possible.' In order to do so, they have to operate.

Time dissolves. I don't know how long has passed. After the surgery, the doctor comes out and tells us the operation hasn't been able to slow the swelling. Hughesy's family are suffering intensely, and the doctor isn't sure that they're able to take in what he's telling them.

'Michael,' he says, 'can we have a word privately?'

He wants to take me aside and spell it out, so that I can pass it on to them. He thinks there's a better chance that they will be able to focus on what I'm saying. The swelling's going up, he explains.

I keep asking, 'Can you give me more information?' I am feeling kind of clear on the outside, but completely empty within, like what he's saying is just echoing around inside me. I need to hear it more than once before I can comprehend it.

The doctor tells me that there is a lot of swelling in Hughesy's brain, and they need to release it. They will operate again, and then place him in an induced coma.

After a few more hours of waiting, we jump to our feet as the doctor reappears. He says the news is better. 'The swelling has slowed down, which is a good sign. We're going to keep him in the coma overnight and see how much more it comes down. We'll keep our fingers crossed, but won't know much until the morning.'

By now it is eight or nine in the evening, about six hours since Hughesy was hit. Inside the waiting room, Greg has arrived and the family go through periods of quiet. Outside, the corridors are silent. I pace up and down the corridor outside Hughesy's room for hours. Hughesy's manager, James Henderson, and Dr Peter Brukner from Cricket Australia are there, but everyone else has been kept out and there's an eerie stillness.

At about 3.30 am, I find my car and drive home. I'm only thinking, *Will he be right to play cricket again?* That's all. I'm still focused on cricket, nothing bigger than that. The next piece of information, that's what I'm looking to.

Maybe it will tell us that he will be right for the Test match.

I lie on my bed, and my mind is still squirrel-wheeling around in this little circle. *Will he be okay for the Test match? If not, will he be right for the Second Test?* I'm not reflecting on Hughesy and our friendship. That would be like allowing too much in. I can only focus on what the doctors will tell us tomorrow morning.

Trying to sleep is pointless. At 5.30 am, I'm back in the car. At St Vincent's, Hughesy's family are where I left them, going through lulls in between bouts of crying.

It's mid-morning when a doctor comes in and tells us there's been a change since the optimistic news last night. They can't control the swelling, and have increased his medication. We don't know what to do or say. But every piece of news that doesn't say, *He'll be okay, he'll be playing again soon,* is shattering.

After staying with the family for a while, I go back in and see him. Last night, his face was swelling up but he was still recognisable, still Hughesy. Now, in the morning, he's much more puffed up.

The nurses are lovely, moving about the room quietly and doing everything with care. To one of them I say, 'Where's he at now?'

She explains that the swelling has now gone up to about five times normal and they have stopped monitoring it.

This is the first time I look back at him and see that it isn't him. He is still breathing, through the tube feeding oxygen into his mouth, but it isn't *him*. He doesn't have that typical warm Hughesy sweat across his forehead and cheeks, like he had yesterday. The beat of his heart and the flow of oxygen – it's like the machine is doing it, keeping him alive, more than his own body is.

I stay in the room with him for a fair while. Hours. I just hold his hand and urge him to come back to us. Am I saying goodbye? No. I'm fogged-up by shock, just saying the same encouraging words over and over again. If I move off from that topic, I talk about cricket: how he's going to play in the Test match, how I've lost my battle with CA, but we're going to get justice because Hughesy's going to go out there as my replacement and score a hundred. No, a double-hundred.

Later, we will be told that on impact, in that split second when the ball hit him, he was effectively gone. I won't be able to accept that. That's too tough for me to take. Right through that first afternoon and evening in hospital, for all the hours I've been talking to him, I've never let anything like this filter into my head. It's only cricket. He might be out of the game for a few weeks. But he can't die.

I know what my friendship with Phillip Hughes was. Over the days following his passing, my role as Australian captain overlapped with my personal grief at losing one of my best mates. It was hard to separate the two. Managing the scene in the hospital, bringing players together, giving a eulogy at his funeral, and then, after long negotiations, taking the field in a Test match two weeks later – I had no chance to retreat into my private space and grieve for the bloke I regard as my little brother.

Like many in Sydney's grade cricket scene, I had heard about Phil Hughes before I met him. In 2006, Neil D'Costa was getting an earful about this prodigious left-hander from the North Coast from one of the young Western Suburbs players, Shariful Islam. Shariful was an under-age representative cricketer who raved non-stop about how Phil Hughes was the best batsman he'd ever bowled to and was going to play for Australia. There's a story that in a New South Wales under-17s dressing room, the boys were asking each other how many centuries they'd made in their careers. One guy would say two, another would say five, another would say six, and then they'd get to Hughesy and he'd mumble, almost embarrassed, 'Seventy.' Up the North Coast, he was already a legend.

Neil made inquiries about getting Phil to the Magpies, and won out against some other Sydney clubs who were on the trail. I didn't know this, but one of the attractions of Western Suburbs for Hughesy was that I was playing there, and he wanted to play with me. This was a bit embarrassing for me. At the time, I had been playing for Australia for three years and had the full Shane Warne-inspired look of blond-tipped hair and an earring. Phil had gone to a hairdresser in Coffs Harbour with a photo of me, saying he wanted the same hair. Over the years, the story – like my haircut! – only made me cringe. But Hughesy, with his typical mischief, loved to play it up for all it was worth.

He still had a year of high school to finish in Sydney, and Neil got him enrolled at Homebush Boys' High. I was living in my townhouse at Breakfast Point, near Concord on the Parramatta River, and a bunch of other Wests players, including Hughesy, would also soon be living in that development. Neil brought Phil along to my place, and immediately he clicked with all the boys.

My mates became his mates. Steve Phillips was my best mate at the time, and Lloyd Andrews had been a friend of mine since junior cricket. They became Hughesy's inner circle, along with Daniel Smith, the New South Wales state right-hander and wicketkeeper. Steve and Hughesy were very, very similar: they spoke similarly and enjoyed the same things off the field, be it watching rugby league, sharing opinions or socialising. Steve had a big brother relationship with Hughesy, but associating with older guys was something that came naturally to this boy. That probably came from the time he had spent up in Macksville with Greg and Jason, who were his real heroes, and the desire to learn from his elders also reflected his ambition to get ahead in the game.

He was cheeky and instantly lovable, though what left the deepest impression on me was how serious he was about his cricket and how determined he was to play for Australia. I had never seen that in any young cricketer, that depth of hunger. Nobody I have known has valued the baggy green more than Hughesy, and it was apparent from the first day we met.

Although I was not playing a lot of grade cricket by that point, when I was around, Hughesy watched me like a hawk. He wanted to imitate my preparation down to the last detail. He asked a lot of questions and listened hard to the answers, reminding me of the way I used to grill Ricky Ponting and Damien Martyn. I was an obsessive worker in my preparation for cricket, particularly in that period when I had had to rebuild my approach to the game after being dropped by Australia in the 2005–06 season. Whether it was gym work-outs, hitting balls or the full range of practice drills, I felt that I had to get a certain amount of work into me before I was properly prepared to play.

Hughesy adopted this fully. It was a big part of his later relationship with Justin Langer as Australian batting coach. For players like us, there is almost no such thing as too much preparation. We were always competing in training, over who was fitter and stronger. I couldn't compete with Hughesy's strength – with that arse and legs, he was such a pocket rocket. So we weren't competing directly, just trying to push each other.

Hughesy hit the state scene with a blast in 2007–08, and my first state game with him was the Shield final that season, against Victoria at the SCG. He made a hundred, of course. They tried to bounce him, and he'd cut and pull them away. They bowled spin, and he hoicked them over mid-wicket. He drove them spare. His celebration was the biggest anyone could remember and, not for the last time, when I saw him make a hundred it felt as sweet as if I had made it myself.

In the New South Wales dressing room, we were Wests boys. To me, he was always the young country kid playing for Western Suburbs. I wanted to help him in his cricket, and look after him as a big brother in the way Shane Warne had looked after me. Tours are special. With more time on your hands, you get to know each other in a more relaxed, distraction-free way than when you are at home. On tour, Hughesy and I would get together every night, just as I'd done with Warney.

The first opportunity to consolidate our friendship in that way came in 2009, when he was picked to tour South Africa with the Australian team, as the opening batting replacement for the retiring Matthew Hayden. That was a huge pair of shoes for Hughesy to fill, but he slipped into life as an Australian Test cricketer as if he was born for it. He was happy and natural and never overawed. Even when the South Africans got him out fourth ball in his first Test innings in Johannesburg, he just shrugged it off and went out and smacked runs in the second dig. Then, on a really difficult pitch in Durban where the rest of us were struggling against Dale Steyn, he made two incredible hundreds.

He didn't need too much personal help from me. He developed friendships with Ricky Ponting and Simon Katich, and in his unique way, he had them thinking he was their personal project. He knew exactly what he needed from each of us. He and I had that Western Suburbs connection, and the common ground in our domestic lives, but Kato loved him as his opening partner. Batting together, they were two stars of that series. When Hughesy ran down the wicket and leapt in the air – after bringing up his first Test hundred with a six! – I had an almost out-of-body experience. I was so excited, I felt like it was me celebrating out there. That's how much I cared for his success.

We were always close when we were on tour together over the next two years. After he was dropped during the 2009 Ashes series and became an irregular member of the Australian team, we were speaking on the phone or texting every day. Hughesy always went back to state cricket and churned out more runs, making his case for reinstatement. He came back into the team as a replacement in January 2010 and stayed with us when we toured New Zealand that autumn, but when it came time to leave a batsman out, the selectors always seemed to find it easiest to omit Hughesy.

I can't say why, as I wasn't a selector at the time, but my guess is that it was two things. One, Hughesy's unorthodox-looking technique always gave the selectors a story they could tell him: that he should work on his leg-side play, that he should stop trying to score so many runs square of the wicket on the off side, that he should improve his footwork against spin. And two, he was such a good bloke, he never moaned or made a big deal of his disappointment. He would sit down and listen to the selectors' explanation very closely, then go off and work harder on his game. If we were on tour, as we were when he was dropped during the Ashes tours of England in 2009 and 2013, he would be the first guy running out gloves or Gatorade to the batsmen who had replaced him.

Which is not to say that he didn't feel the anguish. He felt it as much as anybody I ever knew. On those England tours, he would come to my hotel room and pour it all out. I could only let him talk and give him broad encouragement about making more runs. It wasn't for me to complain about the decisions. As a senior player, I couldn't show disloyalty to the guys who had been chosen in his place. And as his friend, I knew I would only be bringing him down if I grizzled and whinged and said he should have been picked instead of so-and-so. I had to walk a careful line. But Hughesy was always receptive to encouragement, and his record shows his amazingly consistent ability to pick himself up after each disappointment and do exactly what the selectors asked. He was doing it again the day he got hit.

The year 2010 was a watershed for our friendship. Early in the year, I broke up with Lara and Hughesy dislocated his shoulder in a boxing-gym accident. During that winter, we both needed a friend more than ever. Hughesy came to stay at my unit in Bondi for a night, and ended up staying for six weeks. We went out together, exercised together, talked non-stop, and picked up each other's spirits. His shoulder, and my heart, got put back together. We became as close as brothers that year, although the one part of our lives we couldn't share was Hughesy's addiction to caffeine. I didn't drink coffee, and he would guzzle it from dawn through to well after dark. He was on his own there.

When I became Australian captain, our friendship shifted again. It became tighter, but I was more careful in letting people see it, because I didn't want Hughesy to carry the burden of being seen as the captain's favourite. In Sri Lanka in 2011, my first Test tour as captain, Hughesy scored his third Test century, an extremely gutsy innings in Colombo. When he passed his hundred, I promise to God it was like I was in the middle raising my bat.

That's how I'd felt when Hughesy scored his hundreds in Durban two years earlier, but the difference now was that I had that same experience with other young guys. Shaun Marsh also made his maiden Test century on that tour, and later that summer David Warner would do likewise. The 'Hughesy' feeling I had always had – of genuinely getting as much pleasure out of my teammates' achievements as I'd ever got out of my own – was now extended to all of the other players, especially the young ones coming through.

Unfortunately, Hughesy was out of the team four Tests later, after a couple of failures against New Zealand. He was back in again the next summer, making two half-centuries against Sri Lanka before working his butt off in our 4–0 loss in India. On the 2013 Ashes tour, we really did believe he had cemented his place with his unbeaten 81 alongside Ashton Agar in their world record last-wicket partnership at Trent Bridge. This was a new side of Hughesy, the old head batting with the teenager, saying nothing to Ashton between deliveries except 'Next ball, next ball'. He was strongly influenced by our batting coach Justin Langer, another hard little nut.

One Test match later, though, the selectors dropped Hughesy for what turned out to be the last time. He was the victim of a chain reaction of circumstances. Darren Lehmann, newly installed as coach and selector, was determined to give Shane Watson and Chris Rogers a few chances as our opening pair. Ed Cowan was pushed down to number three and Hughesy to number six for the Trent Bridge Test match, so we had effectively four openers in our top six. Ed got sick during the match and missed out with the bat; he was replaced by Usman Khawaja for the next Test match at Lord's. We got beaten comprehensively there, with none of the batsmen making any notable contribution.

For the Third Test at Old Trafford, David Warner was returning from his disciplinary suspension, which he followed with some games for Australia A in Africa. The selectors felt it would be unfair to drop Usman after one Test match, in which he had made a second-innings fifty. They wanted to rush Davey back in, as we were 2–0 down in the series. Steve Smith had done enough to hold on to his number five spot. Darren Lehmann said that he felt, deep down, that Hughesy was an opener, not a middle-order batsman, but at the time he was backing Watson and Rogers as the opening pair. So it ended up that the short straw, as usual, went to Hughesy.

He came to my hotel room, fuming. I was in a tricky situation. I wasn't a selector anymore, having given up that role at the start of the tour. All the same, I had to take accountability for the selectors' decisions as if they were my own. When I had been a selector, in a way it had been easier. I could look Hughesy in the eye, as I would with any other player, and say, 'We had to drop you, so we did.' This time, I couldn't quite own the decision like that, but I couldn't afford to disagree with it either. I never said to Hughesy, 'You should have been picked.' I made it clear to the selectors if I disagreed with them, but I didn't take that to the player.

Hughesy was really pissed off. Instead of giving him the impression that I was taking his side against the selectors, I said, 'Don't be so easy to drop. Make more runs and also make it clear to the selectors, when you've been dropped, that you disagree.'

'They say I'm still young, I can use this time to develop my game.'

'You want to play for Australia right now, don't you? Don't just let them think there'll be time later. If you're too accepting about it, they won't see how hungry you are to play.'

But Hughesy was such a great bloke, even when he had that shit inside him, he wouldn't express it to teammates or selectors. He cared so much about the team, the next day he was running gloves out to guys who'd been picked in front of him, when he knew he trained twice as hard as them and deserved the position more. That's the one-of-a-kind bloke he was.

It's another cricket day, only nobody around our country is playing. People are swarming into St Vincent's: Hughesy's extended family, friends from everywhere, Cricket Australia people. Potentially, it's chaos. My goal is to help Virginia,

Greg, Jason and Megan in any way possible. I'm spending small slices of time at Hughesy's bedside, but for the most part I'm trying to work out what they need, who has to be called, what's got to be organised. I am answering questions non-stop. But I can't tell a single person what they want to hear.

By afternoon, there's mayhem in the hospital. The Hugheses are in a small room, and a few metres down the corridor is a long waiting room heaving with people. The family don't know what to do, and I'm trying to balance the need to protect Hughesy's family with the pressing demand for news. Virginia assigns me a job: she wants me to take people, one by one, into Hughesy's room to see him.

About 30 family members and close friends are allowed to go in. Justin Langer has instantly flown across from Perth to spend hours by Hughesy's bedside. Nobody is allowed to see him unless I or an immediate family member takes them in, and with the state his family's in, that means 95 per cent of these visitors are my responsibility. I have to prepare each of them for how he looks. 'The swelling is major,' I say. 'He won't look like the Hughesy you know.'

But there seem like hundreds of others, milling about, waiting and hoping. They all want to know what will happen next. I repeat that we won't know anything more until the morning, and tell people they ought to go home. Just as the Hugheses are constantly asking me to make sense of the medical news for them, many friends and teammates outside the room are also looking to me for answers. I don't have any, not for them and not for myself. The hospital staff are saying to me, 'The corridors are full, we can't have this, you'll have to take them downstairs.' I say, 'I'm doing my best here.'

On the Wednesday night, a doctor comes into the waiting room where the family are. 'We're going to have one last go at medicating him tonight. We'll let you know more tomorrow morning.' I can tell from his tone that it's not good. No new development has offered us anything to hope for, but we hope all the same. We're swimming against the tide. Our hope seems to be the only thing going Hughesy's way now.

I go home and sit on my bed. Three hours later, I wake up, still in my clothes and shoes; I've been so tired, I conked out. Within seconds, reality wakes up too. *Hell.* I shower, change and drive back to the hospital. It's not going to be a good day.

It's on this third morning, the Thursday, that the doctors tell Hughesy's immediate family and me that it's over. A lot has been done to prepare them, but I will never forget Virginia's cry. The room is a scene of complete devastation, like a hurricane has hit those poor people. I know what it's like to come from a tight-knit family, but the Hugheses are something else. Phillip would talk to his dad several times a day, every day, wherever he was in the world. He talked to his mum once a day too. He and Megan were soul mates. Jason was his best friend and his hero. Other cricketers have always laughed and marvelled about how everything Hughesy does is for his family's benefit.

For 20 minutes after we get the news, I am with them, crying and hugging. It's so horrible, there are no words for it. Finally, we all go back into the adjoining room to tell his extended family and close friends. We don't need to say anything. I can see from their faces that they know, that they've heard the crying and screaming through the wall.

We are allowed to see him one last time before the life support is turned off. As we go to walk in, Greg sees Ricky Ponting standing in the hallway. He turns to me and says, 'Can you take Ricky in?' Punter and I are in there for ten or 15 minutes. We're both in tears. We've been Hughesy's Test captains, and a lot more than that. In the past few years, when they shared James Henderson as their manager, Hughesy and Punter became very close.

Virginia wants the immediate family and me to be the last people to see him, so after Punter goes out, the five of us go in. I just feel so unbearably sad for Hughesy's family. He is everything to them.

The hospital is still packed and my main job is still to manage the flow of people. Most, I hope, get their chance to say goodbye. A gathering is hastily organised at the Sydney Cricket Ground Members' Bar, where a lot of cricket people go. The next morning, I give a press conference where I read a statement:

> Words cannot express the loss we all feel as a team right now. To Greg, Virginia, Jason and Megan, we share in the deep pain that you're feeling.

Apart from when he was home on the farm with his beloved cattle, Hughesy was at his happiest playing cricket for his country with his mates. Our dressing room will never be the same. We loved him, and always will. Things were always put into perspective when Hughesy said, 'Where else would you rather be, boys, but playing cricket for your country?'

We are going to miss that cheeky grin, and that twinkle in his eye. He epitomised what the baggy green is about and what it means to us all.

The world lost one of its great blokes this week and we are all poorer for it. Our promise to Hughesy's family is that we will do everything we can to honour his memory.

Last night I asked James Sutherland if Hughesy's Australian one-day international shirt number, 64, could be retired, to which they agreed. That means so much.

His legacy of trying to improve each and every day will drive us for the rest of our lives. We'd like to thank everyone, both here and overseas, for the touching tributes to Hughesy in recent days.

Our dressing room will never be the same. We loved him, and always will. Rest in peace, Brussy.

The tributes to Hughesy pour in from around the world over the next week, coming from all walks of life, from Queen Elizabeth II to the grassroots campaign to 'Put out your bats', where thousands of people put their bats outside their houses in acknowledgement of Hughesy's passing. For myself, I'm numb and unaware of a lot of it. I have to shove my personal feelings to one side and continue in my role of chief helper to Virginia, Greg, Jason and Megan, as well as prepare for the funeral. The thought of playing cricket again is the furthest thing from anyone's mind.

Along the way, there are negotiations between the players and Cricket Australia over when to recommence playing. The Indian team is still in the country, making ready for the start of a Test series that now seems immaterial to many of us. When consulted, I am hardline. I think the Australian players need as much time as possible. I also believe that it is for the cricketers as a group to make a decision, and it should be one-in, all-in. I know that CA is under pressure to get the Test series with India started, but that is not our responsibility. All I can say to CA is that too many players are unready to even think about cricket, let alone play again.

Hughesy's funeral is going to be in Macksville, with a service at the school gymnasium. I want to drive up a few days before, but am in no state to handle the six-hour trip. Kindly, James Packer lends his helicopter to fly me up, and my personal trainer Duncan Kerr comes along.

When we get there, Megan is the only family member in a fit state to organise the funeral, and has taken on that role. She and Phillip had a very special relationship; they were almost like twins. Upon his death, she had been able to guess the code to his phone, all his passwords: they were like two halves of the one brain. I really want her wishes to be respected. Michael Brown, formerly the operations manager of Cricket Australia, was previously in the funeral business and, using all his experience, is fantastic and efficient in getting the hall how Megan wants it. After taking a look at the hall, I have one suggestion: that Hughesy's Cricket Australia suit be hung up, and his main caps – Australia, South Australia and New South Wales – put on display.

The Hugheses have asked me to make a speech, which I write with the help of two good friends: my commercial director Jim Kelly and Ross Thornton, chairman of my cricket academy. Both are corporate communications specialists who have also worked for senior politicians. I come up with the ideas, and Ross and Jim fine-tune them into a speech. We talk about making it personal, from me to Hughesy, but because of how he passed, playing the game he loved, I want it to be a message to the entire cricket family.

The day is uncomfortably hot and humid for everyone sitting in the hall. My emotions are close to the brink all the way through. Megan, Hughesy's cousin Nino Ramunno, and his cattle-breeding partner Corey Ireland make wonderful tributes, which I hear through the beating of my pulse in my head.

Finally, when my time comes, I'm not worried about how my tribute will come across generally. All I care about is giving Virginia, Greg, Jason and Megan something that they can hold on to – if not today, then at some point in the future.

I am deeply honoured to have been asked by Phillip's family to speak today. I am humbled to be in the presence of you, his family, his friends, and his community. He was so proud of Macksville, and it's easy to see why today. Taken from the game, his family and loved ones at the age of just 25, he left a mark on our game that needs no embellishment. I don't know about you, but I keep looking for him. I know it's crazy, but I expect any minute to take a call from him or to see his face pop around the corner. Is that what they call the spirit? If so, then his is still with me, and I hope it never leaves.

I walked to the middle of the SCG on Thursday night. Those same blades of grass beneath my feet, where he and I and so many of his mates here today have built partnerships and taken chances and lived out the dreams we painted in our heads as boys. The same stands where the crowds rose to their feet to cheer him on, and that same fence he sent the ball to time and time again. And it's now, forever, the place where he fell.

I stood there at the wicket, I kneeled down and touched the grass. I swear he was with me. Picking me up on my feet to check if I was okay. Telling me we just needed to dig in and get through to tea, telling me off for that loose shot I played, chatting about what movie we might watch that night and then passing on a useless fact about cows. And I could see him swagger back to the other end, grin at the bowler, and call me through for a run with such a booming voice a bloke in the car park could hear it. The heart of a man who lived his life for this wonderful game we play, and whose spirit enriched not just our sport, but all of our lives. Is this what indigenous Australians believe about a person's spirit being connected with the land upon which they walk? If so, I know they are right about the SCG. His spirit has touched it, and it will forever be sacred ground for me. I can feel his spirit there, and I can see how it has touched so many people around the world.

The tributes to him from cricket lovers have kept me going. The photos, the words, the prayers, and the sense of communion in this loss from people across the globe have shown me his spirit is in action. It has sustained me and overwhelmed me in equal measure. And the love of my band of baggy green and gold brothers and sisters has held me upright when I thought I could not proceed. His spirit has brought us closer together – something I know must be him at work because it's so consistent with how he played and lived. He always wanted to bring people together, and he always wanted to celebrate his love for the game and its people.

Is this what we call the spirit of cricket? From a little girl in Karachi holding a candlelight tribute to masters of the game like Tendulkar, Warne and Lara showing their grief to the world, the spirit of cricket binds us all together. We feel it in the thrill of a cover drive, or the taking of a screamer at gully, whether by a 12-year-old boy in Worcester or by Brendon McCullum in Dubai.

It's in the brilliant hundred and the five-wicket haul, just as significant to the players in a Western Suburbs club game as it is in a Test. The bonds that led to cricketers from around the world putting their bats out, that saw people who didn't know Phillip lay flowers at the gates of Lord's, and that brought every cricketing nation on Earth to make its own heartfelt tribute. The bonds that saw players old and new rush to his bedside, from wherever they heard the news, to say their prayers and farewells.

This is what makes our game the greatest game in the world. Phillip's spirit, which is now part of our game forever, will always act as a custodian of the sport we all love. We must listen to it. We must cherish it. We must learn from it. We must just dig in and get through to tea. And we must play on.

So rest in peace, my little brother. I'll see you out in the middle.

19

FEAR

This new helmet. I pick it up and heft it in my hands, and it feels strange. I'm all in favour of altering the rules about what helmets we wear, considering the reasons, but it's almost impossible for me, at this stage of my career, to cope with such a dramatic change. It's significantly heavier than the helmets I've played my whole career in. The grille sits closer to the peak than the old helmet, to stop balls getting through. It's got optional neck protectors that chafe at my collar and block my movement. My brain agrees with the changes, but my gut says differently . . . I can't stop feeling it when I'm batting.

Every time I look at it, it reminds me of Hughesy.

His death has taken a toll on all of us. Not until I'm in England in 2015, trying to contribute something to our

Ashes effort, do I gain a full understanding of the toll it's taking on me.

Since Hughesy, I have a fear of dying that I never had before. And the helmet is reminding me of that fear every time I look at it.

Throughout my whole career, I've only ever worn two helmet models: first an Albion one, and a Masuri for the last ten years. Since Hughesy's death, there have been moves to mandate a new helmet, one that is more resistant to impact and bolstered by extra padding over the ears and around the neck. In Australia, it's been voluntary so far. During the 2015 World Cup, I've been sticking with my old helmet. I wear the new Masuri model in the nets, to try to get used to it, but stick with my old one for matches. Comfort is everything to me, and given my obsessiveness, so is keeping the same gear. My comfort *is* my obsessiveness. I like what I like. I have always worn the same batting pads throughout my career. It's the same with my gloves. The specifications of my gear are all quite old-fashioned. I've stuck with a skinny-handled bat, a white bat grip, white boots, the same sweatbands, a long-sleeved shirt. Even when I changed sponsors from Slazenger, I asked Spartan to manufacture pads with identical insides. In fact, one of the reasons I chose Spartan as my gear sponsor in 2012 was that Kunal Sharma, the founder and owner of the company, gave me the chance to design all of my own gear myself – the shape and weight of my bat, what gloves and pads I was most comfortable with – which, with my personality, was a dream come true, and eventually the passionate Kunal became a friend as well, in part because he recognised how obsessive I am about the tiniest things. My security has been in retaining the same gear.

And now, when I'm 34 years old, I have to change my helmet.

When we arrive in the UK for the 2015 Ashes tour, it is made clear to us that we have to change our helmets to the new reinforced model. Out of respect for the other players, I don't make a big deal of fighting the change. But alone, lying awake at night, I'm thinking, *Why? Why are we having to change helmets? It's because you can die in this game. Because Hughesy died. I'm not comfortable with these ear pads, I don't like the weight, but I have to wear it because I can die.*

On this tour, my batting has died.

Nothing has been quite right since Hughesy. I can see that now. I've gone through good moments at times, even such career highs as winning the World Cup and winning a Test match at Lord's. But throughout it all, there was something not quite right with me, and I couldn't put my finger on it.

Maybe it was too obvious. Or too frightening to face.

I never grieved. One minute I was at war with Cricket Australia, with the selectors and the high-performance manager, and the next minute the world came to an end. But then Hughesy's funeral was behind us, CA was anxious to get the Test series with India going, and the world started spinning again. Yet it was all upside-down. The anger had taken a break, but it didn't go away. The annoyance that had been building up inside me had been put on pause for a couple of weeks, but then it turned back on and, if anything, it got worse.

The black cloud is always lurking. During the preparation for Hughesy's funeral, and the service itself, I can distract myself by trying my best to help his family. Outside the Hugheses' house, some bats are lined up on the verandah in tribute. When I pick one up, I suffer a bad reaction, like I am physically sick and nervous at the same time. This is a *cricket bat*, the piece of equipment that has been my first love and an extension of my body since my Pop first cut out that fence paling when I was a tiny child. And now it is sending me into a spin, like it is triggering a rebellion from deep inside me. I am sickened and shocked by the feeling. I put the bat down again. It's too early.

As soon as the funeral is over, and I look up and think about cricket again, the blackness returns. In discussions with Cricket Australia, the Test team is adamant about postponing the Brisbane Test match, scheduled to start on 4 December.

Hughesy's funeral is on 3 December, so CA comes up with an alternative plan to make Adelaide the first Test match instead of the second, and shift the Brisbane game afterwards, sandwiching it between the Adelaide match and Christmas. The Boxing Day Test in Melbourne will run as scheduled, but because we will then have played three five-day matches back-to-back, the New Year's Test in Sydney will be put back by a couple of days. This arrangement gives us only three days to recover from the funeral, get to Adelaide and prepare for the Test match. Individuals are given a no-penalty option if they want to stand aside from the game in Adelaide.

The Test players generally want longer, noting that the Sheffield Shield cricketers are to be given another week to recover. To be asked to perform in the international spotlight, when so many of us were so close to Hughesy, is an enormous demand. Unanimously, we want to play the Adelaide Test match as a tribute to Hughesy and for his family, but the timing has to be right. Eventually an agreement is struck to begin the match on 9 December, six days after the funeral. In retrospect, most of us would agree that it is still too soon. But we feel a responsibility to India and to the Australian cricket public.

By the time this has been agreed, I still haven't trained since the morning Hughesy was hit. I was doing rehab three times a day until 25 November, but since then I've done nothing. In the past nine days, I haven't run, I haven't trained, I haven't done weights. Aside from that one sickening moment at the Hugheses' house, I haven't even touched a cricket bat.

My injured hamstring might have been healing during that time, but I have no strength in it. With all the stress and sleeplessness, I doubt even that it's been healing very well.

At the RSL club in Macksville where everyone has gathered for Hughesy's wake, Darren Lehmann comes up and says, 'Mate, you have to play in this Test. You're captain of this team. This team only has one captain, and it's you. The boys need you, I need you, and Australian cricket needs you.'

As much as I love Boof, after everything we've been through recently I want to resist. He is the messenger for Cricket Australia, and they acknowledge that after my role around Hughesy's passing and the funeral, people will look to me for leadership on the field. But I can't help feeling angry about it. A week ago, when all I was asking was for them to trust me, as they had trusted me for the past ten years, they refused. They are not even trusting me now, really. If Boof had asked, *Can you be fit to play in five days?*, I would say no. On top of the injury in my hamstring, I don't even know if I have the courage to pick up a bat and face fast bowling. None of us will know that until we do it. But that's all put to one side at this moment. Cricket Australia has decided it needs me now, and is more or less telling me to play. At the same function, Boof, along with Rod Marsh and Pat Howard, also front my commercial director Jim Kelly and urge him to get me 'up' for the game. I do want to play, desperately. But instead of feeling excited about it, my blood is boiling again.

After two more days with Hughesy's family in Macksville, I travel to Adelaide and my mind turns to getting ready. It feels like I am seized up with rust and disuse. When I get to Adelaide, the first thing I do when I get alone in my hotel room is pick up a bat. I've been really worried since Macksville. What if I literally can't hold it?

What if I have the same reaction? In my room, just to see what it feels like, I start some shadow batting. *I can do it.* It feels all right.

Late that afternoon, I go to Park 25 near the city and face three Australia A bowlers, just to see if I have the courage to play the game that killed my mate. This session isn't a test of my hamstring, but of whether I am mentally able to bat. When the first short ball comes, I trust my body and it moves. I haven't lost my muscle memory completely. I can do this. Or my body can.

I do some running, though it isn't a proper fitness test. The hierarchy aren't as concerned as they were a few weeks ago about whether I'm fit enough to play in the game. Ironically, this 'test' is the very kind of session I wanted before the scheduled First Test, when they ruled me out. But by now, we have all been overwhelmed by events. A new reality has taken over.

All through this, I should be grieving. I should be left to recover at home with Kyly, to absorb things a little, like a normal person. Maybe my subconscious is trying to grieve, and that's part of what's producing the waves of stress, anxiety and frustration. But so much is going on, with gathering the team and looking after them, making sure they are emotionally fit to play, that I don't even have time to breathe.

Even if my body isn't better, I tell myself I'm fit enough to play. I do two days of full training with the team, going through the motions as normal, although, in my mind, all the training feels rushed. I now have to think about going out and scoring runs against India. I don't do much running, but have a lot of treatment from Alex. He is doing so much for me it's not funny. He looks after me like gold, giving me hands-on massages with stretching and strength work for hours and hours, way above and beyond his normal duties. I can sense that he's also very nervous about me playing this Test match. My left hamstring is fine – not to run a marathon or sprint 100 metres, but good enough to play a Test match. I'm more worried about my back. I would feel more confident if I had had some time on the MedX in the past two weeks. I'm concerned that, if my back goes, my hamstring will follow. That's the way it's been in the past.

Day one is beautiful and sunny. I find that I'm able to control the emotions and let my body take over, do what it knows how to do. We all have Hughesy's Test number, 408, embroidered on our shirts, and it is painted in white on the outfield in front of the members' area. Before play, there is a 63-second pause for the 40,000-plus people to applaud him. It's strange, because the symbolism is heavy but the adrenalin of playing a Test match is taking over, as if cricket has a mind of its own.

When I toss with Virat Kohli, who has replaced the injured M.S. Dhoni as India's captain for the first two Test matches, I feel normal. I have a lot of respect for Virat and the other Indian players who represented their country by coming to Phillip's funeral. It's obvious that we are here to play for Hughesy, but I have also had to look into each of my teammates' eyes and make sure that they are here to play a Test match for Australia, that they're not clouded by what's happened. Their professionalism amazes me and lifts me.

Davey Warner clears the cobwebs in the way only he can: he crashes seven fours, all through the off side, from the first two overs he faces. Eventually, the Indian right-armer Varun Aaron bowls a bouncer, getting that part of the game out of the way. Bouncers are still bowled. Not every ball kills. The crowd cheers, and I take a deep breath.

THE INNINGS

128 versus India, Adelaide, 2014

Chris Rogers is out in the eighth over, and Watto looks good for nearly an hour before nicking to slip. I'm in. I jog onto the field, accustoming my eyes to the bright blue light. It's all routine. Aaron gives me a bouncer first ball, and I dodge it. As in the nets, my body is doing its thing. I have 26 years of muscle memory to carry me through this.

Fortunately, Davey Warner is batting so well he's taking the pressure off. By lunch, he's 77 not out and we are two down for 113. I'm very rusty at first, but find my timing after the resumption. My emotional state is not troubling me – meaning, I feel quite empty in my stomach and clear in my head. There is a numbness about everything. But that's probably a good mental condition for batting.

I am about 50 when Ishant Sharma bowls a bouncer. I go up onto my back foot and twist away as it whistles by.

NO. Instantly, I feel it, like a metal clamp grappling my lower back. *Here we go again*. It's that movement of going onto my back foot and torquing around. My back is in searing pain, and I know what this means, but I'm not saying anything. I'm going to bat on.

A few overs later, when I'm on 60, Ishant bowls another bouncer and I am forced into the same evasive move. The grabbing is the same, but worse. I kneel down and do some stretches on the turf. *I've got to push through this.* But within seconds, Alex is out there by my side, asking me what it is, though he knows already. He helps me off the field. I'm devastated, as I would be if this happened in any Test match. But in the circumstances, it's breaking my heart.

I'm taken from the Adelaide Oval to hospital, where I have a number of injections. The relief they bring is also familiar. As soon as the needle goes in, it feels like a crazy itch inside me, between my back and my stomach, has been scratched and relieved. It's an amazing feeling, so good. *Oh, thank you!* Straight away, I feel better and get back to the ground. In the dressing room, the boys are concerned but welcoming.

The day has been a good one for us. Smithy has batted through the afternoon, but in the last half hour Mitch Marsh gets out. I say to Alex, 'I'm batting.'

He freaks. 'If you bat here and do your back again, you mightn't be able to play another game. Ever.'

I don't care about my career. I'm totally driven by my emotions. My only goal is to make a hundred for my little brother. If that means the end of my career, I'm willing to sacrifice that. Like every other decision in the game, my thinking is driven by a spill-over of adrenalin from the previous ten days.

Nathan Lyon goes in as a night-watchman, but is quickly out. I repeat to Alex that I want to bat. He repeats, 'I don't want you to.'

Hadds goes out to the middle, and is dismissed on the second ball of the last over of the day. I would definitely insist on batting now, but stumps have been drawn. Alex says, 'Sleep on it, and let's see in the morning.'

Every medical decision I make is in consultation with Alex. I tell him the absolute truth the whole time. He is one person I can trust entirely, and I'm not going to break that now.

I sleep in my back brace and have a reasonable night's rest, but when I wake up early the next morning, I feel pain and discomfort. I can't touch my toes, but am sure I can get through some more batting.

Ahead of the team, I travel to the oval and go to the nets while it's still quiet. I hit ten balls for Alex and Peter Brukner. They need to be satisfied that I can move my feet and evade short balls, even more than whether I can hit shots through the field. It's about safety as much as the ability to bat.

By the time the boys arrive, I'm preparing to resume the innings with Smithy, who is 72 not out overnight. We are six down for 354, so while it's a healthy position it's still 100 to 150 runs short of where we want to be on this pitch. I only want to help.

When we walk out for the first ball, the crowd might be cheering, but the world feels silent around me. I don't feel anything, physically or emotionally. I am completely numb. I'm not nervous, not happy or unhappy. Obviously I care about what is happening, but my emotions are not there, like they've been burnt out of me.

But I am free and alone. That may sound strange, given that I'm in front of 45,000 people here and millions more on television. But I'm in my bubble. Ever since I can remember, playing cricket has been my day off. Increasingly so, since I've been Australian captain. With the circus of my life and my commitments, playing cricket is my meditation. Nobody can contact me here. I don't have any other things to do. All the shit that has been going on before and after Hughesy's passing, whatever is going on in my life, it can't touch me while I am playing cricket.

I go into the middle with a clear goal. My mind is entirely focused on improving our team's position and making a hundred for Hughesy. Nothing can get between me and that goal. Every ball seems very simple, only asking me one question: this is where I am, so hit me or leave me. I can sense that my body is stiff and uncomfortable, especially down my lower back into my hamstrings, but I don't feel any pain.

It's an overcast day, unusual for Adelaide in summer, and after about ten overs we have to go off for a rain delay. Smithy is on 98 and I'm 85. He says to me, 'I'm going to walk over to the 408 sign when I make my hundred. Do you want to come with me?'

I decline. Making a hundred will be Smithy's moment, and he deserves to celebrate it in his own way. I let him know that he can do what he wants.

First ball after the resumption, Smithy tucks it away for two and we hug. He runs off to the 408 sign and raises his bat and helmet to thank Hughesy up in the sky. There seem to be a lot of numerical coincidences around. The next run I score takes our innings total to 408. The crowd get on their feet and give Hughesy a standing ovation. He was only living in Adelaide for his last couple of years, but he loved the place and the feeling was mutual.

We're off again for rain, but in due course I get my hundredth run. My celebrations are very low-key. I know Hughesy's family are watching, and I know that they know I'm doing this for him. It doesn't need to be any more demonstrative than that. Like I say, when I'm in the middle today I feel very quiet and very numb. It's not like any other innings.

And it's the last hundred I will make for Australia.

Maybe there's a part of me – maybe it's the spirit of Hughesy inside me – but something in my heart knows that this is the end. Of what? Not of my career. But it's the end of something. I get to 128 and am out just before stumps. We make the declaration overnight at seven for 517, and the next morning I'm able to take the field. I can't do the constant crouching necessary to stand in a catching position, but manage to get through the day fielding at mid-on and mid-off. On such a good batting wicket, we have to work very hard for every dismissal, and I am at the centre of the decision-making, even though there is still that part of me that is elsewhere.

I manage to bat again in the second innings, but the back is grabbing and I don't last long. I just want to win this match and get into rehab again. India are chasing a big target, but we are going to have to work and work on a pitch that is showing no sign of deteriorating. We're into the last day, the 44th over of the second innings, when Virat Kohli pushes a ball from Nathan Lyon to my right-hand side at mid-wicket. I take a few steps and reach out to field it and throw it, and – *pop*. There is no mistaking a hamstring when it goes, but this is unfamiliar. I did my left hamstring in Perth and again in Zimbabwe two months ago, the same hamstring I've strained about six times in the last two years. Not once have I done my right. But I've done it now. Scans will show I've ripped it off the bone. I don't need a diagnosis. It feels like this has been waiting to happen.

For the second time in the match, I've embarrassed myself. I was embarrassed to do my back and retire hurt while batting, and now I'm embarrassed to be walking off on the fifth day with a torn hamstring. I have finished every game I have started. Today, I've let my teammates down. I've let my country down.

Later in the afternoon we win the game, thanks to some fantastic spin bowling from Lyono, who takes seven wickets, and great support from all the bowlers and fielders. As I'm watching from the dressing room, I'm happy, of course, but I don't get the exhilaration I always get from winning a Test match. There is something strange happening inside me. I can't say *I don't care*, but that's what it feels like – or what it doesn't feel like. It's not a specific feeling, but an absence of feeling. I'm watching everything from the outside. Usually I am the most bubbly person in the room in these circumstances, but the numbness has fully set in. In the press conference, I admit that this could be the end of my career. It just comes out. I feel nothing. I'm not going to stop. Far from it, I'm going to put every bit of my being into getting back into this series, or if not, into the one-day series with India, or if not that, the World Cup and the Ashes. That's my aim.

But I can't deny it. Something that has always been in me is not in me any more.

Nine months later, that *something* has not come back. The England tour is turning into a personal and team disaster. We don't make enough runs in the First Test in Cardiff, we bounce back to square the series at Lord's, but then we suffer horrendous first-day collapses in Birmingham and Nottingham. Throughout, I barely contribute a run. I admit publicly that the team is carrying me, something that makes me sick in the guts, but it's true, it's staring us all in the face. I would like to say I can't understand why my batting is off, but that wouldn't be true either. I can understand it all too well.

Between that Adelaide Test match last December and now, I have clawed my way towards my old reality: the pre-Hughesy normality. Through December and January, I threw all my focus into getting myself up for a massive occasion, a World Cup at home. I was privileged to be part of Australia's team that won the World Cup in 2007, in the West Indies. The last time the cup was staged in Australia, though, I was ten years old. My body is giving up on me, but I can't live without this challenge to get myself up for. Shoving all the trauma of Hughesy and getting injured to one side, I force myself into the old tunnel vision, so that all I can see ahead of me is the World Cup and then the Ashes.

After the Adelaide Test match against India, I hold a number of conversations with Alex Kountouris, Peter Brukner and my surgeon. I go into hospital for an operation to repair my right hamstring, and, lying on the couch at home, I watch every ball of the Border–Gavaskar Trophy series, which our boys seal 2–0 with a win in the Second Test in Brisbane. In the final two matches, on dead-flat wickets in Melbourne and Sydney, I see signs that the boys are buggered, especially the bowlers. The lifeless pitches have something to do with it, but I have a feeling that the emotional let-down is catching up with several of them.

My summer is all about rehab. In consultation with Alex and the doctors, I believe I can be fit for the World Cup in 12 weeks. I train a minimum of three times a day. I've never trained so hard in my life. From the day I get out of hospital, I am straight into it, repeating certain exercises 15 times a day.

Throughout all that, I never give myself time to grieve for my mate. I'm thinking about Hughesy 24/7, but my mind hasn't been able to stop and take it all in. I'm still half-expecting a text from him. His number is in my phone. He's still there, in a corner of my mind.

During the Boxing Day Test in Melbourne, I go to the MCG to do some guest commentary duties in the Channel Nine box. Pat Howard comes and we have a sit-down conversation in which he gives me a date I have to be fit by, if I'm to be selected for the World Cup. That date is 4 March, or three months after the injury took place. Australia's first World Cup match, the tournament-opener against England in Melbourne, will be on 14 February. I am ecstatic.

'Mate,' I say to Pat, 'thank you, I will be fit and ready to go by then.'

On 11 January, Rod Marsh calls me with some different news. 'Michael, congratulations, you've been selected for the World Cup and you're captain, but you have to be

100 per cent fit by the Bangladesh game on 21 February.' He's implying that they're doing me a favour by giving me one week's grace after the tournament opener. The date he has given me is ten weeks after my surgery.

But I'm stunned. 'I beg your pardon? That's two weeks earlier than Pat Howard told me last week.'

Rod is firm on it, so I call Alex. 'We've only got until the Bangladesh game,' I say.

'Mate, I don't think you can do it,' Alex says.

'I can do it,' I say, before hanging up and calling Pat Howard.

'What's going on?' I say, quite angry now about the mixed messages.

'We're preparing as if you're not going to make it,' Pat says.

'I'm going to prove you wrong,' I snap.

Throughout January, while our team is playing a one-day series against India and England, I am constantly on the phone with Rod, Pat and Darren Lehmann, arguing. It's gone from them doing this to me before the First Test, then sucking up to me to get me to play in Adelaide when I wasn't ready, to now, as I see it, setting me up for failure.

It's definitely not personal. I don't have any hard feelings against Rod, Pat or Darren, all of whom I respect as individuals. What I can't come to grips with is how the system seems to have changed so radically. My capacity, and the medical staff's, to make decisions about my fitness has been eroded by the changes to the system over the past four years.

I'm up for the fight. If they want to challenge me, I'll take them on. I'm doubly determined to have a red-hot crack at getting myself fit for the World Cup and proving a few people wrong. I intensify my rehab. Alex says, 'Understand that if you break during this, you'll break badly, and you'll be back to the start.'

He means, *Go too hard at this, and there will be no World Cup.*

I accept this. I know the risks. I visit the surgeon for regular testing and talk to him on the phone. He is always most encouraging, giving me confidence. That spurs me on to walk faster, get up the stairs, do everything I have to do. I also start running a little earlier than expected.

As if to push me closer to the brink, CA tells me I can't do my key rehab sessions with Duncan Kerr, my personal trainer. Since I met him when I was 17, Duncan has been like a family member, compassionate and caring and always available when I need to share my concerns over a meal or a session in the gym. CA has always accepted how much I rely on Duncan, but suddenly now there is no trust. I am seething, feeling that they want me to fail. My mind is restless with paranoia. *Have they turned against me because of all the arguments we've been having, or just because they think I'm not a good enough player and there's someone else they want to pick?*

For the sessions where they are measuring my progress, CA send me to Paul Chapman, the physio at Cricket NSW. They give me a list of nine different tests I have to pass. Chappo's a good guy, and I have no issue with him at all.

But it's a sign that they won't take my word and want to oversee every move I make, and tick every box legally in case there is another fight. They're covering their arses. They're not even trusting Alex, their own physiotherapist, I presume because they believe he's too close to me, and I am annoyed because I think they have taken his judgment out of the equation.

There is not going to be any room for subjectivity. I am not going to be asked about my sense of my improvement or well-being. Nor is Alex, and nor is my surgeon. It's going to be very black-and-white. I can either pass these tests and I'm in, or fail them and I'm out. I ask Chappo for the description of the tests, so I can train towards them privately and see where I'm at. It's a long list: I have to do a set of six 'run-a-threes', each within 11 seconds; complete a two-kilometre time trial in under 7 minutes 30 seconds (a time I've never done before – the fastest I've ever done is 7:34); and a lot more involving strength, speed and distance. There is a strength test on a machine in Melbourne that I have never done before in my life. It's a long list, with clearly set requirements at the outer limits of my capacity.

Nobody at CA has asked me the simple question, 'Michael, what do *you* think?' It's a courtesy I'm sure Ricky Ponting, Steve Waugh, Allan Border or Greg Chappell would have been offered. It's a courtesy *I* would have been offered for the past ten years.

Throughout those weeks I am an angry man. My guts feel like they're full of bile. I have had enough. I feel that the inconsistency, the arbitrary change to policy, is directed at me personally. After all these years, this is an absolute mockery. They have always taken unfit players on tours, and into tournaments and series, and let them work their way into fitness in the early stages. Andrew Symonds in 2007 and Mike Hussey in 2011 were both taken to World Cups when unfit, but got themselves right as the tournaments proceeded. Why have they changed these processes, just for me?

I'm hell for Kyly to live with, and I'm a pain in the butt to a lot of people who are phoning me, with the best intentions, wanting to help. My back has reached the state where Kyly has to help me put my shoes and socks on; I can't do it myself. When Alex can't do it, she will give me a massage. She can see what's happening: I've been so set on doing my job for the Hughes family and my teammates, I haven't been allowing myself some peace and quiet to grieve. But I can't yet see that for myself.

I feel that my only way through this is to build a forcefield.

I'm on my own. This is why I batted again in Adelaide – for Hughesy. This is why I had the surgery. This is why I'm putting myself through torturous, tedious rehab. I don't care about what anyone says, or how anything looks. I don't know how Kyly is putting up with me. Any activity that doesn't help me get to my goal, I am not touching. To regain my focus, I send myself into a state of frenzied, stubborn determination. In my mind, I picture Tiger Woods when he was preparing for a big putt: he would crouch down and block the world out with his hands, look down a tunnel where he existed alone, so there was just him and the ball he had to get into the hole. That's how I feel, every day. Cricket Australia and others are throwing rocks at me. I'm going to let them bounce off.

Anyone with any distance, or objectivity, would be able to see what I am going through. It would be clear as day. It *is* clear as day to me, once the Ashes are over, once I've retired from international cricket. Through that period from November 2014 to August 2015, I am burnt out by a lifetime of cricket and unable to stop and take in the enormity of Hughesy's passing.

I can understand this now, looking back. It's so obvious. But due to the situation swirling around me, and my own personality flaws, I will not step back and understand this until after I have retired. Then, it will be like a room with the light suddenly turned on. But until then, my stubbornness and combativeness, which have served me so well in cricket that I rely on them like a drug of addiction, are burying me deeper and deeper into my siege mentality. It's me against the world, and I rely on that to bring out my best.

Seeking comfort from my teammates is not an option. I confide in Shane Warne, but as far as the current team is concerned, I maintain my facade of confidence. I pass the fitness tests and make it into the World Cup, but the last thing I want is for them to know what shit I am going through. When you're captain, you don't want your team to feel they need to help you or take your side. They're all recovering from Hughesy's death in their own ways, getting over their own burn-out from the toughest summer of their lives, and picking themselves up for the World Cup. They have their own battles. I am so deeply immersed in my own problems, I don't realise how clearly they can see what's happening to me. Hard as I try to be normal, my teammates know that I'm not. Behind closed doors, some of them are doing their best to look after me. I don't make it easy for them.

The World Cup seems to make it all worthwhile. We get to the big stage, the final at the MCG, and produce our most thorough performance of the tournament. I have Hughesy constantly in my mind. Through Cricket Australia, I am asked to wear his one-day shirt, number 64, in the final. Another player suggests we all wear Hughesy's number.

Hughesy's family have made it clear to me, however, that they want the least amount of publicity possible, so as players we agree to drop those plans. All the drawn-out focus on Hughesy through the summer has been extremely hard on Greg, Virginia, Jason, Megan and the rest of their family. Steve Smith and David Warner were making hundreds almost every time they batted against India, and of course they felt they had to keep on saluting Hughesy at every milestone, as it might have been noticed, and over-interpreted, if they stopped. But for the Hughes family, accolades are not going to change anything.

Having been absent from the summer's cricket since Adelaide, I want to pay my own tribute to my mate, but at the same time I don't want to intensify his family's hurt. I carry my black armband with Hughesy's name and number on it in my pocket, and in the final, I wear it.

I make my decision about retiring from one-day cricket the night after the semi-final, in which we beat India at the SCG. I tell Kyly that night, and the next day, before giving a press conference, I let the players know.

Scoring 74 in the final, to help steer our chase safely past New Zealand, is gratifying, after all the boys have done to get us into that position. It is also my last chance to walk onto an Australian oval and say thank you to the fans.

At that point, I have no set plan to quit Test cricket. I am contemplating doing it after the Ashes series, but haven't made up my mind yet. I am on a high after the World Cup and can see that the team is building so well towards the Ashes.

I have never won a Test series in England, either as a player or as captain. In 2005, 2009 and 2013, we came home empty-handed. Every time was shattering. Now, in 2015, I think we have a very strong squad. After the Ashes, win or lose, I will take some time off and contemplate retirement. But after the World Cup final, I am hell-bent on that one last frontier.

I should see the writing on the wall, but part of the problem of my state of mind is my inability to have any insight into myself. Through December and January, I put on the blinkers: *I have to get ready for the World Cup.* Through February and March, it's: *We have to win the World Cup.* In March and going up to our departure in late May, the obsession has become: *We've won the World Cup, that's awesome, and now we have to win the Ashes.* The drive that has kept me going throughout my career has mutated into a kind of angry, ambitious mania. Throughout it all, I am unable to stand back and think about the main thing, which is that the game I love has killed my mate. I can't afford to stop and let myself think about that. It might divert me from the next battle I've got myself into.

We go to the West Indies for a two-Test tour on our way to England. The wickets and conditions are poor, but in practice and on the field I try to be my usual self. It is off the field that the darkness catches up with me.

Kyly can't come on that tour, as she has work commitments. She has also just fallen pregnant with our first child, which only she and I know about at this stage. Her absence hits me hard. Previously, if Kyly wasn't on tour – or even if she was – I would spend time with Hughesy every night. Often, we formed a trio. I think of our last dinner together, in the Emirates during the Pakistan series a month before Hughesy passed away. Kyly and I were on our way out to dinner together, and as we were leaving, she said, 'Have you invited Phillip?' She was not the only wife in the team who sometimes looked forward to Hughesy's presence at dinner more than her husband's. A bit of light-hearted conversation at the end of the day, with someone we trusted absolutely, was always the best tonic.

Knowing that Hughesy isn't going to be in the West Indies, I beg Kyly to come, and when she says she can't, I say, 'I don't know how I'm going to get through this tour.'

During the days in the Caribbean, I try to be my normal self in team meetings and training and matches, but when the night-time comes, the sadness builds up and I am not in the mood for being with my teammates. I don't want them to see how low and lonely I am.

I end up sitting in my room each night watching every episode of every season of *Sons of Anarchy*. I don't leave my room for dinner once. I have room service and fall asleep. I have no inclination to do what I've been so keen to do on past West Indies tours – go to the beach, have a drink, talk cricket, hang out with teammates. I'm just numb and empty. I go through my daily routines like a robot: play, recovery, back to the room, order food, *Sons of Anarchy*, sleep.

The worst tour of my life? No contest. Most tours felt like the best of my life.

So then we go on to England, and while I am constantly lifted and enthused by the preparation my teammates put in, while I am ecstatic to have my wife – and her baby bump – with me, while I am more determined than ever to retain those Ashes . . . there is still something bleak and heavy sitting inside me. It sets off a chain reaction. The helmet is driving me nuts. Every setback around the team, from the career-ending injury to Ryan Harris at the beginning of the tour through to my losing the toss at Trent Bridge, feels like another lead weight. I can't shake it off, but I can't see it clearly either. I feel personally to blame when we don't win the series. For the first time in my life, cricket feels like a trap I have to get out of.

Uncharacteristically, I am brought down by every bad omen. Before the Second Test, Brad Haddin has to leave the team when his daughter Mia suffers health problems relating to the neuroblastoma she has had since the start of her life. His deputy Peter Nevill stands in for him at Lord's and plays very well. For the Third Test, the selectors decide to stay with Peter, which causes some confusion in the group. Is Hadds being left out for form reasons and, if so, what is the effect of his family situation? Has he been effectively penalised for taking time out to be with Mia and his family? For years, cricketers have not wanted to risk losing their place, so they let family dramas unfold in their absence. We live in more enlightened times – or do we? Since Boof became coach, he has made a big deal of putting families first. But when Hadds is not reinstated for the Third Test, lots of guys are scratching their heads and wondering.

I see both sides of the Haddin decision. There is a certain logic, but there is also an emotional fall-out. I don't think the selectors expected the emotional side. They thought that because Boof had talked to some of the senior players and they said they understood, then it would be completely fine with the entire group. The selectors said, 'Hadds, we were thinking of dropping you in the West Indies and not bringing you to England. You didn't perform in Cardiff and that forced the issue.' If Mia's setback hadn't happened, they might still have gone ahead and dropped him. It was a performance-based decision.

But I don't think the consequences were fully thought through. If Hadds, our vice-captain, was in any danger of being dropped, he should not have been in England.

Same with Shane Watson, who was dropped after our loss in Cardiff. If they were only going to get one Test match to prove themselves, they shouldn't have come in the first place. Picking teams on performance is absolutely 100 per cent fine, but it's a bad thing for team harmony to have your senior men given one Test match and then spending the tour running Gatorades. They don't have to grizzle; it's going to be evident in their morale, and it's going to affect the morale of those who replace them.

Nev is pumped to have his opportunity, but out of respect to Hadds, who has been his mentor, he doesn't want to show it too much. I think Nev feels he has to walk on eggshells. Everyone knows that it is devastating to sportsmen of Hadds's and Watto's experience and pride to be told their Test careers are effectively over so early in such an important tour.

I wonder what I can do. First and foremost, I am focused on winning. I want the selectors to give me a team to win. That's all that matters. If omitted senior players are pissed off, we can try to deal with that. I speak to Hadds about whether he wants to go home, and say I will support him either way. He wants to stay and help. The option doesn't arise so much with Watto, who needs to be there on standby if Mitchell Marsh, his replacement, or another batsman gets injured.

All up, it is just another thing to add to the list of setbacks. After the First Test loss, we have two of our three most experienced players on the bench, Rhino gone, and Mitch Johnson showing some effects of burn-out.

And then there's my batting. Whether I want to accept it or not, every time I put that new model of helmet on I am thinking about Hughesy. I go out to bat in Cardiff, wearing it in a Test match for the first time. My vision is impaired, compared to when I was wearing my old helmet, and my movements are tentative. With my personality, my gear and routines honed to such a fine point in 12 years of international cricket, I can't cope with the change.

My batting is sheepish. When the bowlers are running in, I go onto the back foot to defend, but my head isn't over the ball. On the front foot also, I'm not getting there. It's only a few inches out, and a few milliseconds off the pace, but that makes all the difference. The wicket at Lord's is a belter, and I pull a ball from Mark Wood straight to square leg. When I need one of those little things to go my way and throw the switch and relax me again, it's not to be found.

At Edgbaston and Trent Bridge, the change in pitch conditions is mind-blowing. Having previously being presented with dry pitch after dry pitch, suddenly we have spring-like English conditions. I win the toss at Edgbaston and bat first. The ball will swing early, but my view is that if we make 240 in the first innings, we will win the game. We just have to get through to lunch on the first day. Instead, we barely get into the afternoon session – all out for 136 in 36 overs. England bowl and catch superbly, and we don't bat well.

I contribute 13 runs for the match. In practice sessions over the past few months, I've been preparing for days like this, when the ball is moving around, but none of it matters, because my head isn't in the right place.

Trent Bridge is the worst wicket I have seen in 12 years as an international cricketer. This game should not start. The pitch needs four hours of sunshine on it before it's playable. I am sure that whoever wins the toss will bowl the opposition out for less than 120. I don't say that, of course, particularly when I call incorrectly. My teammates are no doubt thinking, *I wish he'd won the toss.*

David Warner and Steve Smith are out within the first over. I'm in, wearing this helmet. For my entire career, my helmet was part of my own skin, totally natural. Now I can't stop feeling it and seeing it.

But I have a plan. Always, what has worked for me is this: the more dangerous the bowling, the more positively you have to bat. There is no point in waiting for them to get me. I won't be a sitting duck. I will play with intent and if they get me, they get me.

But no matter what I try, it refuses to work. It's cricket, and I am caged up inside my own mind. I urge myself to watch the ball, but thoughts buzz around in my head like a cloud of flies blurring my vision. I'm not watching the ball. I think I am, but I'm not. Everything seems faster. Stuart Broad is bowling at 135 km/h, and it feels like 150 km/h. When your mind is clear, none of those things matter. You just watch the ball, have a smile on your face, and react.

Instead, I go too hard at the ball and nick it to second slip. My mind is gone. I can't let go of the fear of getting hit, because sitting on my head, heavy and cumbersome, is an object that couldn't be a more stark reminder if it was a tombstone. On 27 November last year, we all realised, *Oh my f—ing God, in the sport we've loved all our lives, we can die. Not just get hurt, but die.*

Did we pick the wrong team? We'll never know. When things get chaotic in the first innings at Edgbaston and Trent Bridge, experienced players would have had plans and stuck to them without second-guessing. Hadds would have thought, *I've seen this before, my mind is clear, I'll hit the first ball for six.* Watto would have had a set plan and stuck to it. But would it have worked? To have Hadds and Watto in there playing the way they play, it may not have changed the outcome, but it would have created a different atmosphere in the changing room.

I take accountability. I should have been stronger with the selectors in demanding the team I wanted, and in sticking with it. I didn't push hard enough to have Peter Siddle in the team, and when he storms back in at The Oval, making a huge difference, it is too late for the Ashes. Once we lost Ryan Harris, we should have replaced him with a similar type of bowler.

But these things are always overtaken by the circumstances. Mitch Marsh scored three first-class hundreds in the first three games. How could they not choose him ahead of Watto? Mitchell Starc was outbowling everyone in the nets, and Josh Hazlewood was a lot faster than Sidds. We were asking every batsman coming out of the nets, 'Who's bowling best?' Always the answer was 'Starc and

Hazlewood'. The selectors went for speed over accuracy and consistency, and practice performance over experience.

My responsibility is in not pushing an alternative view, so there's no point trying to dodge that now. I became so bitterly disappointed with my own form, trying so hard to fix it, that I wasn't thinking straight in all those other areas.

I retire after the Fifth Test, which we win, making the series result 3–2 in England's favour. I go on holidays with Kyly. I slow down, finally.

I begin to see clearly.

The Australian cricket team is in a fantastic place, with lots of talented young guys working extremely hard under Steve Smith's captaincy. It's their time. I can walk away, as one of six retirees this year – with Brad Haddin, Shane Watson, Mitchell Johnson, Chris Rogers and Ryan Harris – knowing that we are passing the Australian team to a generation who can own this next era. They need fresh ideas and a new leader.

It's time for me to go.

20

OBSESSIVE AND COMPULSIVE

I wish I knew then what I know now. By the time I'm retired, that is a recurring theme. I wish I knew *myself*, when I was playing, with the insight I gained once I found peace and distance from cricket, and fatherhood. I might have enjoyed those last years more.

Fatherhood helps loosen me up and soften me. I've had a niece and nephew for several years and have been looking forward to becoming a father since I was young. When Kelsey Lee is born on 16 November 2015, several weeks premature and just 2.1 kilograms, so that she has to stay in hospital for five weeks, she is so tiny and delicate. She melts me. She has me wrapped around her finger, and I have such admiration for the maternal love coming from Kyly, handling all this while still being the great person she is. She's the perfect mother. I don't know if anyone can ever be ready for kids, but she is as ready as anyone could be. She never complained once during a sometimes difficult pregnancy, and very soon she and Kelsey Lee have become thick as thieves. I've always respected women, but it goes to a new level now. Seeing Kyly as a mother makes me think of Mum, who taught me so much about love, and of Leanne, who is such a great mother to her two kids. If I can be half as good a parent as Mum, Dad and Leanne, I will be proud. I'm now as passionate about being the best father and best provider I can be as I was about being the best cricketer I could be.

I wonder, if I had this experience earlier, this softening and humanising, whether it might have made me a more compassionate captain.

After becoming a father, I finally press PAUSE, and look at the day, the moment, to soak it up. I wish I did that more during my career, stop to enjoy the journey as it was happening. I got to play with some of the greatest cricketers to play the game, win World Cups, win Test series, meet fantastic people . . . It was not just what I'd dreamed of back in my bedroom at Liverpool, it was *better* than the dream.

When it was good, I couldn't get enough cricket. In 2012, I started the year with 329 against India in the New Year's Test match at the SCG. It felt like I could bat another ten hours. The only thing that would stop me was when I felt we had enough runs to win the game. Two Test matches later, I made 210 against the Indians at the Adelaide Oval and we completed a 4–0 series win.

I scored another hundred in the one-day series at home, and then went to the West Indies, where we won the Tests 2–0. I couldn't get enough cricket; I played my only season of the Indian Premier League, a six-match stint with the Pune Warriors. With the Australian team, I toured England and the United Arab Emirates for one-day series with England and Pakistan.

Somewhere in the middle of it, I slipped away to Wolgan Valley for our wedding.

Is there another cricket match on somewhere? I'll be in it. Days after getting back from the Emirates, I play a one-day domestic match and then three back-to-back Sheffield Shield matches for New South Wales. Then it's into a Test series with South Africa at home. The runs are just flooding out of my bat. I make 259 not out in Brisbane, and then 230 in Adelaide. My year ends with 106 in the Boxing Day Test match against Sri Lanka. By now, my hamstrings are barely connected with my legs, my back is killing me, and the year has exhausted Punter and Huss into retirement. What just happened?

I don't stop to smell the roses – I want them to keep on sprouting. When I make the triple-hundred in Sydney, the highest score in 130 years of Test cricket on my home ground, do I sit back and reflect on it? Not for a moment. I am not content; I focus on how I can get better.

After the next three double-hundreds, I always think my game can improve. My goal isn't to maintain that form, but to get better still. I never take a moment to reflect on what I've done. I fear that if I stop and look back, I will seize up.

Every morning, I get out of bed with the sparrows and say to myself, *You can get better every day*.

It's a lot of stress to put on yourself, every single day of your life. And it's only when I'm married and living with Kyly, and she's getting to know me better and better, she tells me, 'You're obsessive-compulsive.' It's not a medical diagnosis, but it might as well be. She can see that for everything I'm achieving, I am unable to press PAUSE on life, and if I continue this way it's going to damage me in the long run.

The signs have been there since the beginning. When I was a kid, my room was spotless. I made my own bed and packed my own school bag, had to have everything just so. I wouldn't even let my own mum pack my lunchbox. What kind of boy is that fussy about having things a certain way?

There's a story my parents tell about my neat-freakness that goes right back to when I was a toddler. I was given a set of Tonka trucks. They were my pride and joy – so much so that I would not take them outside the house, in case they got a speck of dirt on them. One of my cousins came over once, and, surprise surprise, took my Tonka trucks out to the sandpit in the back yard. I blew my top, got them back inside, and made sure they didn't go out again.

I was obsessive in my fears, too. There was my fear of someone breaking into the house and my bedroom being near the front door – one reason why I slept with my cricket bat. I was afraid of flying. I liked the beach, but didn't like the sand. I was afraid of sharks, and had regular nightmares that they were chasing me. There was a physical dimension to it: as a child, I regularly broke out in sweats, and at night I would walk around and talk in my sleep. The physical symptoms seemed to go hand in hand with my impatience and my incessant need to be active.

If I was like that naturally, as a kid, don't even ask about my cricket kit. It's immaculate in its neatness. I pack it exactly the same way every time and have to know where everything is. I drink a certain amount of hydrolytes before every game. I wear the same brand of shoes for nine-tenths of my career. I carry my helmet on flights; I won't allow it to travel in the cargo hold. Once, when I was at the Australian Cricket Academy, Rod Marsh took my dad into the team changing room while we were out in the field.

'Take a look around,' Rod said. 'Now, guess who owns that corner.'

Dad could see what he meant. The entire room was a mess, total chaos, but in this corner, every bit of equipment and clothing was laid out perfectly. It was spotless and well organised.

'Where does this kid come from?' Rod said.

'I don't know,' Dad said, 'that's the way he is.'

These are not superstitions, as such. I don't have to step onto the field left foot first, or count a certain number of steps in the middle, or place my faith in some lucky talisman. But it might be worse than having superstitions. It is the absolute rigid need to stick to certain routines. When I'm in the middle, I mark my guard every single over: centre twice, leg stump twice. Every single over, whether I'm playing for Western Suburbs, New South Wales or Australia.

It might have more widespread effects than simply following superstitions, because my need for these routines is hyper-rational and is who I am. You can't tamper with it. It's what made me me. I always wore inner gloves inside my batting gloves, but inners inside-out, because I didn't like feeling the seams against my skin. If a changing room attendant found my inners and turned them the right way out, I changed them back. If I marked my guard and a fieldsman came and scuffed it out, I re-marked it. These things were what made me me. It limited my social life when I was young. My friends would be going out on Friday or Saturday night, and I would say, 'Not me – cricket tomorrow.' I was totally disciplined about being in bed by 8.30 pm. I was full-on, and insatiable. I wanted to play every day. Indoor cricket, outdoor cricket, playing games was the best type of preparation for playing more games. Play and play and play.

After I got dropped from the Australian team in late 2005, it only became more frenzied. I scolded myself for letting my focus drift. From now on, my training routines were made of iron. There was no sponsor commitment, no friendship, nothing in the world that I would allow to interfere with my dedication. I enclosed myself in my bubble and saw only what I wanted to see. I needed that discipline if I wanted success. Always the next thing, and always more.

Part of being who I was, was never to stop to reflect on little achievements and find some inner peace. I loved winning and scoring runs, and celebrated those achievements, but I kept and relied on that fanaticism about success. This manic self-discipline, this obsession with getting better, this compulsion for certain routines, was more than a set of habits, it was an addiction, because I believed I would be better with it and lost without it.

During a Test match, the routine cannot be changed. The night before a Test match, I have room service. Then I'm asleep by ten o'clock, for eight hours, rising at six in the morning. As captain, I exude this obsessiveness through the team. My phone is never turned off. Whenever a teammate wants to text or call, 24 hours a day, I will answer it. I go to bed with my phone switched on.

In the changing room, waiting to bat, I am nervous, usually on my feet talking with anyone who will put up with me. During most breaks, I have a shower to freshen myself up. It's what has worked for me since I was a child, and if you even think of persuading me to change it now, I'll bite your head off.

During those years of captaincy, I am less and less tolerant of anyone going outside the team program. In their spare time, I am more than happy for my teammates to do whatever the hell they want. That's what I've always done: when I switch off, I run my own race. But when it comes to cricket, I am obsessed with the team doing everything as a team.

That year of 2012, when I score all those runs, is the highlight of my career but also, in a way, the worst thing for me; *because it vindicates all this obsessiveness and compulsiveness.* It tells me that I am right to follow this course in the way I have. And it tells me that I need to intensify my efforts if

I want to get better still. There's no little voice in me saying, *You need to limit this.* I'm thinking, this is how successful people operate. They throw every ounce of energy into what they're doing, and they switch off later. I will be the best I can be, and then walk out of cricket.

I have a bet with Steve Bernard in the West Indies in 2003 that I will retire by the time I'm 30 – this is before I've even played one Test match. But that's the cut-and-dried, impatient quality of my mind. I feel that if I fail to be the best cricketer I can be, I will never forgive myself. When in doubt, work harder, train more, the answer is always more.

It's not my brain but my body that eventually cries, *Stop!*

When I am 17 years old, playing for New South Wales Colts, suddenly my lower back feels like it's being grabbed by a vice. The pain is eye-watering. We go to hospital, where a scan shows two bulging discs and degeneration in the lower part of my back. Every now and then, through the years, I tear a part of the disc lining, which causes the disc to bulge out between the vertebrae. That's what causes the pain. It's an incurable condition and will only get worse while I am pushing my body to the max. A disc can pop out whether I'm running in training, twisting to get out of the way of a bouncer, or just getting out of bed. I can merely shift my weight from one side to the other, and a spasm will bring me to my knees.

The solution, early in my career, is to have bed rest for four or five days, and then slowly get back into full movement. Through force of will and a fair bit of good luck, I don't miss many matches. But it's like a ticking time bomb inside me, and it feeds my helter-skelter mentality. I have to go out and get everything I can right now, because soon I'm going to be a crock.

I don't let myself contemplate the possibility that the two things might be linked: my obsessiveness and my back problems.

As my career goes on, there are generally two different types of days. Eighty per cent of the time, I wake up with stiffness in the lower back. In my morning shower, it's impossible to pick up the soap if I drop it. Early in the morning, I'm stiff and sore moving around. The hardest part of my day is putting on my shoes and socks in the morning. To lift my foot up and get a sock or shoe on it, I have to reach down awkwardly with one hand, get a grip on the foot, and bring it up as I lean back. Then I can work the sock on with the other hand.

My back hates flexion – bending forwards – and rotation, pretty much the main movements for a batsman. On the other hand, the more extension, or bending backwards, the better. I learn to sleep on my stomach or my back, never my side.

If I bat or field for several hours, the next morning my back will be so stiff that I think, *I'm not rolling out today, I'm staying in bed*. But I am playing a game and I want to win and the greatest point of pride in my entire life is that I get through the first nine years of my Test career without missing a single Test match through injury. So I get up, and it starts again.

Those are the good days.

The other 20 per cent are the days when I have had an episode. I do it playing a cut shot or dodging a bouncer, moving into flexion and twisting while I go at the ball. I'm most vulnerable after fielding all day, flexing and bending in slips. I have Alex Kountouris treat me for 45 minutes before every playing day. He tries taping me, putting me in Thermoskin, and asks everyone in the industry for new ideas. He treats me again for 45 minutes after play. For ten years, I have treatment every breakfast and every evening, and sometimes also another session in mid-morning, after training.

Then there is nerve pain down through my hamstrings, a pins-and-needles feeling, because the hamstrings are connected to the lower back. I get a burning sensation down the back of my right leg. When my back is feeling it, my hamstrings work overtime to compensate, and soon they're gone too. The nerve damage echoes down my limbs. I lose sensitivity through my right shin, and my right big toe is almost totally numb. I lose strength and definition in my right calf.

Injections relieve the pain. I lose track of how many cortisone injections I receive to clear up the hamstring pain, the back pain, the glute pain, injections simply to neutralise the pain in the nerve root sleeve. When Kyly is about to have our baby daughter, I'm gleefully telling her all about the epidural she is going to have. I'm a veteran of anaesthesia.

Knowing I have this condition from such a young age, I prepare my mind to retire at 30. But I make it to that age, and soon after I turn 30 I am given the captaincy of Australia.

Later that year, 2011, I go with Alex to see a surgeon on the Gold Coast. My back and hamstrings are in a bad way, possibly related to the amount of family stress we've been through during the year, and it looks like I may not be able to go to Sri Lanka for the Test and one-day tour. The New South Wales team doctor, John Orchard, supports an idea that the surgeon puts forward, of an operation that goes in through my stomach and replaces the worst of the discs. He says that's what will be needed if I injure it again. I resist, not wanting to risk the possible complications of such a major procedure. I am the captain of my country; I cannot risk six months out of the game, or even the possibility of it all ending. Now that I have made it to 30, I am not prepared to let go. There's too much at stake.

Having refused the operation, I defy all expectations and get myself fit enough to play. From Sri Lanka onwards, I go out and have the best year of my life with the bat.

But it comes at a cost, which I'm just putting off day by day, pushing into the future.

I take anti-inflammatory tablets regularly, and often other painkillers as well. We try to use the least amount of medication. I know there's a risk of developing a dependency on the painkillers, and John Orchard and Alex keep a close eye on everything that I'm taking. From 2012, when the pain begins to mount up and the injuries compound,

John Orchard warns me that there's a risk of tolerance – needing more and more to get the same effect. But if I don't take the medication, I can't get on the field. I say to John, 'Let me take what I can to play the next game, and we'll deal with it later.'

'You might need to miss this series,' he cautions.

'Just keep me going for now, and if it blows out, it blows out.'

John suggests I save up those cortisone injections for special occasions, due to the limit on how much I can take before it loses its effectiveness, but my view is that every game for Australia is equally important. I don't try to 'pace out' my career in that sense. I only think of getting through today, and I'm pig-headed about it.

In a Shield game against Victoria in 2014, I do my back on 70 and come off. The New South Wales physio says, 'You can't go back out there.' I reply, 'I'm going back out there.' I can't move, I can barely run – but the team needs me in this situation, and I go out and bat on.

It affects my game and my whole life, but I battle on to adjust to it. I lose the back-foot strength to get up on my right foot. By 2015, I am moving into the back-foot position against the short ball, but my weight is on my front foot, because I've lost the strength in my right calf. Finally, my performances reach breaking strain.

My mood suffers too. I am not trying to use it as an excuse: in fact the opposite. My view is that I made the choice to continue my career in this condition, so I can't complain about the consequences, a lot of which are actually positive. People might wonder if I would have been a better cricketer without the bad back, but I see it the other way. Without needing to care for my back, I wouldn't have trained as hard, wouldn't have taken as good care of myself, wouldn't have kept that focus. It might even have made me a better cricketer. But at the same time, anyone with serious back pain knows that it's not just a localised feeling, it infiltrates your entire outlook on life and your relations with people. Mostly, what that means is that you lose patience quickly and you are terser than you would like.

It peaks at different times, and mostly I am able to disguise it in public. An exception is just before the 2013–14 Ashes series, when I give the captain's press conference on the eve of the First Test at the Gabba. I'm annoyed that someone in the media has been having a go at me, and give cranky 'Yes' or 'No' answers, leaving them in no doubt about my mood. What they don't know is that at a net session at the Allan Border Field, I have had another painful occurrence and for a little while there has been some doubt over whether I will be able to play. My back is giving me hell, and Cricket Australia are asking me to make public appearances on days when I can barely even walk.

This is the whole cocktail: my back, my obsessiveness, all coming together. I'm a terrible waiter, and I am consumed by this First Test. We have lost three Ashes series in a row. We didn't win a game in England. Last time Australia lost the Ashes at home, four years ago, the captain got sacked. In Brisbane I'm thinking, *If we beat these guys once, we'll win this series.* I am so fired up. I don't want to do any media or sponsor appearances, I just want to get my back right for this game.

Patience is not my strength, and time is crawling. I have been training so hard, working for six weeks on this plan of how I am going to deal with England's bowlers, and now I am sick of talking. Usually I am expansive in these press conferences, but it's all boiling up inside me. Behind every monosyllabic grunt, I'm thinking, *I've got nothing else to say to you people, whatever I say you're going to twist and turn it, you f—ing pricks who built me up in my first few years as the next Australian captain after one Test match. You pricks built me up, and now you take every possible opportunity to smash me.*

Talk about not enjoying my journey as much as I could! When we win the match and the Ashes, I celebrate with a vengeance. Literally. I haven't just got over the top of England, but all my enemies outside and all the demons inside. It's a joyous celebration, of course, but it has an edge of *F— you*.

The anger is a symptom of the last phase of my life as an international cricketer. Other Australian captains have talked about it, and I know I'm not the first. The back and hamstring pain, which is either constant or constantly shadowing me for my whole career, piles in on top of all the other irritations in the last two or three years. I respond in the old way, obsessively. I still drive myself to do more. I know it's stopped me from enjoying my journey as much as I could and should enjoy it, but inside the bubble, all I care about is sticking to my routines and fighting off my number one enemy, this physiological condition inside me.

During the 2015 Ashes tour, when I have failed with the bat in the first two Test matches, Darren Lehmann offers some wise counsel. 'Take the next county game off,' he says. I refuse. All through my career, I have answered every challenge by doing more, not less. I can't let up. More has always worked for me. I play against Derbyshire, and fail in the first innings. I still want to play every game and train in every session, even when the life is ebbing out of my batting. I don't know any other way.

Until I retire, when the fog lifts.

MY WORLD TEST 12

I'm lucky to have been a cricketer in the current era. Aside from all the other joy the game has brought me, I have played with and against some of the greatest cricketers of all time. Now is my chance to be a selector again! This is a Test team of the best I have shared a cricket field with.

MICHAEL SLATER

My first cricket hero. Like so many kids growing up in the early 1990s, I fell in love with the refreshing, exuberant attitude Slats brought to the game. It's easily forgotten in the Twenty20 era, when attack is much more the way of top-order batsmen, how Michael Slater changed the opener's role. He wasn't a slogger, he was an orthodox, solid, tight, dependable opening batsman who was also looking for every opportunity to score runs. Cracking fours off Phil deFreitas to start the 1994–95 Ashes series is one of many great memories he left. If you look up 'positive intent' in the dictionary, you would find a picture of Slats. I didn't play international cricket with him, but was lucky to share the field with him on a number of occasions for New South Wales.

MATTHEW HAYDEN

Having certain players in a team makes everyone walk taller. Matthew Hayden was like that in the Australian team I came into. Physically and psychologically, he could dominate the best attacks. He had a strong mental approach which he used to teach me many memorable lessons. He had been through his own struggles, and turned himself into one of the all-time greats. When I was struggling with my own form, he showed me a way forward.

RICKY PONTING

I have said a lot throughout this book about how much I admire Punter. He led Australian cricket from the front for so much of my career, it was hard to imagine life in the Test team after he retired in 2012. During my time, it was never possible to replace him. He was such a supreme batsman and mentor to young players, but if I could put his legacy in a nutshell, I would say that I most admired him for his performances with the bat when his country needed him most.

SACHIN TENDULKAR

The Indian master had the best batting technique I have ever seen. He played so straight, there were times when you thought you could bowl at him forever and never find a way through. His discipline to stop playing the cover drive while scoring a double-century at the SCG early in my career is something that left me awestruck. Sometimes you know that you have met your superior, and that was what Sachin was for me, and pretty much everyone who played with or against him.

BRIAN LARA

My other boyhood hero along with Michael Slater. Brian Lara had a glorious individual style, full of flourishes, beautiful to watch. He also had the mental toughness to score runs in any conditions, against the best bowling, all around the world. I came to value that most highly of all: his determination and his versatility. I only played against him in the last years of his career, but he had been my idol since I was a little boy. I still pinch myself to think that he was kind and generous enough to offer me the hand of friendship.

JACQUES KALLIS

For the all-rounder's position, I was tempted to pick Andrew Flintoff, the most difficult bowler I faced in Test cricket and an excellent middle-order batsman. But seriously? Jacques Kallis ended his career with a better batting average than Sachin Tendulkar and more wickets than Brett Lee. He took more catches than Mark Waugh. He batted number three and four, and bowled with the new ball, old ball, second new ball, whatever his team needed. The complete cricketer, he could not be left out of any World Test 12.

ADAM GILCHRIST

I saw a lot of great wicketkeeper-batsmen – M.S. Dhoni, Kumar Sangakkara, A.B. de Villiers, Brad Haddin and Brendon McCullum to name a few – but Gilly topped them all. Such a destructive batsman, he was a match-winner for Australia time after time. Early in my career, I was fortunate to have the best seat in the house, being up the other end during some big partnerships with him. Because his batting revolutionised the game and drew all the attention, people underrated him as a wicketkeeper, and he was also the best vice-captain I ever knew.

MITCHELL JOHNSON

The greatest athlete I played with. Give him a football, put him in the gym, and he'll achieve freakish things. He will win swimming races and hundred metre sprints, thrash you at tennis, and don't even mention table tennis – he is a prodigy. As cricketers, we went to the Australian Cricket Academy together and shared the field for much of our careers. He scored Test centuries and took many great catches, as well as being a great all-round fielder. He was a very quiet individual, but when he walked on the field he gave everything. His bowling, at its best, was terrifying, unplayable. We became closer as we got older, and he hit his peak when his efforts did so much to lift us to world number one after the 2013–14 Ashes and our away win over South Africa. I hope I got the best out of him as captain. I always knew how important he was to our success, and let him know how much we all valued him.

SHANE WARNE (Captain)

Enough said. It doesn't take me to say he was the greatest spin bowler of all time. Every respected poll of cricketers and cricket watchers would say the same. But I also think he was the best captain Australia never had. His insight into the game, from every aspect – tactical, physical, psychological – is second to none. He was a superb mentor and man-manager too. I count myself lucky to have had the benefit of his friendship and his cricket wisdom since the early days of my career.

DALE STEYN

I admired the way the South African spearhead grew through his career. He was extremely fast and hostile, but developed great control and the intelligence to bowl differently in different conditions. As skilful with reverse swing as anyone, he could also crank it up to over 150 km/h. We had some great battles on the field as we gave everything to get our countries on top. I value the runs I scored against him more highly than any others.

GLENN MCGRATH

The best fast bowler I've ever played with or against. Not the fastest, but definitely one of the smartest and most skilful. He was also a great friend to me and I'll never forget the intelligence he offered. When he bowled at me in the nets, I asked him to try to get me out, and he told me what he was trying. My cricket education went on a steep upward curve whenever he shared his knowledge. I feel sorry for any team who had to bat against Australia when McGrath and Warne were bowling.

MUTTIAH MURALITHARAN (Twelfth Man)

His tally of 800 Test wickets, a world record, speaks for itself. He was a tough competitor who never let up. When conditions were hard for him he was tight and persistent. When they favoured him, he was a nightmare. I loved facing spin and that was a strength of my game, but Murali challenged my skills to the utmost with every ball he bowled.

CAREER RECORDS

OVERVIEW

PROFILE

Full name:	Michael John Clarke
Born:	2 April 1981
Height:	178 cm (5 foot 10 inches)
Batting:	Right-hand batsman
Bowling:	Slow left-arm orthodox
Nicknames:	Pup, Clarkey
Role:	Middle-order batsman Australian captain
Test cap no:	389
ODI cap no:	149
ODI shirt no:	23

DOMESTIC TEAMS

New South Wales (2000–2016)
Hampshire (2004)
Pune Warriors India (2012–2013)
Kowloon Cantons (2016)

STATISTICS LEGEND

A	Played Away (opposition home ground)
Ave	Average
BBI	Best Bowling Innings
BF	Balls faced
Ct	Catches
D	Drawn
DNB	Did Not Bat
DNP	Did Not Play
Econ	Economy Rate
H	Played at Home
HS	High Score
Inn	Innings
L	Lost
Mat	Matches
N	Played at a Neutral Ground
NO *or* *	Not Out
NR	No Result
P	Played
Runs	Batting – runs scored; Bowling – runs conceded
SR	Strike Rate
T	Tied
W	Won
Wkts	Wickets taken
W/L	Win/Loss ratio
4s	Number of 4s scored
4w	Four wickets taken in an innings
6s	Number of 6s scored
5w	Five wickets taken in an innings
50	Number of half-centuries (50-plus but fewer than 100 runs) scored
100	Number of centuries (100-plus runs) scored
%D	Percentage Drawn
%L	Percentage Lost
%W	Percentage Won

DEBUTS & LAST MATCHES

TYPE	DEBUT	LAST MATCH
First-class	New South Wales v Tasmania at Sydney, 9 December 1999	Australia v England at The Oval, 20-23 August 2015
ODI	Australia v England at Adelaide, 19 January 2003	Australia v New Zealand at Melbourne, 29 March 2015
T20	Essex v Hampshire at Chelmsford, 2 July 2004	Pune Warriors v Kolkata Knight Riders at Pune, 19 May 2012
Test	Australia v India at Bangalore, 6–10 October 2004	Australia v England at The Oval, 20-23 August 2015
T20I	Australia v New Zealand at Auckland, 17 February 2005	Australia v Sri Lanka at Perth, 31 October 2010

INTERNATIONAL CRICKET: BATTING

CRICKET	MAT	INN	NO	RUNS	HS	AVE	BF	SR	100	50	4s	6s
Tests	115	198	22	8643	329*	49.10	15456	55.92	28	27	978	39
ODIs	245	223	44	7981	130	44.58	10104	78.98	8	58	665	53
T20Is	34	28	5	488	67	21.21	473	103.17	0	1	29	10

INTERNATIONAL CRICKET: BOWLING

CRICKET	MAT	INN	BALLS	RUNS	WKTS	BBI	AVE	ECON	CT	4w	5w
Tests	115	65	2435	1184	31	6/9	38.19	2.91	134	0	2
ODIs	245	106	2585	2146	57	5/35	37.64	4.98	106	1	1
T20Is	34	15	156	225	6	1/2	37.50	8.65	13	0	0

AWARDS

Allan Border Medal	2005, 2009, 2012, 2013
Australian Test Player of the Year	2009, 2012, 2013, 2014
***Wisden* Cricketer of the Year**	2010
***Wisden* Leading Cricketer in the World**	2012
ICC Cricketer of the Year	2013
ICC Test Player of the Year	2013

TEST PLAYER OF SERIES

SERIES	FIRST MATCH	WINNER
Trans-Tasman Trophy (Aus/NZ) in Australia, 2008/09	20/11/08	Australia 2–0
The Ashes (Aus/Eng) in England, 2009	08/07/09	England 2–1
Border–Gavaskar Trophy (Aus/Ind) in Australia, 2011/12	26/12/11	Australia 4–0
South Africa in Australia, 2012/13	09/11/12	South Africa 1–0
Warne–Muralitharan Trophy (Aus/SL) in Australia, 2012/13	14/12/12	Australia 3–0

ODI PLAYER OF SERIES

SERIES	FIRST MATCH	WINNER
Australia v Pakistan ODI Series in UAE, 2009	22/04/09	Australia 3–2
Australia in Sri Lanka, 2011	10/08/11	Australia 3–2
NatWest Series (Aus/Eng) in England, 2013	06/09/13	Australia 2–1

CAREER RECORDS: CAPTAINCY

TEST KEY STATISTICS: AS CAPTAIN

Matches Played:	47
Tosses Won:	24 (51.06%)
Not Outs:	10
Aggregate Runs:	3946
Highest Score:	329*
100s:	14
Batting Average:	51.92
Best Bowling Innings:	5/86
Bowling Average:	36.20
Win–Loss–Draw:	24–16–7

TEST RESULTS: AS CAPTAIN

MATCHES	P	H	A	N	W	L	D	%W	%L	%D	W/L
v England	16	6	10	0	7	7	2	44%	44%	12%	1.00
v India	8	5	3	0	5	3	0	62%	38%	0%	1.67
v New Zealand	2	2	0	0	1	1	0	50%	50%	0%	1.00
v Pakistan	2	0	0	2	0	2	0	0%	100%	0%	0.00
v South Africa	8	3	5	0	3	3	2	38%	38%	25%	1.00
v Sri Lanka	6	3	3	0	4	0	2	67%	0%	33%	–
v West Indies	5	0	5	0	4	0	1	80%	0%	20%	–
TOTALS	**47**	**19**	**26**	**2**	**24**	**16**	**7**	**51%**	**34%**	**15%**	**1.50**

ONE-DAY INTERNATIONAL KEY STATISTICS: AS CAPTAIN

Matches Played:	74
Tosses Won:	30 (40.54%)
Not Outs:	9
Aggregate Runs:	2745
Highest Score:	117
100s:	5
Batting Average:	45.75
Best Bowling Innings:	3/15
Bowling Average:	30.66
Win–Loss–No Result:	50–21–3

ONE-DAY INTERNATIONAL RESULTS: AS CAPTAIN

MATCHES	P	H	A	N	W	L	NR	%W
v Afghanistan	2	1	0	1	2	0	0	100.00%
v Bangladesh	6	3	3	0	6	0	0	100.00%
v England	21	10	11	0	14	6	1	70.00%
v India	4	3	1	0	2	2	0	50.00%
v Ireland	1	0	1	0	0	0	1	–
v New Zealand	3	2	1	0	1	2	0	33.33%
v Pakistan	9	1	0	8	6	3	0	66.67%
v South Africa	4	1	3	0	3	1	0	75.00%
v Scotland	3	1	2	0	3	0	0	100.00%
v Sri Lanka	14	9	5	0	7	6	1	53.85%
v West Indies	6	4	2	0	6	0	0	100.00%
v Zimbabwe	1	0	1	0	0	1	0	0.00%
TOTALS	**74**	**35**	**30**	**9**	**50**	**21**	**3**	**70.42%**

TWENTY20 INTERNATIONAL KEY STATISTICS: AS CAPTAIN

Matches Played:	18
Tosses Won:	8 (44.44%)
Not Outs:	3
Aggregate Runs:	369
Highest Score:	67
50s:	1
Batting Average:	28.38
Best Bowling Innings:	1/2
Bowling Average:	72.00
Win–Loss–Tied–No Result:	12–4–1–1

TWENTY20 INTERNATIONAL RESULTS: AS CAPTAIN

MATCHES	P	H	A	N	W	L	T	NR	%W
v Bangladesh	1	0	0	1	1	0	0	0	100.00%
v England	2	0	1	1	0	1	0	1	0.00%
v India	2	1	0	1	2	0	0	0	100.00%
v New Zealand	3	1	2	0	2	0	1	0	83.33%
v Pakistan	5	1	0	4	3	2	0	0	60.00%
v Sri Lanka	2	1	0	1	1	1	0	0	50.00%
v West Indies	3	2	1	0	3	0	0	0	100.00%
TOTALS	**18**	**6**	**4**	**8**	**12**	**4**	**1**	**1**	**73.53%**

CAREER RECORDS: TESTS

BATTING

KEY STATISTICS: BATTING

Matches Played:	115
Innings Played:	198
Not Outs:	22
Aggregate Runs:	8643
Highest Score:	329*
50s:	27
100s:	28
200s:	4
300s:	1
Ducks:	9
Scoring Rate:	55.92
Batting Average:	49.10
Batting Average as Captain:	51.92

TEST MATCH RUN TOTALS

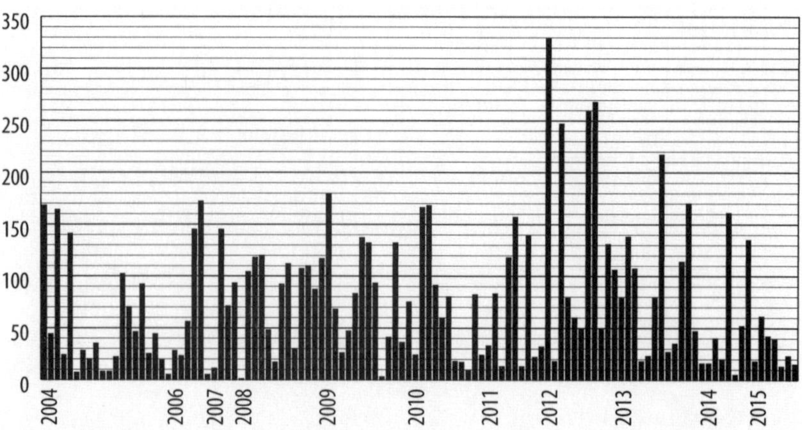

BATTING: THE MATCH LIST

★ – Not Out; DNB – Did Not Bat; DNP – Australia did not play a second innings.

#	MATCH DATE	OPPONENT	GROUND	RUNS BY MC	RESULT	MARGIN
1	06/10/04	India	Bangalore	151 & 17	W	217 runs
2	14/10/04	India	Chennai	5 & 39★	D	–
3	26/10/04	India	Nagpur	91 & 73	W	342 runs
4	03/11/04	India	Mumbai	17 & 7	L	13 runs
5	18/11/04	New Zealand	Brisbane	141 & DNP	W	inn & 156 runs
6	26/11/04	New Zealand	Adelaide	7 & DNB	W	213 runs
7	16/12/04	Pakistan	Perth	1 & 27	W	491 runs
8	26/12/04	Pakistan	Melbourne	20 & DNB	W	9 wickets
9	02/01/05	Pakistan	Sydney	35 & DNB	W	9 wickets
10	10/03/05	New Zealand	Christchurch	8 & DNB	W	9 wickets
11	18/03/05	New Zealand	Wellington	8 & DNP	D	–
12	26/03/05	New Zealand	Auckland	22 & DNB	W	9 wickets
13	21/07/05	England	Lord's	11 & 91	W	239 runs
14	04/08/05	England	Birmingham	40 & 30	L	2 runs
15	11/08/05	England	Manchester	7 & 39	D	–
16	25/08/05	England	Nottingham	36 & 56	L	3 wickets
17	08/09/05	England	The Oval	25 & DNB	D	–
18	14/10/05	ICC World XI	Sydney	39 & 5	W	210 runs
19	03/11/05	West Indies	Brisbane	5 & 14★	W	379 runs
20	17/11/05	West Indies	Hobart	5 & DNB	W	9 wickets
21	09/04/06	Bangladesh	Fatullah	19 & 9	W	3 wickets
22	16/04/06	Bangladesh	Chittagong	23★ & DNP	W	inn & 80 runs
23	23/11/06	England	Brisbane	56 & DNB	W	277 runs
24	01/12/06	England	Adelaide	124 & 21★	W	6 wickets
25	14/12/06	England	Perth	37 & 135★	W	206 runs
26	26/12/06	England	Melbourne	5 & DNP	W	inn & 99 runs
27	02/01/07	England	Sydney	11 & DNB	W	10 wickets
28	08/11/07	Sri Lanka	Brisbane	145★ & DNP	W	inn & 40 runs

MICHAEL CLARKE

#	MATCH DATE	OPPONENT	GROUND	RUNS BY MC	RESULT	MARGIN
29	16/11/07	Sri Lanka	Hobart	71 & DNB	W	96 runs
30	26/12/07	India	Melbourne	20 & 73	W	337 runs
31	02/01/08	India	Sydney	1 & 0	W	122 runs
32	16/01/08	India	Perth	23 & 81	L	72 runs
33	24/01/08	India	Adelaide	118 & DNP	D	–
34	30/05/08	West Indies	North Sound	110 & 10	D	–
35	12/06/08	West Indies	Bridgetown	0 & 48*	W	87 runs
36	09/10/08	India	Bangalore	11 & 6	D	–
37	17/10/08	India	Mohali	23 & 69	L	320 runs
38	29/10/08	India	Delhi	112 & DNB	D	–
39	06/11/08	India	Nagpur	8 & 22	L	172 runs
40	20/11/08	New Zealand	Brisbane	98 & 9	W	149 runs
41	28/11/08	New Zealand	Adelaide	110 & DNP	W	inn & 62 runs
42	17/12/08	South Africa	Perth	62 & 25	L	6 wickets
43	26/12/08	South Africa	Melbourne	88* & 29	L	9 wickets
44	03/01/09	South Africa	Sydney	138 & 41	W	103 runs
45	26/02/09	South Africa	Johannesburg	68 & 0	W	162 runs
46	06/03/09	South Africa	Durban	3 & 23*	W	175 runs
47	19/03/09	South Africa	Cape Town	0 & 47	L	inn & 20 runs
48	08/07/09	England	Cardiff	83 & DNP	D	–
49	16/07/09	England	Lord's	1 & 136	L	115 runs
50	30/07/09	England	Birmingham	29 & 103*	D	–
51	07/08/09	England	Leeds	93 & DNP	W	inn & 80 runs
52	20/08/09	England	The Oval	3 & 0	L	197 runs
53	26/11/09	West Indies	Brisbane	41 & DNP	W	inn & 65 runs
54	04/12/09	West Indies	Adelaide	71 & 61*	D	–
55	16/12/09	West Indies	Perth	11 & 25	W	35 runs
56	26/12/09	Pakistan	Melbourne	28* & 37	W	170 runs
57	03/01/10	Pakistan	Sydney	3 & 21	W	36 runs
58	14/01/10	Pakistan	Hobart	166 & DNB	W	231 runs
59	19/03/10	New Zealand	Wellington	168 & DNB	W	10 wickets
60	27/03/10	New Zealand	Hamilton	28 & 63	W	176 runs

CAREER RECORDS: TESTS

#	MATCH DATE	OPPONENT	GROUND	RUNS BY MC	RESULT	MARGIN
61	13/07/10	Pakistan	Lord's	47 & 12	W	150 runs
62	21/07/10	Pakistan	Leeds	3 & 77	L	3 wickets
63	01/10/10	India	Mohali	14 & 4	L	1 wicket
64	09/10/10	India	Bangalore	14 & 3	L	7 wickets
65	25/11/10	England	Brisbane	9 & DNB	D	–
66	03/12/10	England	Adelaide	2 & 80	L	inn & 71 runs
67	16/12/10	England	Perth	4 & 20	W	267 runs
68	26/12/10	England	Melbourne	20 & 13	L	inn & 157 runs
69	03/01/11	England	Sydney	4 & 41	L	inn & 83 runs
70	31/08/11	Sri Lanka	Galle	23 & 60	W	125 runs
71	08/09/11	Sri Lanka	Pallekele	13 & DNP	D	–
72	16/09/11	Sri Lanka	Colombo (SSC)	6 & 112	D	–
73	09/11/11	South Africa	Cape Town	151 & 2	L	8 wickets
74	17/11/11	South Africa	Johannesburg	11 & 2	W	2 wickets
75	01/12/11	New Zealand	Brisbane	139 & DNB	W	9 wickets
76	09/12/11	New Zealand	Hobart	22 & 0	L	7 runs
77	26/12/11	India	Melbourne	31 & 1	W	122 runs
78	03/01/12	India	Sydney	329* & DNP	W	inn & 68 runs
79	13/01/12	India	Perth	18 & DNP	W	inn & 37 runs
80	24/01/12	India	Adelaide	210 & 37	W	298 runs
81	07/04/12	West Indies	Bridgetown	73 & 6	W	3 wickets
82	15/04/12	West Indies	Port of Spain	45 & 15	D	–
83	23/04/12	West Indies	Roseau	24 & 25	W	75 runs
84	09/11/12	South Africa	Brisbane	259* & DNP	D	–
85	22/11/12	South Africa	Adelaide	230 & 38	D	–
86	30/11/12	South Africa	Perth	5 & 44	L	309 runs
87	14/12/12	Sri Lanka	Hobart	74 & 57*	W	137 runs
88	26/12/12	Sri Lanka	Melbourne	106 & DNP	W	inn & 201 runs
89	03/01/13	Sri Lanka	Sydney	50 & 29	W	5 wickets
90	22/02/13	India	Chennai	130 & 31	L	8 wickets
91	02/03/13	India	Hyderabad (Deccan)	91 & 16	L	inn & 135 runs

#	MATCH DATE	OPPONENT	GROUND	RUNS BY MC	RESULT	MARGIN
92	14/03/13	India	Mohali	0 & 18	L	6 wickets
93	10/07/13	England	Nottingham	0 & 23	L	14 runs
94	18/07/13	England	Lord's	28 & 51	L	347 runs
95	01/08/13	England	Manchester	187 & 30*	D	–
96	09/08/13	England	Chester-le-Street	6 & 21	L	74 runs
97	21/08/13	England	The Oval	7 & 28*	D	–
98	21/11/13	England	Brisbane	1 & 113	W	381 runs
99	05/12/13	England	Adelaide	148 & 22	W	218 runs
100	13/12/13	England	Perth	24 & 23	W	150 runs
101	26/12/13	England	Melbourne	10 & 6*	W	8 wickets
102	03/01/14	England	Sydney	10 & 6	W	281 runs
103	12/02/14	South Africa	Centurion	23 & 17*	W	281 runs
104	20/02/14	South Africa	Port Elizabeth	19 & 1	L	231 runs
105	01/03/14	South Africa	Cape Town	161* & 0	W	245 runs
106	22/10/14	Pakistan	Dubai (DSC)	2 & 3	L	221 runs
107	30/10/14	Pakistan	Abu Dhabi	47 & 5	L	356 runs
108	09/12/14	India	Adelaide	128 & 7	W	48 runs
109	03/06/15	West Indies	Roseau	18 & DNB	W	9 wickets
110	11/06/15	West Indies	Kingston	47 & 14*	W	277 runs
111	08/07/15	England	Cardiff	38 & 4	L	169 runs
112	16/07/15	England	Lord's	7 & 32*	W	405 runs
113	29/07/15	England	Birmingham	10 & 3	L	8 wickets
114	06/08/15	England	Nottingham	10 & 13	L	inn & 78 runs
115	20/08/15	England	The Oval	15 & DNP	W	inn & 46 runs

BATTING: BY OPPONENT

OPPONENT	RUNS	MAT	AVE	SR	HS	50s	100s
Bangladesh	51	2	25.50	46.78	23*	0	0
England	**2241**	**35**	40.74	56.23	187	**7**	**7**
ICC World XI	44	1	22.00	57.89	39	0	0
India	2049	22	53.92	56.57	**329***	6	**7**
New Zealand	823	11	58.78	54.68	168	2	4
Pakistan	534	10	33.37	51.49	166	1	1
South Africa	1487	14	67.59	59.59	259*	3	5
Sri Lanka	746	8	**74.60**	**60.94**	145*	5	3
West Indies	668	12	39.29	47.61	110	3	1

AGGREGATE RUNS BY OPPONENT

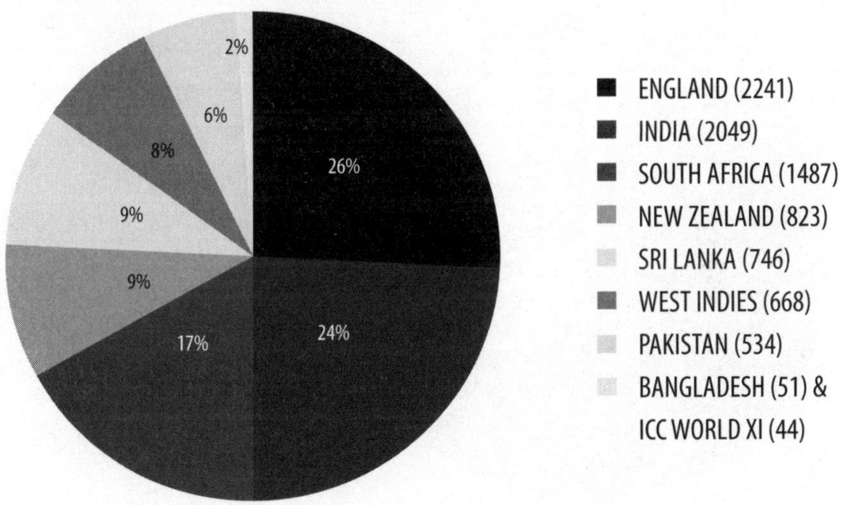

BATTING: BY COUNTRY

COUNTRY	RUNS	MAT	AVE	SR	HS	50s	100s
Australia	**4654**	**53**	**62.05**	57.92	**329***	**13**	**17**
Bangladesh	51	2	25.50	46.78	23*	0	0
England	1435	22	39.86	56.01	187	6	3
India	972	13	40.50	49.74	151	4	3
New Zealand	297	5	49.50	58.69	168	1	1
South Africa	528	8	40.61	57.76	161*	1	2
Sri Lanka	214	3	42.80	**61.67**	112	1	1
UAE	57	2	14.25	60.63	47	0	0
West Indies	435	7	39.54	46.52	110	1	1

AGGREGATE RUNS BY COUNTRY

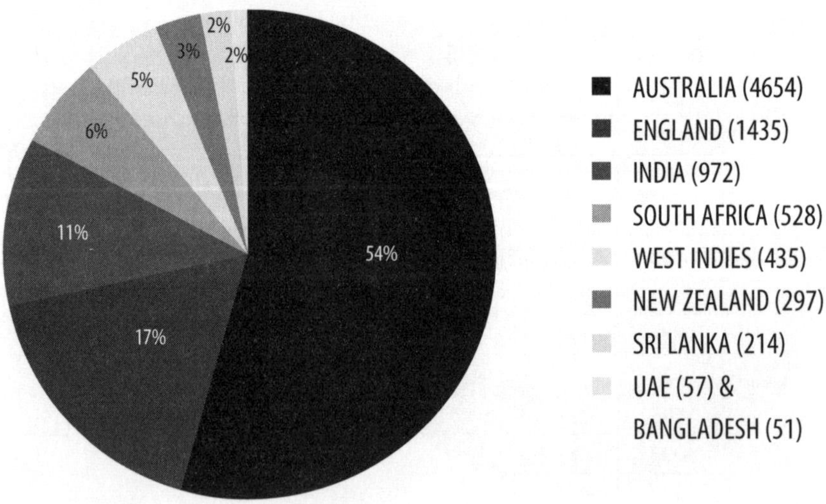

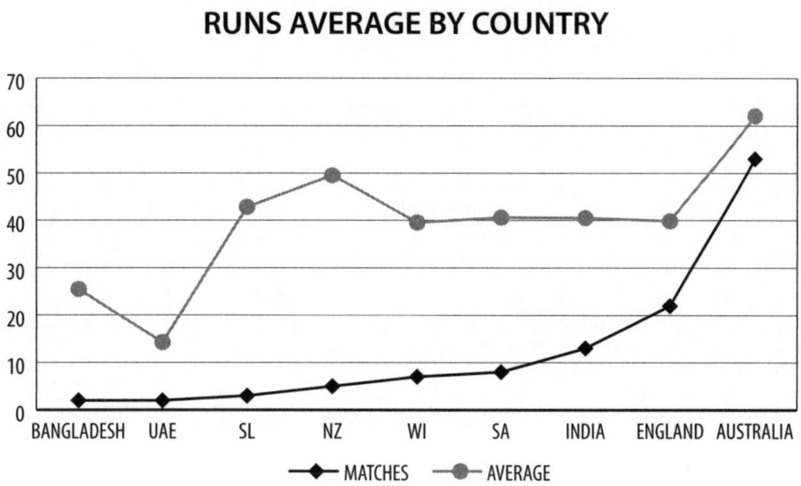

BATTING: BY YEAR

YEAR	RUNS	MAT	AVE	SR	HS	50s	100s
2004	596	8	49.66	57.08	151	2	2
2005	476	12	28.00	52.48	91	2	0
2006	429	6	71.50	61.11	135*	1	2
2007	320	4	80.00	56.23	145*	2	1
2008	1063	**13**	50.61	46.64	118	**5**	4
2009	1042	**13**	54.84	55.60	138	**5**	3
2010	771	12	36.71	51.64	168	3	2
2011	618	9	38.62	58.52	151	1	3
2012	**1595**	11	**106.33**	**65.96**	**329***	3	**5**
2013	1093	**13**	47.52	56.39	187	3	4
2014	429	7	35.75	56.74	161*	0	2
2015	211	7	21.10	50.23	47	0	0

AGGREGATE RUNS BY YEAR

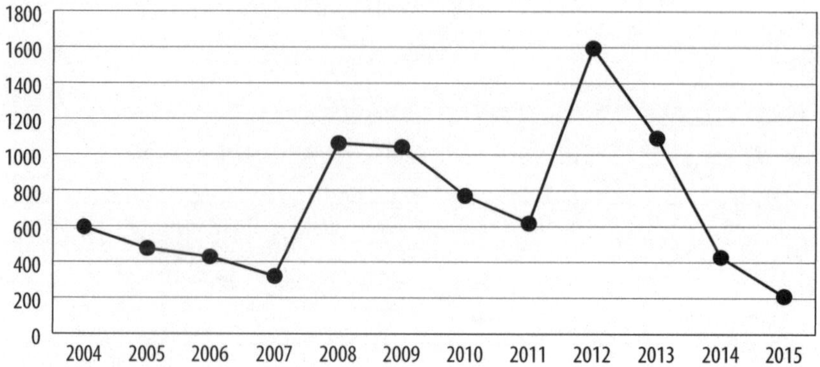

AGGREGATE RUNS BY YEAR

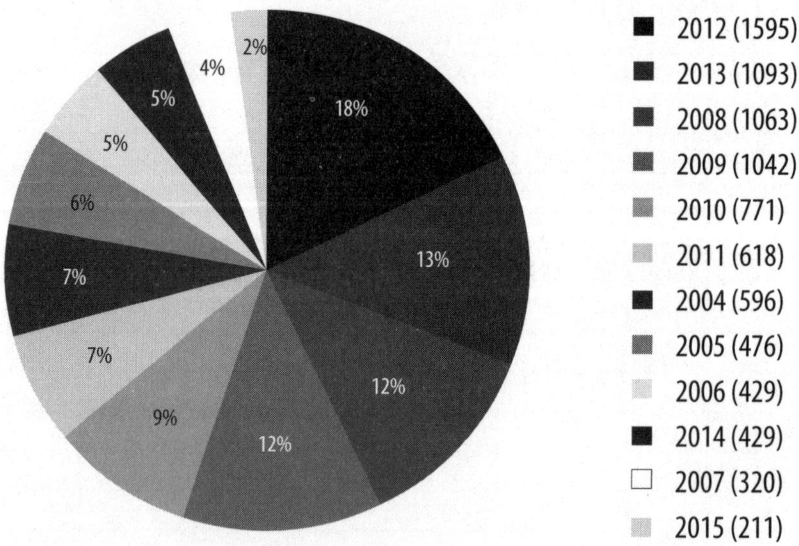

BATTING: BY POSITION

POSITION	RUNS	MAT	AVE	SR	HS	50s	100s
No. 3	25	2	12.50	40.32	25	0	0
No. 4	1745	38	30.61	53.72	187	4	5
No. 5	**5959**	**72**	60.80	56.41	**329***	**20**	**20**
No. 6	829	17	48.76	**59.00**	151	3	3
No. 7	78	3	**78.00**	48.44	39*	0	0
No. 8	7	1	7.00	38.88	7	0	0

AGGREGATE RUNS BY POSITION

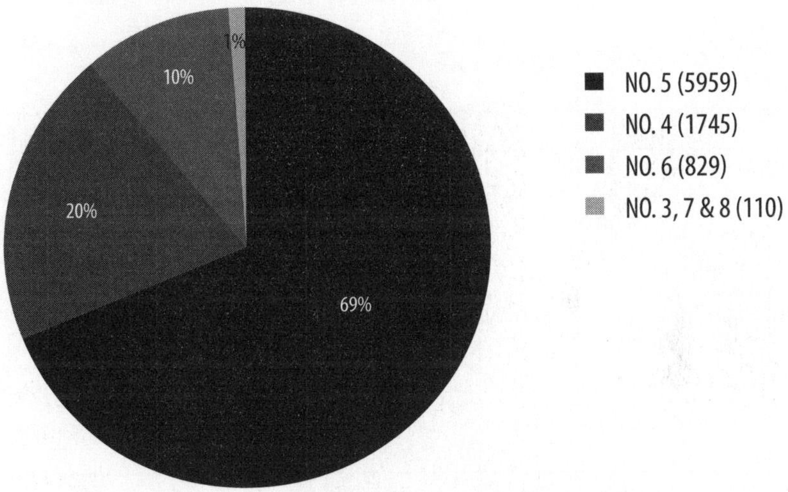

BATTING: CENTURIES

#	DATE	RUNS	BALLS FACED	OPPONENT	GROUND	SERIES
1	06/10/04	151	248	India	Bangalore	Border–Gavaskar Trophy
2	18/11/04	141	200	New Zealand	Brisbane	Trans-Tasman Trophy
3	01/12/06	124	224	England	Adelaide	The Ashes
4	14/12/06	135*	164	England	Perth	The Ashes
5	08/11/07	145*	249	Sri Lanka	Brisbane	Warne–Muralitharan Trophy
6	24/01/08	118	243	India	Adelaide	Border–Gavaskar Trophy
7	30/05/08	110	187	West Indies	North Sound	The Frank Worrell Trophy
8	29/10/08	112	253	India	Delhi	Border–Gavaskar Trophy
9	28/11/08	110	239	New Zealand	Adelaide	Trans-Tasman Trophy
10	03/01/09	138	250	South Africa	Sydney	South Africa tour of Australia
11	16/07/09	136	227	England	Lord's	The Ashes
12	30/07/09	103*	192	England	Birmingham	The Ashes
13	14/01/10	166	328	Pakistan	Hobart	Pakistan tour of Australia
14	19/03/10	168	253	New Zealand	Wellington	Trans-Tasman Trophy
15	16/09/11	112	178	Sri Lanka	Colombo (SSC)	Warne–Muralitharan Trophy
16	09/11/11	151	176	South Africa	Cape Town	Australian tour of South Africa
17	01/12/11	139	249	New Zealand	Brisbane	Trans-Tasman Trophy
18	03/01/12	329*	468	India	Sydney	Border–Gavaskar Trophy
19	24/01/12	210	275	India	Adelaide	Border–Gavaskar Trophy
20	09/11/12	259*	398	South Africa	Brisbane	South Africa tour of Australia

CAREER RECORDS: TESTS

#	DATE	RUNS	BALLS FACED	OPPONENT	GROUND	SERIES
21	22/11/12	230	257	South Africa	Adelaide	South Africa tour of Australia
22	26/12/12	106	187	Sri Lanka	Melbourne	Warne–Muralitharan Trophy
23	22/02/13	130	246	India	Chennai	Border–Gavaskar Trophy
24	01/08/13	187	314	England	Manchester	The Ashes
25	21/11/13	113	130	England	Brisbane	The Ashes
26	05/12/13	148	245	England	Adelaide	The Ashes
27	01/03/14	161*	301	South Africa	Cape Town	Australia tour of South Africa
28	09/12/14	128	163	India	Adelaide	Border–Gavaskar Trophy

CENTURIES SCORES

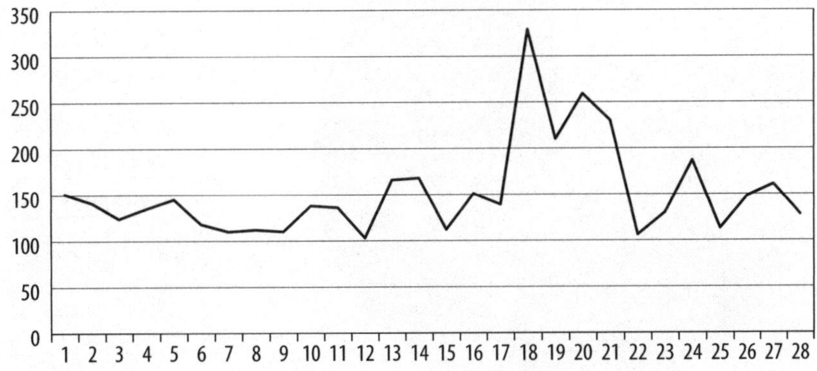

NUMBER OF CENTURIES: BY YEAR

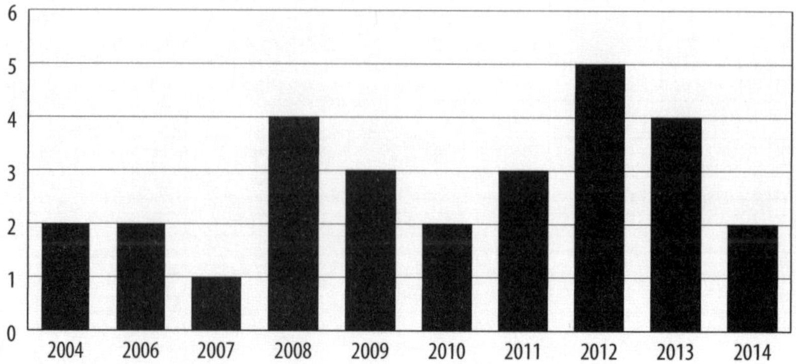

NUMBER OF CENTURIES: BY OPPONENT

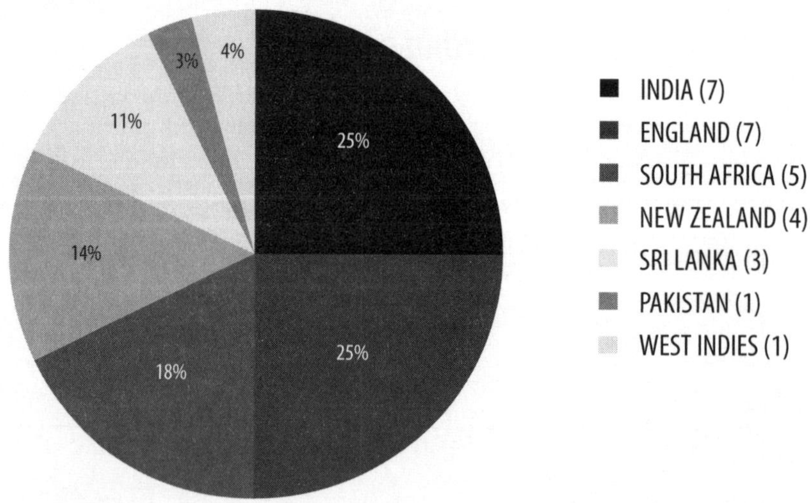

BATTING: HIGHEST PARTNERSHIPS

PARTNERS	RUNS	WICKET	OPPONENT	GROUND	MATCH DATE
RT Ponting & MJ Clarke	386	4th	India	Adelaide	24/01/12
RT Ponting & MJ Clarke	352	4th	Pakistan	Hobart	14/01/10
MJ Clarke & MEK Hussey	334*	5th	India	Sydney	03/01/12
RT Ponting & MJ Clarke	288	4th	India	Sydney	03/01/12
MJ Clarke & MEK Hussey	272	5th	South Africa	Adelaide	22/11/12
EJM Cowan & MJ Clarke	259	4th	South Africa	Brisbane	09/11/12
MJ Clarke & MJ North	253	5th	New Zealand	Wellington	19/03/10

BATTING: DISMISSALS

HOW DISMISSED	NO.	PERCENTAGE
Bowled	37	21.0%
Caught	73	41.5%
Caught Behind	35	19.9%
LBW	19	10.8%
Stumped	8	4.5%
Run Out	4	2.3%

BOWLING

KEY STATISTICS: BOWLING

Overs:	405.5
Balls:	2435
Maidens:	62
Runs Conceded:	1184
Wickets:	31
Bowling Average:	38.19
Bowling Average as Captain:	36.20
5 Wickets in Innings:	2
Best Bowling Innings:	6/9
Economy Rate:	2.92
Strike Rate:	78.55

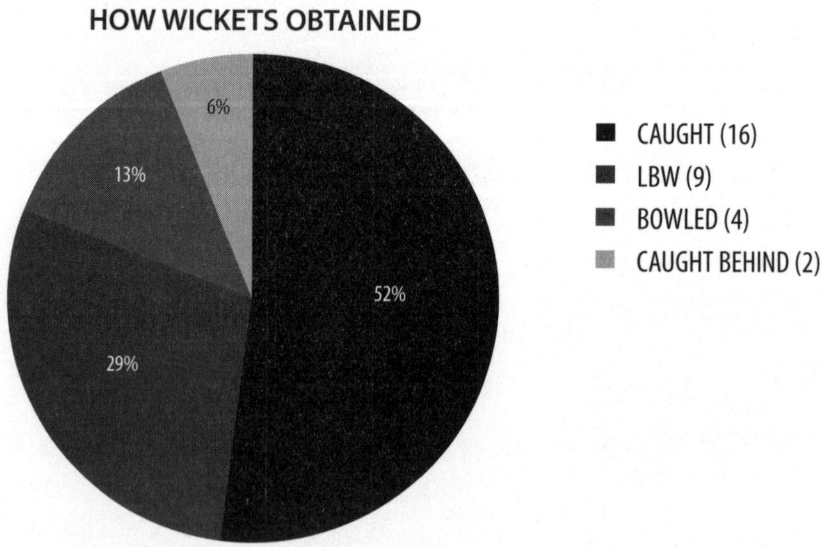

BOWLING: THE WICKET LIST

O – Overs bowled; M – Maidens; R – Runs conceded; W – Wickets taken; Econ – Economy rate of runs conceded.

#	MATCH DATE	OPPONENT	GROUND	O	M	R	W	ECON
1–6	03/11/04	India	Mumbai	6.2	0	9	6	1.42
7	10/03/05	New Zealand	Christchurch	5	0	16	1	3.20
8	18/03/05	New Zealand	Wellington	3	1	8	1	2.66
9–11	02/01/08	India	Sydney	8.5	1	33	3	3.73
12	24/01/08	India	Adelaide	11	0	41	1	3.72
13-14	30/05/08	West Indies	North Sound	21	10	36	2	1.71
15-16	12/06/08	West Indies	Bridgetown	19	1	41	2	2.15
17–18	09/10/08	India	Bangalore	37	10	78	2	2.10
19	16/07/09	England	Lord's	8	1	27	1	3.37
20	27/03/10	New Zealand	Hamilton	16	4	27	1	1.68
21	09/10/10	India	Bangalore	8	0	27	1	3.37
22–23	17/11/11	South Africa	Johannesburg	6	2	8	2	1.33
24	03/01/12	India	Sydney	9	0	22	1	2.44
25–29	23/04/12	West Indies	Roseau	25	1	104	5	4.16
30	22/11/12	South Africa	Adelaide	25	6	56	1	2.24
31	20/02/14	South Africa	Port Elizabeth	7.5	2	16	1	2.04

FIELDING

KEY STATISTICS: FIELDING

Catches:	134
Catches per Match Average:	1.16
Most Caught Batsman:	DPMD Jayawardene (5)
Most Caught Country:	England (33)
Most Balls Caught Off Bowler:	MG Johnson (21)
Most Catches In:	Australia (63)
Most Catches Away:	England (20)
Most Catches (Innings):	3
Most Catches (Match):	4

CATCHES BY OPPONENT

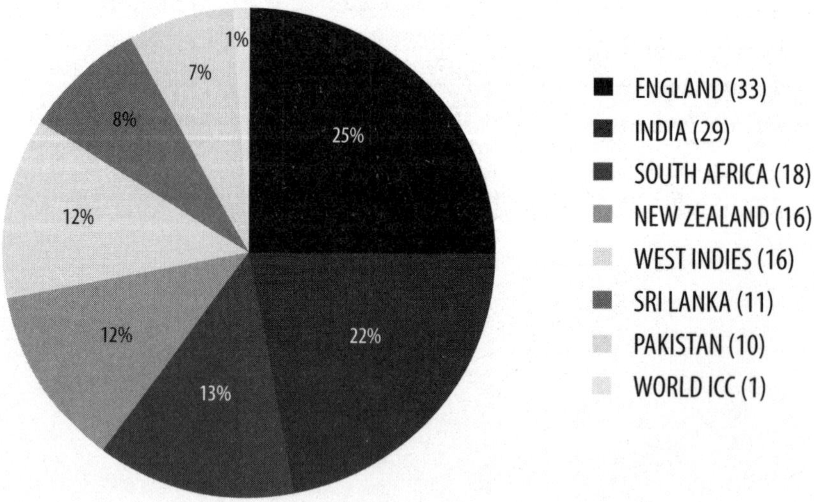

CAREER RECORDS: ONE-DAY INTERNATIONALS

BATTING

KEY STATISTICS: BATTING

Matches Played:	245
Innings Played:	223
Not Outs:	44
Aggregate Runs:	7981
Highest Score:	130
50s:	58
100s:	8
Ducks:	10
Opened Batting:	21
Scoring Rate:	78.98
Batting Average:	44.58
Batting Average as Captain:	45.75

BATTING: THE SERIES LIST

** – Not Out; HS – High Score.*

SERIES	MAT	TOTAL BY MC	HS	AVE	WINNER
VB Series (Aus/Eng/SL) in Australia, 2002/03	1	39	39*	–	Australia
Australia in the West Indies, 2003	4	170	75*	85.00	Australia
TVS Cup (Aus/Ind/NZ) in India, 2003/04	5	118	70	39.33	Australia
VB Series (Aus/Ind/Zim) in Australia, 2003/04	10	248	63	31.00	Australia
Australia in Sri Lanka, 2003/04	5	83	36	20.75	Australia
Australia in Zimbabwe, 2004	3	126	105*	126.00	Australia
Videocon Cup (Aus/Ind/Pak) in Netherlands, 2004	2	43	42	21.50	Australia
NatWest International (Aus/Pak) in England, 2004	1	31	31	31.00	Australia
ICC Champions Trophy (Aus/BD/Eng/Ind/Ken/NZ/Pak/SA/SL/USA/WI/Zim) in England, 2004	3	42	42	42.00	West Indies
Chappell–Hadlee Trophy (Aus/NZ) in Australia, 2004/05	2	42	36	21.00	–
VB Series (Aus/Pak/WI) in Australia, 2004/05	8	411	103*	68.50	Australia
Australia in New Zealand, 2004/05	5	147	71*	49.00	Australia
NatWest Series (Aus/BD/Eng) in England, 2005	5	184	80*	46.00	–
NatWest Challenge (Aus/Eng) in England, 2005	3	2	2	2.00	Australia
ICC Super Series ODIs (Aus/ICC) in Australia, 2005/06	3	26	17*	13.00	Australia

CAREER RECORDS: ONE-DAY INTERNATIONALS

SERIES	MAT	TOTAL BY MC	HS	AVE	WINNER
Chappell–Hadlee Trophy (Aus/NZ) in New Zealand, 2005/06	3	184	82*	92.00	Australia
VB Series (Aus/SA/SL) in Australia, 2005/06	11	341	80	56.83	Australia
Australia in South Africa, 2005/06	5	86	53	21.50	South Africa
Australia in Bangladesh, 2005/06	3	70	54	35.00	Australia
DLF Cup (Aus/Ind/WI) in Malaysia, 2006/07	4	169	81	42.25	Australia
ICC Champions Trophy (Aus/BD/Eng/Ind/NZ/Pak/SA/SL/WI/Zim) in India, 2006/07	5	63	47	31.50	Australia
Commonwealth Bank Series (Aus/Eng/NZ) in Australia, 2006/07	10	268	75	33.50	England
ICC World Cup (Aus/BD/Ber/Can/Eng/Ind/Ire/Ken/NL/NZ/Pak/SA/Sco/SL/WI/Zim) in West Indies, 2006/07	11	436	93*	87.20	Australia
Australia in India, 2007/08	7	222	130	37.00	Australia
Chappell–Hadlee Trophy (Aus/NZ) in Australia, 2007/08	3	55	48	27.50	Australia
Commonwealth Bank Series (Aus/Ind/SL) in Australia, 2007/08	10	314	79	39.25	India
Australia in West Indies, 2008	5	117	56	29.25	Australia
Bangladesh in Australia, 2008	3	40	25	13.33	Australia
South Africa in Australia, 2008/09	2	19	19	9.50	South Africa
Chappell–Hadlee Trophy (Aus/NZ) in Australia, 2008/09	4	188	98	47.00	–

SERIES	MAT	TOTAL BY MC	HS	AVE	WINNER
Australia in South Africa, 2008/09	5	157	66	31.40	South Africa
Australia v Pakistan ODI Series in UAE, 2009	5	235	100*	78.33	Australia
Australia in Scotland, 2009	1	16	16	16.00	Australia
NatWest Series (Aus/Eng) in England, 2009	6	253	62*	50.60	Australia
Pakistan in Australia, 2009/10	4	173	80	43.25	Australia
West Indies in Australia, 2009/10	4	138	47	46.00	Australia
Chappell–Hadlee Trophy (Aus/NZ) in New Zealand, 2009/10	2	33	22	16.50	Australia
Australia in Ireland, 2010	1	0	0	0.00	Australia
NatWest Series (Aus/Eng) in England, 2010	4	220	99*	110.00	England
Australia in India, 2010/11	1	111	111*	–	India
Sri Lanka in Australia, 2010/11	3	102	50*	51.00	Sri Lanka
England in Australia, 2010/11	6	206	82	34.33	Australia
ICC Cricket World Cup (Aus/BD/Can/Eng/Ind/Ire/Ken/NL/NZ/Pa/SA/SL/WI/Zim) in Sri Lanka/India/Bangladesh, 2010/11	7	233	93	77.66	India
Chappell–Hadlee Trophy (Aus/NZ) in India, 2010/11	1	24	24*	–	Australia
Australia in Bangladesh, 2011	3	148	101	74.00	Australia
Australia in Sri Lanka, 2011	5	242	58*	121.00	Australia
Australia in South Africa, 2011/12	3	71	44	23.66	Australia
Commonwealth Bank Series (Aus/Ind/SL) in Australia, 2011/12	6	311	117	55.16	Australia
Australia in Ireland, 2012	1	0	0	–	–

CAREER RECORDS: ONE-DAY INTERNATIONALS

SERIES	MAT	TOTAL BY MC	HS	AVE	WINNER
NatWest Series (Aus/Eng) in England, 2012	4	115	61	28.75	England
Afghanistan v Australia ODI Match in UAE, 2012	1	75	75	75.00	Australia
Pakistan v Australia ODI Series in UAE, 2012	3	135	66	45.00	Australia
Sri Lanka in Australia, 2012/13	2	29	20	14.50	–
West Indies in Australia, 2012/13	4	68	37	22.66	Australia
Australia in Scotland, 2013	1	4	4*	–	Australia
NatWest Series (Aus/Eng) in England, 2013	4	202	105	67.33	Australia
England in Australia, 2013/14	4	102	43	25.50	Australia
Zimbabwe Triangular Series (Aus/SA/Zim) in Zimbabwe, 2014	1	68	68*	–	South Africa
South Africa in Australia, 2014/15	1	11	11	11.00	Australia
ICC Cricket World Cup (Aus/BD/Eng/Ind/Ire/NZ/Pak/SA/Sco/SL/UAE/WI/Zim) in Australia/New Zealand, 2014/15	7	219	74	36.50	Australia
Chappell–Hadlee Trophy (Aus/NZ) in New Zealand, 2014/15	1	12	12	12.00	New Zealand

BATTING: BY OPPONENT

OPPONENT	RUNS	MAT	AVE	HS	50s	100s
Afghanistan	75	2	75.00	75	1	0
Bangladesh	392	12	49.00	101	3	1
Canada	16	1	–	16*	0	0
England	**1430**	**44**	43.33	105	**11**	1
ICC World XI	26	3	13.00	17*	0	0
India	858	30	39.00	**130**	4	**2**
Ireland	0	3	0.00	0	0	0
Kenya	93	1	**93.00**	93	1	0
Netherlands	93	1	–	93*	1	0
New Zealand	1018	31	40.72	98	8	0
Pakistan	939	21	55.24	103*	6	**2**
Scotland	82	4	27.33	47	0	0
South Africa	566	22	28.30	92	5	0
Sri Lanka	1279	34	60.90	117	**11**	1
West Indies	775	26	38.75	81	5	0
Zimbabwe	339	9	67.80	105*	2	1

AGGREGATE RUNS BY OPPONENT

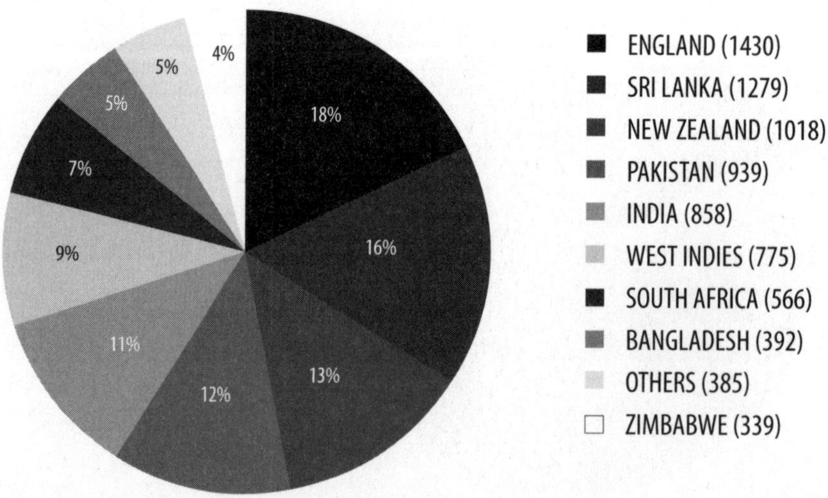

BATTING: BY COUNTRY

OPPONENT	RUNS	MAT	AVE	HS	50s	100s
Australia	**3358**	**107**	38.60	117	**23**	**2**
Bangladesh	218	6	54.50	101	1	1
England	972	27	54.00	105	8	1
India	713	23	54.85	**130**	4	**2**
Ireland	0	2	0.00	0	0	0
Malaysia	169	4	42.25	81	2	0
Netherlands	43	2	21.50	42	0	0
New Zealand	376	11	47.00	82*	3	0
Scotland	20	2	20.00	16	0	0
South Africa	314	13	26.17	66	3	0
Sri Lanka	359	12	51.29	58*	2	0
UAE	445	9	63.57	100*	3	1
Wales	77	3	25.67	54	1	0
West Indies	723	20	65.73	93*	7	0
Zimbabwe	194	4	**194.00**	105*	1	1

AGGREGATE RUNS BY COUNTRY

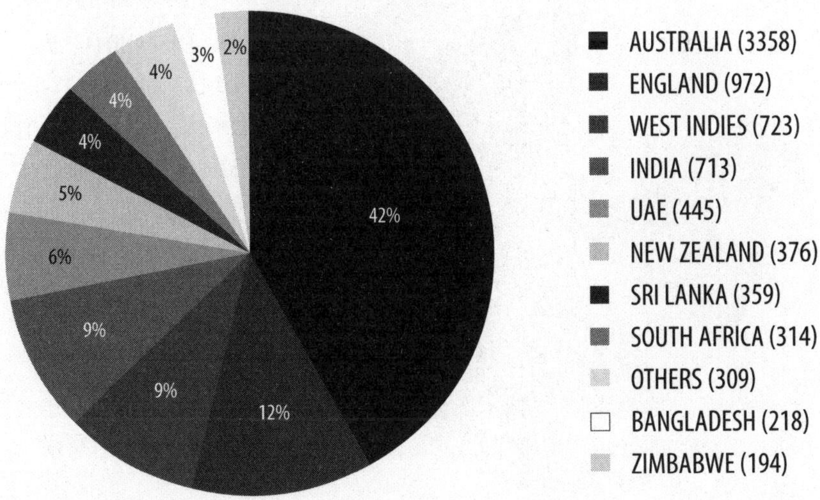

BATTING: BY YEAR

YEAR	RUNS	MAT	AVE	HS	50s	100s
2003	327	10	**65.40**	75*	3	0
2004	615	26	32.37	105*	1	**1**
2005	954	27	53.00	103*	**8**	**1**
2006	729	28	40.50	81	7	0
2007	**981**	**31**	46.71	130	7	**1**
2008	471	18	31.40	79	4	0
2009	868	23	43.40	100*	**8**	**1**
2010	777	19	55.50	111*	5	**1**
2011	900	24	56.25	101	6	**1**
2012	656	15	46.86	**117**	5	**1**
2013	303	11	37.88	105	1	**1**
2014	181	6	36.20	68*	1	0
2015	219	7	36.50	74	2	0

AGGREGATE RUNS BY YEAR

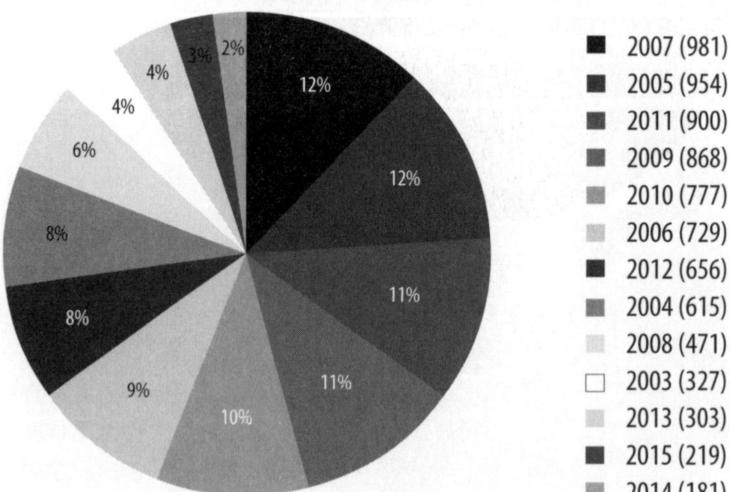

BATTING: BY POSITION

POSITION	RUNS	INNINGS	AVE	50s	100s
Opening	829	21	43.63	6	2
No. 3	850	24	40.48	5	1
No. 4	**4223**	**111**	46.41	**32**	**5**
No. 5	751	17	**62.58**	8	0
No. 6	977	33	46.52	7	0
No. 7	351	17	23.40	0	0

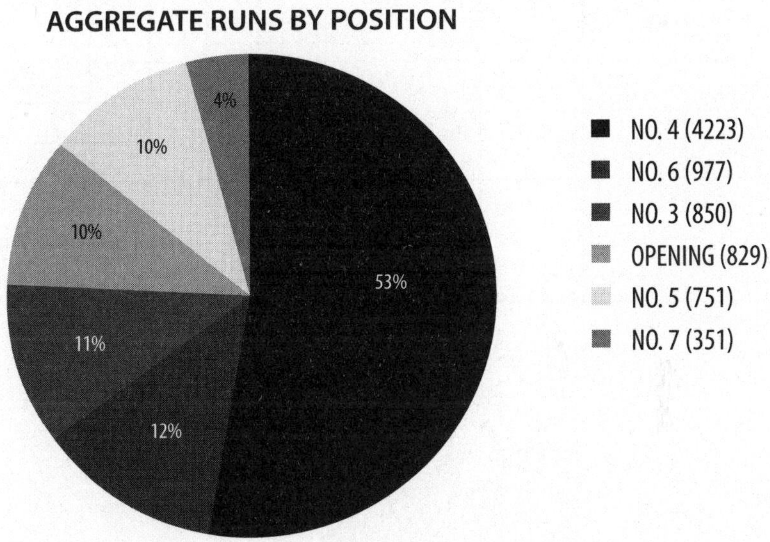

BATTING: CENTURIES

DATE	RUNS	BALLS FACED	OPPONENT	GROUND	SERIES
29/05/04	105*	102	Zimbabwe	Harare	Australia in Zimbabwe, 2004
23/01/05	103*	107	Pakistan	Sydney	VB Series (Aus/Pak/WI) in Australia, 2004/05
29/09/07	130	132	India	Bangalore	Australia in India, 2007/08
01/05/09	100*	122	Pakistan	Abu Dhabi	Australia v Pakistan ODI Series in UAE, 2009
20/10/10	111*	139	India	Visakhapatnam	Australia in India, 2010/11
09/04/11	101	111	Bangladesh	Dhaka	Australia in Bangladesh, 2011
06/03/12	117	91	Sri Lanka	Adelaide	Commonwealth Bank Series (Aus/Ind/SL) in Australia, 2011/12
08/09/13	105	102	England	Manchester	NatWest Series (Aus/Eng) in England, 2013

BATTING: HIGHEST PARTNERSHIPS

PARTNERS	RUNS	WICKET	OPPONENT	GROUND	MATCH DATE
A Symonds & MJ Clarke	220	5th	New Zealand	Wellington	07/12/05
MJ Clarke & BJ Hodge	204	4th	Netherlands	St Kitts	18/03/07
SR Watson & MJ Clarke	197*	3rd	Pakistan	Abu Dhabi	01/05/09
SR Watson & MJ Clarke	163	4th	England	Southampton	16/09/13
MJ Clarke & GJ Bailey	155	4th	England	Manchester	08/09/13
MJ Clarke & MEK Hussey	144	3rd	India	Visakhapatnam	20/10/10
MJ Clarke & MEK Hussey	136*	6th	New Zealand	Auckland	26/02/05
BJ Haddin & MJ Clarke	129	1st	South Africa	Port Elizabeth	13/04/09
MJ Clarke & A Symonds	123	4th	India	Hyderabad	05/10/07
MJ Clarke & MEK Hussey	105	5th	England	Bristol	19/06/05
MJ Clarke & A Symonds	86*	5th	Bangladesh	Canterbury	30/06/05

BATTING: DISMISSALS

HOW DISMISSED	NO.	PERCENTAGE
Bowled	34	19.0%
Caught	77	43.0%
Caught Behind	29	16.2%
LBW	14	7.8%
Stumped	7	3.9%
Run Out	18	10.1%

BOWLING

KEY STATISTICS: BOWLING

Overs:	430.5
Balls:	2585
Maidens:	7
Runs Conceded:	2146
Wickets:	57
Bowling Average:	37.64
Bowling Average as Captain:	30.66
4 Wickets in Innings:	2
Best Bowling Innings:	5/35
Economy Rate:	4.98
Strike Rate:	45.30

HOW WICKETS OBTAINED

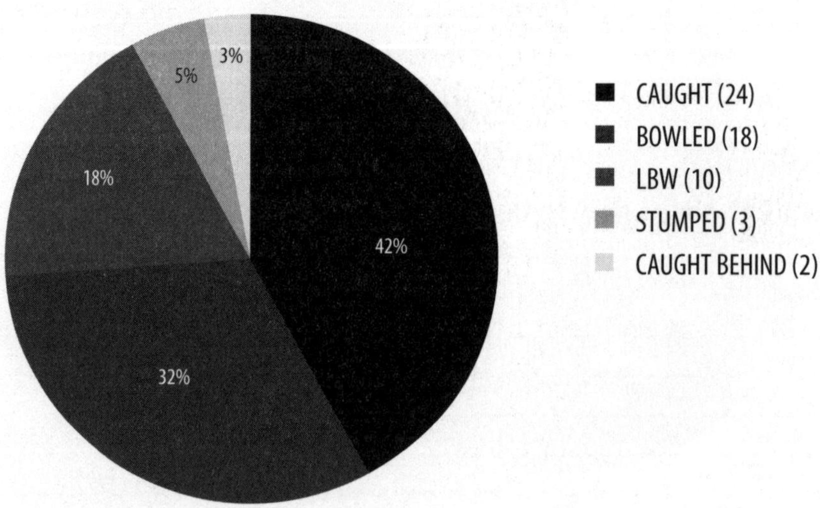

FIELDING

KEY STATISTICS: FIELDING

Catches:	106
Catches per Match Average:	0.43
Most Caught Batsmen:	Kamran Akmal, IR Bell & EJG Morgan (3)
Most Caught Country:	England (17)
Most Balls Caught Off Bowlers:	GB Hogg & B Lee (9)
Most Catches In:	Australia (51)
Most Catches Away:	South Africa (9)
Most Catches (Innings):	4

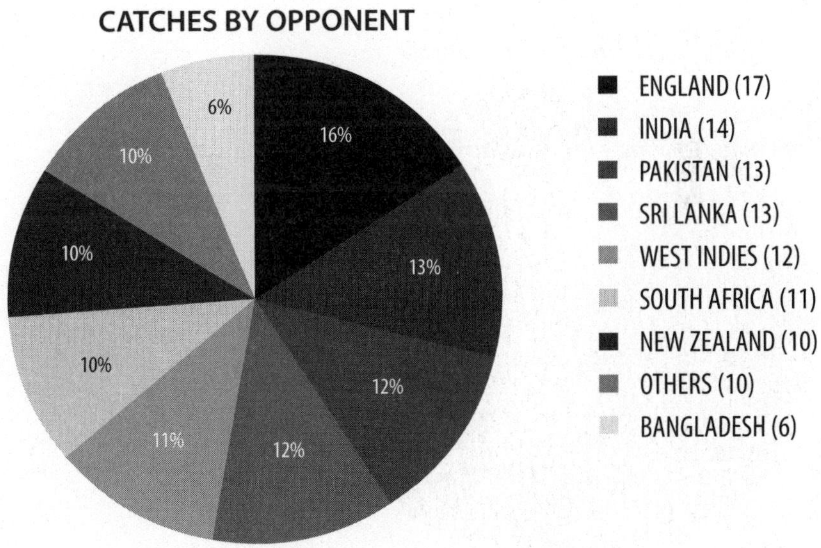

CAREER RECORDS: TWENTY20 INTERNATIONALS

BATTING

KEY STATISTICS: BATTING

Matches Played:	34
Innings Played:	28
Not Outs:	5
Aggregate Runs:	488
Highest Score:	67
4s:	29
6s:	10
Ducks:	2
Opened Batting:	7
Scoring Rate:	103.17
Batting Average:	21.21
Batting Average as Captain:	28.38

BATTING: THE SERIES LIST

★ – *Not Out; HS – High Score.*

SERIES	MAT	TOTAL BY MC	HS	AVE	WINNER
Australia in New Zealand, 2004/05	1	7	7	7.00	Australia
Australia in England, 2005	1	0	0	0.00	England
South Africa in Australia, 2005/06	1	0	0★	–	Australia
Australia in South Africa, 2005/06	1	37	37	37.00	South Africa
England in Australia, 2006/07	1	5	5	5.00	Australia
ICC World Twenty20 (Aus/BD/Eng/Ind/Ken/NZ/Pak/SA/Sco/SL/WI/Zim) in South Africa, 2007/08	5	3	3	1.50	India
Australia in India, 2007/08	1	25	25★	–	India
New Zealand in Australia, 2007/08	1	33	33	33.00	Australia
India in Australia, 2007/08	1	37	37★	–	Australia
Australia in West Indies, 2008	1	0	–	–	West Indies
Australia in South Africa, 2008/09	2	29	27	14.50	South Africa
ICC World Twenty20 (Aus/BD/Eng/Ind/Ire/NL/NZ/Pak/SA/Sco/SL/WI) in England, 2009	2	13	11	6.50	Pakistan
Australia in England, 2009	1	27	27★	–	–
Pakistan in Australia, 2009/10	1	32	32	32.00	Australia
West Indies in Australia, 2009/10	2	12	12	12.00	Australia

SERIES	MAT	TOTAL BY MC	HS	AVE	WINNER
Australia in New Zealand, 2009/10	2	85	67	85.00	–
ICC World Twenty20(Aus/ BD/Eng/Ind/Ire/NZ/Pak/ SA/SL/WI/Zim) in West Indies, 2010	7	92	27	15.33	England
MCC Spirit of Cricket T20I Series (Aus/Pak) in England, 2010	2	35	30	17.50	Pakistan
Sri Lanka in Australia, 2010/11	1	16	16	16.00	Sri Lanka

ACKNOWLEDGEMENTS

I wrote this book thinking, if I was to die today, what would my daughter know about me and what I stood for?

Many people have helped me answer that question in my 35 years, and to them I give sincere thanks.

To the game of cricket – you changed my life. I'd hate to think where I'd be in this world without you. To all the boys and men who have played this great game alongside me and against me. To the coaches, umpires, scorers and helpers. And to everyone out there who threw a ball to me over the years.

To my family – Mum and Dad, you gave me everything I ever needed and were always my greatest inspiration. I only hope I can be as good a parent to my children as you were to me. To my sister, Lea – blood is thicker than water. I'm here 24/7 for you, as you have always been for me.

To Kyly – talk about a life changer! Thank you for putting up with me, for helping me chase my dream and for standing beside me – day in, day out – through the highest of highs and lowest of lows. You taught me to stop and smell the roses. What a journey it's been so far and what a journey we still have ahead of us.

To Kelsey Lee, my angel, you melt my heart. Chase your dreams. Don't fear failing – you learn so much by being knocked down. Get back up and take the world on. And be nice to your mother. Thank you for coming into my life at the perfect time. You have changed me for the better. I love you with all of my heart.

To my friends – you know who you are. Thanks for having my back through the tough times and for having the balls to look me in the eye and set me straight when I needed it most.

To Pan Macmillan – I've always loved working with you and I'm so proud of what we've achieved with this book. To Angus Fontaine and his team, and to Malcolm Knox, who told my story like no one else could.

And to all the people who told me 'You can't', 'You won't', and 'You're not good enough' – you got me out of bed every day and drove me to accomplish things in life I didn't think I could do.

Thank you.

Michael Clarke

INDEX

INDEX

INDEX

INDEX

INDEX

INDEX

INDEX

INDEX

INDEX

INDEX

QANTAS